ADVANCE PRAISE F[

MURDER ON FEDERAL STREET

"Nothing—not politics, not industry, not pop culture, not the four major sports—provides the rich and irresistible stories routinely found in professional boxing. In *Murder on Federal Street*, Sean Nam details the tragically short life of former Philadelphia boxer Tyrone Everett with impeccable research and crisp, clean prose. That doesn't surprise me; Nam has been one of this era's best boxing writers for quite some time.

"I've always rated Philadelphia as America's best boxing city, at least in its prime. And in Nam's book, Philly is a central character. Combine Everett's journey, Philadelphia, and the impact of the city's Black Mafia and you have non-fiction that reads like a novel.

"Until now, only hard-core boxing fans were aware of Everett's story—minus perspective and large chunks of critical and significant facts. Now, thanks to Nam, the picture has gone from cloudy to clear and complete."

—STEVE FARHOOD,
boxing analyst for Showtime, 2017 inductee into the International Boxing Hall of Fame, and former editor of *The Ring* magazine

"In *Murder on Federal Street*, Sean Nam burrows deep into a career and life cut short under tragic circumstances and, on a much grander scale, into the dystopian intersection of boxing and the Philadelphia underworld. It's investigative reporting and storytelling at its finest with a touch of a *Goodfellas* meets *Raging Bull* narrative."

—HARVEY ARATON,
New York Times best-selling author

"*Murder on Federal Street* is about the killing of Tyrone Everett, a sadistically vain, bisexual fighter in 1970s Philadelphia. If there's a hero, it's Sean Nam, whose obsessional reporting and evocative style turn a true story into a noir worthy of a Gamble and Huff soundtrack. Whodunit? Maybe the guys who stole a decision the night of Everett's biggest fight. Maybe a boyfriend. Or a girlfriend. Or the girlfriend's drug dealer husband. Then there's the diabolical criminal consortium lurking behind everything, the Black Mafia. It's a wonderfully nasty business. And for the same unfortunate reasons you might be drawn to boxing, you'll love it."

—MARK KRIEGEL,
ESPN analyst and *New York Times* bestselling author of
The Good Son: The Life of Ray "Boom Boom" Mancini

"Sean Nam has written a compelling, page-turning history of Tyrone Everett which will appeal to boxing and true crime fans alike. His comprehensive research is mind-boggling, covers everything from urban and racial politics to the boxing scene to the underworld, and his writing is top-notch. Nam exhaustively details a complex and controversial story in colorful, gripping prose, and the result is a full and rewarding assessment of Everett's shortened life."

—SEAN PATRICK GRIFFIN,
Professor of Criminal Justice at The Citadel
and author of *Black Brothers, Inc.: The Violent
Rise and Fall of Philadelphia's Black Mafia*

"In death, as in life, Philadelphia lightweight Tyrone Everett remains a colorful, controversial character whose story deserves the kind of in-depth examination as is so ably provided by author Sean Nam. In the ring, Everett was the victim of one of the most outrageous and egregious decisions in boxing history, one that almost certainly was the result of deliberate chicanery. Out of the ring, Everett was a victim of another sort, murder, a crime tinged in sex and drugs, and which continues to resonate in his hometown."

—BERNARD FERNANDEZ,
2020 inductee into the International Boxing Hall of Fame and
author of the *Championship Rounds boxing anthology series*

MURDER ON
FEDERAL STREET

Tyrone Everett, the Black Mafia,

Fixed Fights, and the Last Golden

Age of Philadelphia Boxing

RUSHCUTTERS
BAY BOOKS

MURDER ON
FEDERAL STREET

Foreword by Carlos Acevedo   SEAN NAM

Interior book design: Najdan Mancic
Cover design: Sunjin Nam
Front cover photograph courtesy Peltz Boxing Promotions, Inc.

ISBN 979-8218137298

To Sam and Sumi

It's perversion. Don't you see what it is? It's not natural. To go to great expense for something you want, that's natural. To reach out to take it, that's human, that's natural. But to get your pleasure from not taking? From cheating yourself deliberately [...] from not getting, from not taking? Don't you see what a black thing that is for a man to do?

JOHN GARFIELD

in *Force of Evil*

Life throbbed so strong,
How should they dream that Death in a rosy clime
Would come to thin their shining throng?
Youth feels immortal, like the gods sublime.

HERMAN MELVILLE,

"Balls Bluff"

Billy Giles, the trainer of Hector Camacho: *He's (Camacho) a fighter, but he'll never be someone for kids to look up to. He gets guys in the street mad at him, the wrong guys.*

Michael Katz: *How will he end up?*

Giles: *Like Tyrone Everett, maybe worse.*

THE NEW YORK TIMES,

January 18, 1985

TABLE OF CONTENTS

FOREWORD

SURELY ONE OF only a few prizefighters to inspire a hopscotch rhyme, Tyrone "The Butterfly" Everett seemed on the verge of stardom when he stepped into the Spectrum on November 30, 1976, to challenge Alfredo Escalera for the WBC super featherweight title. Undefeated, talented, handsome, controversial—Everett was twenty-three years old and seemingly destined for glory. In less than six months, on May 26, 1977, he would be dead, murdered under mysterious circumstances. Carolyn McKendrick, the woman who confessed to fatally shooting Everett in her bedroom, claimed she had blasted him with a .30 Carbine Ruger Blackhawk in pre-emptive self-defense after enduring months of physical abuse.

That much, at least, is public record. So is the presence of thirty-nine packets of heroin at the crime scene and, in one of the most startling twists of all, an eyewitness named Tyrone "Terry" Price, a cross-dressing drug runner who may or may not have been caught in flagrante with Everett on the day of the shooting.

What is less known is how the shadow of the Philadelphia underworld obscured the death of Everett and may have even altered its aftermath. In *Murder on Federal Street*, Sean Nam delves into the murky Philadelphia drug scene of the 1970s to reveal, for the first time, the events behind one of the most lurid crimes of its day.

Murder on Federal Street highlights how boxing is rotted from the inside (the ubiquitous corruption typical of unregulated industries) and beyond (the street culture that leads so many underprivileged men to fight for a living). Everett suffered from both ends of this crooked overlap as well as the severe judgment of the ornery Philadelphia fight crowd. "A southpaw who preferred to box his way to a decision, Tyrone Everett ignored the stylistic shibboleths of his day," Nam writes. "This made him persona non grata to many fans, especially among the oldsters of the previous generation, whose hearts were naturally aligned with home-grown sluggers such as Bennie Briscoe, the archetype of the style Philadelphia was famous for: come-forward, brain-bashing bravado."

In his only title shot, Everett dropped a bewildering split decision to Alfredo Escalera that triggered chiaroscuro images of the boys in the backroom of an earlier era. Yet even in the 1970s, years after its sporting kingpins had been sentenced to long stretches in prison, organized crime still had a presence in boxing. Indeed, some of the shady figures that appear in *Murder on Federal Street* are holdovers from the mafioso heyday of the 1940s and 1950s: Frank "Blinky" Palermo, pop-eyed ex-sidekick of fight-racket capo Frankie Carbo, and "Honest" Bill Daly, for years a moving target of athletic commissioners and congressional committees. To escape the criminal dragnet that eventually ensnared Carbo and Palermo in the early 1960s, Daly conveniently relocated to Puerto Rico.

Although Everett seemed to dominate Escalera for fifteen rounds, the final scorecards—including one submitted by a local judge named Lou Tress—seemed to undermine reality, as boxing often does. "Never in our wildest dreams did we think that we were going to get screwed by the guy from Philly," J Russell Peltz, who promoted the fight, tells Nam. "If I had just done a little bit of homework I would have been aware that he had been involved in a lot of bullshit decisions over the years."

Tress fled ringside before the scores were read. Escalera-Everett remains one of the most infamous results in boxing history—almost certainly a fix—and one of the last frame-ups attributable to the mafia old guard.

But as treacherous as boxing was to Everett, the urban chaos of Philadelphia was even worse. A Casanova in pigtails, Everett was irresistible to women—even if stories of his alleged bisexuality multiplied in the wake of his death—and yet he chose the estranged wife of a homicidal drug dealer named Ricardo McKendrick for his steady. "That's like messing with Scarface's girl or the Godfather's wife," Eddie Everett tells Nam. "You're between two mafia families. They were vicious families."

Carolyn McKendrick, née Swint, came from a family driven (and riven) by the drug trade. Several of her brothers had either been imprisoned or slain as a result of their hustling. Even so, the Swints were small-time compared to Ricardo McKendrick, who had ties to bloodthirsty royalty: the Black Mafia, a ruthless organization that not only controlled heroin trafficking in Philadelphia but also participated in several other acts of bloody mayhem. With a criminal record that went back to his teens, McKendrick was also suspected of participating in one of the most gruesome gangland slayings of the early 1970s. "The victim in this case was fellow Black Mafia member George 'Bo' Abney," writes Nam, "whose body was found on a highway, but his head was discovered swaddled in a pillowcase on the footsteps of a downtown Philadelphia bar."

According to Eddie Everett, Tyrone had been nervous for days leading up to his death, right after a sit-down with Ricardo McKendrick. Did McKendrick have something to do with the murder of Tyrone Everett? Were the rumors of hitmen nothing more than idle street talk? Where did all the heroin at the crime scene come from, and how did it factor into the shooting? Did Carolyn McKendrick take the fall for her husband, Ricardo?

A downtown courtroom would eventually expose a shocking tale of drugs, jealousy, cross-dressing, sex, betrayal, and domestic abuse, with Carolyn mounting a defense based on the nascent battered woman syndrome. Of the Black Mafia and the possibility that Ricardo McKendrick was somehow involved—hardly a word.

To shed light on the labyrinthine career and death of Everett, Nam tracked down several key figures involved, including his manager, Frank Gelb; his promoter J. Russell Peltz; his brother Eddie Everett; and several other significant players. For months, Carolyn McKendrick, who served five years in prison on a third-degree murder conviction, remained elusive. Eventually, Nam caught up with McKendrick, receiving a phone call from her that can only be considered inscrutable.

Sean Nam has written for *The Cruelest Sport, Hannibal Boxing, The Sweet Science, Boxing News, USA Today,* and *Boxing Scene,* but he has also been a contributor to the *Dublin Review of Books, Cineaste,* the *Brooklyn Rail,* and *Atlas Obscura.* These broad cultural interests underscore his vivid portrait of a complex time. *Murder on Federal Street* is a panoramic view of urban decay, organized crime, race relations, and boxing history. At its heart is the lost promise of a young man named Tyrone Everett, who understood just how fleeting his chances of fortune in boxing were. "I figured I'd win the title by the time I was twenty-two or twenty-three," Everett told a sportswriter the day before he died. "But now I'm twenty-four and I'm still not there. It worries me. After a while your legs don't move like you want them to. You have so many disappointments you begin to lose the desire to succeed. You don't want to go to the gym that much anymore. In this game, a twenty-five or twenty-six-year-old man can be old when he's fighting a kid of nineteen."

In the end, Tyrone Everett never reached the grand old age of twenty-six. And the girls on the Philadelphia streets with their "Ty, Ty, Butterfly" rhyme? How long did they chant his name?

CARLOS ACEVEDO

New York City
November 2022

INTRODUCTION

I T W A S O N L Y a boxing match, to be sure, but the fate of a city seemed to hang in the balance on the night of November 30, 1976, when Tyrone Everett challenged Alfredo Escalera for the WBC super featherweight title at the Spectrum arena in Philadelphia. The 16,019 fans who showed up that night—a record for an indoor boxing match in the state of Pennsylvania— were starving for a new sporting hero on whom they could hang their most impossible dreams, and Everett, a brash and handsome twenty-three-year-old African American lefty with a high school diploma in welding from the blighted neighborhood of South Philadelphia, was more than eager to fill in the vacancy.

It was not a particularly buoyant period for the city of Philadelphia, or the country at large, for that matter. Inflation was skyrocketing, racial tensions were cresting, and it was evident that the nation was still reeling from the merry-go-round of scandals from the past decade: MLK and RFK, My Lai and Kent State and, of course, Watergate. But in 1976, the trade winds were starting to pick up in Philadelphia, at least in the cultural realm. That October, the 76ers had signed ABA star Julius Erving to a landmark deal that would, in short order, spark a sea-change for the struggling basketball franchise. Almost two months later, Sylvester Stallone premiered *Rocky*, introducing millions to a slack-jawed, Italian American debt collector turned boxing underdog from Philadelphia, an unabashed pop culture avatar for a defeatist age. One week later, Tyrone Everett, with thirty-four straight wins under his belt, stepped into the ring at the Spectrum to attempt what the Eagles, the Flyers, the Phillies, and the 76ers were not expected to do that year. He was going to bring the city, his home, a championship.

Or so he thought.

Today, the Escalera-Everett bout is mostly a forgotten affair, a footnote for check-listing boxing aficionados. But at the time, it was a tentpole event, the first world title fight to land in the City of Brotherly Love since Joey Giardello traded punches with Rubin "Hurricane" Carter in 1964. For the lead promoter J Russell Peltz, a precocious, twenty-nine-year-old dyed-in-the-wool boxing fanatic from the suburbs of Bala Cynwyd, the show was the crowning achievement of six years of relentless toil to reinstate a tradition of competitive fighting in his hometown. Boxing in Philadelphia had an illustrious history dating back to the turn of the 20th century, but it had been in a tortured rut for more than two decades. That all changed in the 1970s, thanks mostly to Peltz, whose bold matchmaking and consumer-oriented focus brought about what would later be referred to as the last golden age of Philadelphia boxing. And there was no stronger symbolism in support of this total reversal of fortune than the fact that, in 1976, a world championship fight was taking place within city limits once again.

The irony, however, was that a significant swath of the public had mixed feelings about the man tasked with winning a boxing title for the city. A southpaw who preferred to box his way to a decision, Tyrone Everett ignored the stylistic shibboleths of his day. This made him persona non grata to many fans, especially among the oldsters of the previous generation, whose hearts were naturally aligned with home-grown sluggers such as Bennie Briscoe, the archetype of the style Philadelphia was famous for: come-forward, brain-bashing bravado. Everett also had a few personality quirks that rubbed the local denizens the wrong way, chief among them was his inclination for show-boating and gloating at his opponents, something that may seem benign and routine today but was at that time considered verboten by the upright cognoscenti. Still, for a time, outside of Briscoe, nobody was drawing better in Philadelphia than Everett. His support hailed chiefly from his stomping grounds, the Black locales of South Philadelphia, which included, uniquely, a significant number of sloe-eyed, heart-throbbing female fans. To the male audience, Everett was "The Mean Machine," and for the little girls who would hopscotch on the sidewalks, he was "Ty, Ty … little butterfly." [1] As the oldest of five boys, raised improbably by a single mother within gang-infested, poverty-stricken environs, Everett never quite had the chance to convert the rags of his youth into untold riches, but his short life was nothing if not memorable.

If Everett failed to endear himself to certain circles, a victory over Escalera, he figured, would make him respected, irreproachable. They would have to love him at that point. No doubt, there was a lot on the line for Everett on November 30. A win on that night would have put him alongside Muhammad Ali, his stylistic and attitudinal forebear, as the only other

---

[1] Everett's delicate moniker, mentioned in newspaper articles at the time, is disputed by his brother and promoter, neither of whom have ever heard it be applied to Everett.

U.S.-born fighter at the time to hold a world title; it would have made him only the second 130-pound fighter from Philadelphia to win a title (Benny Bass being the first when he defeated Tod Morgan in 1928); finally, a win would have ensured him the kind of posthumous recognition that entirely eludes him today. Of course, as the record shows, Everett would go on to lose a bitterly contested decision, one that still stirs the bile in those who witnessed it.

After watching Everett rake the Puerto Rican Escalera with right-hand counters through fifteen rounds, countless observers could fathom no other conclusion than a clear points win for Everett. It was as clinical a vivisection as one could expect in Philadelphia, where fighters approached the pugilist's craft with far more brutish methods. Everett had barely been touched, save for a handful of solid rights. In fact, the biggest blow that Escalera landed was the one he delivered with his teeth, one of which chipped off of Everett's forehead in the pivotal 13th round, requiring the challenger to finish out the final three rounds of the fight through a mask of blood. Barring a knockout, however, boxing verdicts are always produced at the discretion of three individuals, and in this case, two of the judges indicated on their scorecards that Escalera had turned in the superior performance. Most controversially, one of them, Lou Tress, was from Philadelphia. Alas, the championship would return to San Juan. In a list of the twelve worst decisions in boxing history, the late Harold Lederman put Escalera-Everett at the top of the heap, ahead of such infamous blunders as Pernell Whitaker vs. Julio Cesar Chavez and Lennox Lewis vs. Evander Holyfield.

The ensuing outrage was both swift and, sadly, all too ineffectual. No matter how much the Everett camp protested, the original decision would stand pat, a stone slab over the controversy. A pernicious fog hung over the boxing establishment in Philadelphia for months, years. Nobody could quite shake off the feeling that they had been swindled, as if they had been pawns in an elaborate con. Eventually, some clues here and there would turn up, like seashells in the sand, suggesting that there were more than just a few shenanigans afoot before, during, and after that bout, enough, at least, for Peltz to claim, years later, that the fight had been fixed. "There's no doubt in my mind that it was rigged," Peltz would say.

There were calls for an immediate rematch, and here the Everett camp had more luck. After the usual hemming and hawing of boxing negotiations, Escalera-Everett II was scheduled for June, this time in Puerto Rico. But the day for redress would never come. On May 26, 1977, Everett was discovered in a pool of blood in the bedroom of his girlfriend's clapboard home in South Philadelphia. He had been shot in the head with a single bullet. Parked outside the home was his prized beige Cadillac Coupe de Ville. Inside, on the dining room table, were a panoply of drugs, including thirty-nine neatly packaged glassine bags of heroin, whose ownership would never be determined. The murder weapon, assumed to be a Ruger Blackhawk pistol, would never turn up. His manager Frank Gelb, who had to identify the body at the hospital morgue, would have nightmares "for many, many years." Everett was twenty-four. "A Dream Died at 2710 Federal Street," read the headline the next day in the *Philadelphia Daily News*.

The girlfriend was named Carolyn McKendrick, a married woman who had fallen head-over-heels for the hotshot boxer two years prior. Pretty, well-spoken, and impeccably dressed, McKendrick would confess to the crime of shooting her live-in boyfriend—but not without justification. During a two-week trial that had the whole city rapt with suspense, McKendrick claimed that she had shot her lover because she believed she caught him cheating on her with a gay drug pusher, Tyrone Price. The top witness for the prosecution, Price was allegedly inside the home that day. In many ways, there could not have been a more dissonant assertion made about Everett, who, in addition to his well-noted reputation as a boxer, was also a notorious Casanova who seemingly treated the whole of South Philadelphia as an extension of his boudoir. At the time of his death, he left behind three children (with one more on the way). He was a ladies' man, his closest friends and family would say in his defense; Carolyn should have known better than to harbor any feelings of jealousy. By the same logic, his supporters brushed aside any imputation of homosexuality. Although Price, who was also a crossdresser, swore on the stand that he never had sexual relations with Everett, the association would henceforth brand the fallen boxer with a searing scarlet letter. Bring up Tyrone Everett today to those who are familiar with him and more times than not, the most common response is along the lines of, "He's the one that was in bed with another guy, right?"

It was more than a crime of passion, however. In alleging that McKendrick had been the subject of domestic violence, the defense found its trump card. Multiple witnesses, including one of Everett's brothers, took the stand to relate the number of times they had seen Everett subdue McKendrick with his hands. Wracked by love and jealousy, with welts on her face and body, Carolyn McKendrick, so went the defense, was a "love slave" who had finally decided she was not going to suffer any longer. (This was around the time that public awareness of the rights of female murderers reached a fever pitch, thanks to the landmark trials of Joan Little and Francine Hughes. Incidentally, the latter case was litigated the same year as McKendrick's and was responsible for ushering into the general lexicon the term "battered woman syndrome.") The message stuck with the jury. In the end, McKendrick wound up with a third-degree murder verdict, a far lesser penalty than the first degree sought by the prosecution, netting her a relatively meager five-year stint in prison. Given the circumstances, her defense attorney would later wonder if the outcome was not, in effect, a victory.

But as with the Escalera decision, the conclusion of the trial left his loved ones in a state of gnawing bitterness. Everett's mother Doris and his brother Eddie were never satisfied by the official story, going so far as to claim that McKendrick may not have been the trigger-person, that there had been far more insidious forces working behind the curtain, pulling the strings. The two sourced their alternative narrative from the fact that McKendrick's husband was a renowned drug dealer, who kept dangerous company. They were "cold-blooded and vicious drug people," Doris would say years later. "When [Everett] took up with her, I said that is not good news. I told him to leave her alone. I never did like her." Unbeknownst to many at the time of the trial and in the decades to come, the Everett family was essentially voicing concern about the Black Mafia, one of the most vicious criminal organizations in the Philadelphia underworld of the 1970s. The tantalizing intersections between that group and the circumstances of the Everett murder were never clearly delineated, only hinted at, and are described here for the first time.

A crooked decision, a tragic death, and, finally, obscurity. A simple search for "Tyrone Everett" on YouTube will turn up exactly one fight under his name, a blotchy rendering of an otherwise dull mismatch. His other fights remain shut away in 16mm film cans, in private collections, undigitized, decaying. Fighters today from Philadelphia love to bring up their city's rich ancestral past, like Briscoe, but they rarely mention Everett in their reminiscences. Perhaps things would have been different had Everett hung on for a bit longer. After all, the late 1970s saw the sport swept up by a television boom and the rise of Atlantic City as a boxing hotbed. Most of all, Everett had the adversaries he needed to create a legitimate fighting legacy. Given his lofty spot atop the rankings, there is every reason to believe that he would have had opportunities to trade punches with some of the greatest champions of the era, like Alexis Arguello (whom Escalera would go on to face twice, losing both times), Bobby Chacon, Rafael Limon, and Cornelius Boza-Edwards to name a few. One of the stipulations in the contract for his Escalera fight, in the event of a win, was a four-bout contract with Top Rank, perhaps the most successful boxing promotional company in history. There was talk that his final fight in that partnership could lead to a showdown against the Panamanian dynamo Roberto Duran. We will never know.

PROLOGUE

A DEATH IN THE FAMILY

I've been dreaming a lot lately. I see myself coming into the ring, I have the championship belt around my waist, I wear a different colored robe for every fight, tomorrow it'll be rose pink, not baby pink, rose pink, and when I step into the ring in something like that, and the lights go down, and the spotlight hits me, I hear all the girls in the audience screaming, 'Whoo-eee, look at Tyrone Everett.' Then I dream, 'How can I lose hearing those girls screaming for me like that?' What a dream.

—TYRONE EVERETT
to the *Philadelphia Inquirer*, Nov. 29, 1976

May 31, 1977.

T HE GIRLS WERE screaming again. This time they wore starchy black dresses with white cloche hats and sat elbow-to-elbow along weather-beaten pews of the New Light Beulah Baptist Church. A handsome, 19th-century building made of serpentine stone, the New Light Beulah Baptist Church stood on the northwest corner of Bainbridge and 17th streets, a busy artery in South Philadelphia. It was a sweltering Tuesday evening, and though the sun hung low on the skyline, the acrid summer air lingered unabated, like a weekend morning hangover. It was, in other words, hardly an ideal day to congregate in a limited indoor space with questionable air conditioning, but the roughly 1,100 men and women who were packed inside the New Light Beulah Baptist Church, a number that far exceeded the usual Sabbath attendance, were not thinking about the potential for heatstroke or the fact that their very gathering, as they stewed in conditions that were subtropic, posed a distinct fire hazard. There were other things on their mind, things that blunted their usual responsiveness to such risks.

No one would ever forget the heat, but they would also never forget the noise. It was one collective moan that ebbed and flowed with disturbing uniformity, punctuated only by piercing caterwauls that skirted the edge of sanity. The girls were screaming, yes, as were their mothers, sisters, aunts, and cousins. They rocked from side to side, wailing, as they fanned themselves off and dabbed away at the sweat and tears smearing their faces. The men, meanwhile, looked on in silence, their stoicism betrayed only by a moist glaze in their eyes. South Philadelphia had never experienced a tragedy like this. It was a threnody for the ages.

There was not an empty seat in sight, not on the main floor, not on the balcony. From runty schoolchildren to local barflies, from the city's top brass—mayor Frank Rizzo—to heavyweight emeritus Joe Frazier, it seemed all of Philadelphia had descended on this point, all gathered pell-mell to secure a final glimpse at Tyrone Everett, resting inside the casket at the front of the chapel. His hands were placed over a pocket-sized Bible. A diamond ring adorned his right index finger. Towering over the body were large baskets containing bursts of white carnations and camellias. Farther behind stood a resplendent all-female choir draped in robes of red, beige, blue, black, and maroon belting out the lines to a hymn by Joseph Medlicott Scriven.

> *What a friend we have in Jesus,*
> *all our sins and griefs to bear!*
> *What a privilege to carry*
> *everything to God in prayer!*
> *O what peace we often forfeit,*
> *O what needless pain we bear,*
> *All because we do not carry*
> *everything to God in prayer!*

Propped up by an easel, off to the side, was a charcoal portrait of Everett wearing boxing trunks and posing in the familiar fighter's stance: hands curled into fists and held at chin level, while his eyes penetrated the picture plane with a glare. It would have been a standard boxing portrait, the kind often seen catching dust in old mahogany bars, were it not for the pair of conspicuous celestial accessories adorning the subject. Two plumes serving as wings sprouted behind his shoulders and above his modest afro, a halo. Tyrone, the angel.

Yet pictures often have a way of contorting their meaning to fit the circumstances, and this one was no exception. For one, it was completed some three years earlier, back when

Everett was still alive and busy tenderizing the calloused faces of hard-bitten men with hair-trigger right hooks; when he was considered by most observers to be one of the world's top lightweight contenders and the best on the East Coast; when he could still be spotted prowling the city in his off-yellow Cadillac Coupe de Ville and dancing away nights at Palumbo's with lovelorn girls. The angelic embellishments in the portrait were meant to underscore how he had challenged the received image of the prototypical Philadelphia prizefighter. Amid the backdrop of drugs, violence, and urban decay that characterized so much of life south of South Street, Everett did practically seem like an angel.

> *Can we find a friend so faithful,*
> *Who will all our sorrows share?*
> *Jesus knows our every weakness,*
> *Take it to the Lord in prayer.*

But there was nothing angelic or peaceful or nostalgic about this valediction at the New Light Beulah Baptist Church. A cadre of fleet-footed nurses in white garb shunted up and down the aisles trying to lend a hand to the bone-tired and unsteady, while helmeted police officers were scattered about like chess pieces, attempting to keep the peace. It was a scene that could have belonged on the Western Front. For the girls, in any case, it was a far, far cry from those Tuesday night fights at the Spectrum when they would show up in frill-laden cashmere coats to root for their man, screaming as he made his way out of the dark tunnel and into the ring—and into their hearts.

Outside, traffic slowed to a tugboat pace. A crowd reported to be as large as 3,000 milled desperately in front of the church, spilling out onto the street. The ones closest to the entrance waved five-dollar bills furiously at the doorkeeper's face, as if Marvin Gaye or the O'Jays were just beyond the threshold. But Frank Talent, an emcee whose day job consisted of fielding complaints for the municipal courthouse, was not the type to be greased. He held his ground like a solitary seawall against a tidal surge. He thought it a shame that these folks had to linger out here and wondered why the funeral was not being held at the Spectrum, where only three days earlier, Elvis, lady-killer incarnate, had dashed off one of his final, drug-debauched performances. Not only would the Spectrum have been able to accommodate everyone, but the venue would also have carried the proper symbolic significance. After all, it was at the Spectrum where Everett first got all those girls to scream, "where he got his name and fame."

Bedlam continued to roil inside the church. In a way, Mike Everett was partly to blame. Mike had insisted on an open casket for the occasion, which seemed like the appropriate thing to do since his brother was known for his pretty face, the prime object of his intractable vanity. Pretty faces were hard to come by in South Philadelphia, where the men had mugs as rough-hewn as the cast iron molds pounded out at the local foundries. That Everett was able to keep his visage unmarred in a profession that routinely invited such aftereffects was a source of unfailing pride. But what Mike really wanted to communicate to the world was that his brother, even in the moment of his brutal death, had somehow managed to escape disfiguration, despite the fact that it was his face that had been the target of a single bullet fired from a Ruger Blackhawk pistol. The bullet that ended his life should have smattered his forehead, gouged his eye, cleaved through his cheekbone, and left him looking like a Francis Bacon portrait. Instead, the bullet traveled through his right nostril and exited the back of his skull, thus preserving the natural proportions of his face. Even in death, Tyrone Everett looked virtually untouchable.

But the funeral was getting out of hand. Far from quelling the collective sorrow, the open casket seemed to amplify it. The wails reached another octave midway through the viewing, just as the Everett family—the mother Doris and her four remaining sons—filed into the chapel and seated themselves in the front pew. Doris was wrapped up in the arms of Jerry, one of the youngest of the Everett brothers. A few more women collapsed to the floor. One nearly met her own death after losing her footing near the low balustrade on the balcony. In an effort to restore some semblance of order, one junior pastor from the church read from the 9th Psalm—Have mercy upon me, O Lord; consider my trouble which I suffer of them that hate me, thou that liftest me up from the gates of death—and a family friend belted out the lyrics to "It's So Hard to Say Goodbye to Yesterday," but neither succeeded in tempering the surging heartache of the mourners.

Another pastor tried shaming them instead. "Save it for tomorrow," he intoned. "One day death is coming at your door. You going to be stretched out. Somebody got to come to your funeral … let's throw our arms around this mother.

You had a mother. It hurts. You don't know how it hurts."
Clearly, though, something else had to be done—something
had to give. So Mike, now the oldest Everett brother, decided
to shut the casket. The sound of a dry thud cast a momentary
chill in the room. The wailing receded. They moved on with
the service. In his monologue, Reverend Taylor C. Killebrew
read from a eulogy penned by the Everett family. "He always
had a smile for everyone he came in contact," he said. "Always
giving and doing something for everyone."

When the service was over, when all the necessary rites
had been completed, the casket was opened once more for
viewing, but only on the condition that the attendees behave
themselves. The family was up first.

Eddie, the third oldest, broke down in a heap as he lifted
the black veil from his brother's face and left a kiss. "You
taught me everything I know," he cried. "You gave me a
will to live. You were like a father to me. I'm going to miss
you, Tyrone."

His mother followed. Doris walked gingerly to the casket,
her body leaning against Mike. Like Eddie, she lifted the
veil and planted a kiss. Moments later, in the hallway, Doris
crumbled to the floor, shouting her dead son's name.

The burial took place the next morning. Chaperoned by
a cavalcade of fifty cars, the body was whisked away from
the New Light Beulah Baptist Church to Eden Cemetery
in Collingdale, a small town some ten miles away from
Philadelphia. It was another sunbaked day. Reverend
Killebrew made his last liturgical pronouncements as three

hundred people watched the casket lowered into the seething dark of the earth.

• • •

ON AND OFF for the past several years, Eddie Everett has organized The Family of Boxers Award ceremony, a humble but inspired grassroots function honoring local Philadelphia fighters, old-timers, and up-and-comers alike. Among the half-dozen or so awards that are handed out is the Tyrone Everett Award, a prize given to a young fighter, usually a prospect or rising contender, of promising vintage, just like the eponymous figure himself. Past recipients of this distinction have included Jesse Hart, who won it in 2012. At the time, Hart—who would twice go on to challenge, unsuccessfully, for a super middleweight title—was just starting out as a professional, yet that did not mean he was a complete unknown. As the son of Eugene "Cyclone" Hart, one of the middleweights responsible for sparking the resurgence of the Philadelphia boxing scene in the 1970s, Hart was of distinguished pugilistic stock. Indeed, on the day of the ceremony, it was his father Eugene who went up to the podium to receive the plaque on his behalf, thus bringing a certain symmetry to the proceedings. And that, clearly, was the point of this modest assembly. Not so much to build prestige—no one will ever confuse the Family of Boxers with the International Boxing Hall of Fame or the more local Bennie Briscoe Awards—but to bring together fathers and sons, to bridge the present to the past. For Eddie, moreover, the awards were one way for him to stay tied to the sport that had defined much of his early life and, most of all, to help him keep alive the memory of his late brother, an effort one imagines is not dissimilar to a man standing on a street corner trying to light a cigarette on a blustery night.

"All of his history is with me," Eddie said one afternoon. "Michael has a bit of dementia, so he don't really remember much about Tyrone's career." Michael, who goes by Mike, was for the first two decades of his life the second oldest Everett brother and the second-best boxer in the family. Although he was not as gifted a fighter as Tyrone, Mike was a competent professional and even once fought for the junior welterweight title, in Thailand, no less, just three months after the death of his brother. Mike ended up succumbing to the champion in six rounds. That was the beginning of the end of his fight career. Without the stewardship of his older brother, his taste for combat drastically dissipated. Mike lost four of his next five fights and retired in 1979, shortly before his twenty-fifth birthday. Eddie, on the other hand, had soured on the fight game much earlier, quitting after only three professional fights. Unlike his brothers, Eddie could not stomach the paltry remuneration that the sport offered to its unheralded prospects. "I loved boxing, but I didn't think it was worth the risk," he said. "It's the best decision I made at that age." Instead, Eddie went into the public sector. He retired recently after decades of employment under the Southeastern

Pennsylvania Transportation Authority. Now, he is the de facto custodian of his brother's legacy.

"Growing up, everybody had a hero," Eddie remembered fondly. "Doctor J, whatever. My hero was Tyrone. He was amazing. I was proud to be his brother. To me, he was bigger than life. Tyrone was the Elvis Presley, the Michael Jordan of South Philly. For him to be my brother was an honor to me. If Tyrone wanted to be a gang member, I would've joined a gang. I followed him. They still talk about him in South Philly.

"I learned everything from him. I wanted to be like him. Everything he did, I did. He was good with the girls; I became good with the girls. He taught me how to fight, taught me how to dress. He molded me and carried me when I wasn't as strong as him."

Their father was mostly absent during their childhood, so, naturally, the Everett brothers looked to the eldest for paternal direction. When Tyrone Everett started boxing, the others followed suit. It was in boxing that the brothers found self-worth, dignity, structure. In boxing, the oldest Everett was peerless.

"There was nobody in the gym that could handle Tyrone," Eddie said. "I don't care what size you were. He was vicious. He would get in the ring, and he would knock people out. He would box four or five guys in a day in the gym and he would hurt everybody. He was exceptionally strong. And he could take a punch. You couldn't be as good as he was unless you can take punishment. As good as he was, his strongest thing was that he could take punishment. He didn't like getting hit.'

"We was in the store one time and a kid came up to him and asked him if he liked boxing and he looked at him crazy, like, 'No!' He didn't like getting hit. People thought he loved boxing. He did, he just didn't like getting hit. But he could take a punch better than anybody in the gym, than anybody I know. He knew he had the talent. But he didn't like it. He knew the danger of getting hit. Even though he could take his punch, he had a style where he didn't get hit a lot. He didn't want to end up punchy at the end of his career. Everett wanted a short career; he wanted to get in and out."

In the Everett household, boxing died along with Tyrone.

"The thing about it is that none of our sons got into boxing," Eddie said. "It ended with us. We didn't introduce them to it at all. [Tyrone's] youngest son is identical to him, but he sells cars. He's like a millionaire. His oldest son is doing well, too. And he has two daughters. So, they're doing well. But I know that not having a father has left their life empty."

PART ONE

CHAPTER ONE

Love of the chase is an inherent delight in man.

—CHARLES DARWIN

Norristown, Pennsylvania, 1969.

LEROY ROBERTS CAUGHT himself doing it again. He was staring at the clock, wishing the hands would twitch a little quicker. It was another day on the beat for Roberts, one of the few Black patrolmen on the Norristown police force, and the long hours of the afternoon were starting to grate on him. He nodded at the usual faces as he made his way down the sidewalk, his tall and muscular frame exuding the placid might of the Law. On the inside, though, he was all ruffled. Roberts was twenty-seven years old, and he had not anticipated that his new profession would be so under-whelming. For most of his adult life he plugged away as a moonlighting boxer, earning extra money by sinking his fists into the skulls of other men. Now, this sudden shift to a more conventional nine-to-five lifestyle was proving to be a more difficult adjustment than he had ever expected. Often, out of the blue, Roberts would start shadowboxing. The old habits were coming back to haunt him.

Roberts had boxed for nearly a decade, and during that time he had cultivated a reputation as a puncher. He went by the moniker "Hurricane." For a while, he was even considered hot goods. In fact, it was only three years prior, in 1966, when he was twenty-four, that *The Ring*, the self-styled "Bible of Boxing," had Roberts pinned as high as seven in the welterweight rankings, when Roberts had upset undefeated contender Ted Whitfield in Portland, Maine. Whitfield, at the time, was ranked third. The win put Roberts on the map. Roberts was soaring. Of all the pugs out there laboring at this godforsaken craft, he, Leroy Roberts of Norristown, Pennsylvania, was heralded as the number seven welterweight by the greatest authority in the land. Roberts was 12-2 and his future seemed to blaze ahead of him. Then, just two fights later, he ran into Joe Shaw, a Brooklynite with kettlebells for hands, who dropped him four times before the referee waived off the bout in the fifth round. Before Roberts even had a chance to dry off, *The Ring* bumped him off its vaunted list.

But Roberts would rebound, winning his next two fights. He hopscotched to Paris and pulled off a stoppage over local hero Robert Gallois. Roberts liked Paris so much that he went back again to face former European champion Jean Josselin, but he was not so lucky this time. The fight was stopped on cuts, and Josselin was declared the winner. His fortunes hardly improved. The next time he ducked through the ropes was at the Forum in Inglewood, California, and staring across from him was the great Cuban-Mexican welterweight Jose Napoles. At the opening bell, Napoles rushed at Roberts and never let up. It was a back-alley mugging. Roberts never made it out of the first round. From there, the losses simply snow-balled. He capped a five-fight slide with a brutal second-round kayo loss at the hands of Brazilian champion Joao Henrique in Sao Paolo. The dream was over. Roberts swore off boxing, went back to Norristown, and signed up with the local police department. His record stood at thirteen wins against eight losses with four knockouts.

In many ways, it should have been an ideal setup. Unlike other boxing journeymen, Roberts was a natural homebody. Now he could settle down in Norristown, spend time with his family, and draw a decent salary. But what he did not expect after a few months of being on the police force was how much of the sport was still churning inside of him. Boxing, admittedly, was a grueling career choice, but Roberts felt more at peace in the ring than anywhere else in the world. In the ring, he knew who he was. In the ring, he had some semblance of control, whatever the outcome. And now, barely six months into his retirement, Roberts was beginning to feel the hand of some atavistic demiurge working on him, bewitching him, pleading with him to give the sport another shot. Before he knew it, Roberts was back to doing his road work at dawn, before his shift, trotting down the same well-worn psychic path as thousands of would-be boxing retirees before him.

Roberts unburdened his concerns to his friend Frank Gelb, a tall, gregarious family man who owned a furniture store that Roberts frequently passed by on his daily rounds. Frank dressed to the hilt and wore oversized tinted glasses à la the film producer Robert Evans. The two hit it off from the start. On his off days from the force, Roberts would come by the shop and help Frank with truck deliveries. They would have long conversations on any number of topics, but they usually circled back to Roberts recounting one of his zany boxing tales as a rapt-eyed Frank listened. Boxing was an exotic country to Frank, and Roberts was his Rudyard Kipling, a natural raconteur whose recollections reminded him that there was more to life than the sleepy habitat that he occupied in Northeast Pennsylvania. Roberts knew that if he was going to make a second run at the sport, he would need some bureaucratic support. For most of his career, Roberts had handled his own business, with an occasional assist, he would often joke, from his five-year-old son. But he was tired of having to arrange his own bouts, making around-the-clock calls to crabby matchmakers. He needed a manager, and he thought Frank was the man for the job.

◆ ◆ ◆

FRANK GELB GREW up in the postwar milieu of suburban Wynnefield, an idyllic Jewish stronghold on the northern edge of West Philadelphia. He was conscripted into the family furniture business at an early age, learning the rudiments of the trade at every level. The idea, of course, was that he would one day take over the shop from his father Maurice, who in turn had inherited it from his own father. That was the way things were done in the Gelb household. It was a close-knit family with close-knit ambitions.

The original store, Newmore Home Furnishings, was located in the commercial district of West Philadelphia on 61st and Market, a predominantly Black neighbor-hood that had once been, until the 1950s, mostly white. Less than two miles away from the store was Overbrook High, where Gelb attended school and was classmates with Wilt Chamberlain. After classes, Gelb would help out at the store, usually taking charge of the most thankless of menial tasks: going door-to-door to collect payments from customers on the installment plan. It was work that would instill in Gelb a bare-bones business sensibility. That sensi-bility would not only serve him well in his future capacity as the future owner of the store but also, when the time came, as a manager in the freewheeling, outlaw country of boxing. By 1969, when he was thirty-two, Gelb was running the furniture store in Norristown, a suburb half an hour north of Philadelphia. Married to his high school sweetheart, and with four children, Gelb, who turned down college to serve in the Navy, had carved out a solidly white-picket-fence existence for himself, enjoying all the Baby Boomer trappings that came with it. But with every sale of a teak table or wicker chair, Gelb's outlook dimmed, and he felt more and more the disquiet that creeps up in those with unfulfilled ambitions. Furniture provided a fine safety net, sure, but Gelb, who saw his future laid out like a smooth, unruffled rug, shuddered nonetheless at the prospect of having to flip through upholstery swatches for the rest of his life. In the back of his mind, he wanted out, out of the tedium that threatened to chain him down to a humdrum existence. Luckily for Gelb, the local patrolman on the beat was daydreaming just as hard on the job as well.

Roberts was an object of endless fascination for Frank, whose station in life was not conducive to meeting journeyman boxers or other "off the grid" members of the citizenry. Frank never tired of listening to Roberts spin yarn about his career and those trips to Paris and Sao Paolo. Wanderlust, unlike Roberts, coursed through Frank's veins. When Roberts approached him about becoming his manager, Gelb hardly batted an eye. He had found his ticket out of Norristown.

"Roberts just happened to say to me one day, 'I'm not getting anywhere, Frank, maybe you can help me. You look like a good businessman,'" Gelb recalled. "I was young, aggressive, and I liked boxing, so I said, 'Why not.' My family loved Roberts. He was an unusual character. He was a family member to us. That's how I got into the meat of the boxing business."

"We got together more as pals looking for a chance to travel than as business associates," Gelb would later say.

Next on the agenda was to find a fight for Roberts, but with local shows becoming scarcer in recent years, this was a more challenging task than it appeared. Gelb was scouring the paper one day, in September 1969, when he turned the page to a story touting the arrival of a new college-aged promoter on the Philadelphia boxing scene who had apparently decided to ditch his staff position at the *Philadelphia Bulletin* after he was turned down for the boxing beat. The name flashed at Gelb like a neon billboard in Times Square: J Russell Peltz. Somehow it rang a bell, even if Gelb, judging from the accompanying photograph, had trouble placing this upstart with his horn-rimmed glasses and snazzy peacoat and whose dark moustache and deadpan stare could hardly conceal the almost ridiculous fact of his youth. The boxing business was an old man's game, full of the old man's irascibility. Peltz looked like he belonged on Carnaby Street with the rest of the Swinging Sixties set. Gelb flipped through the Yellow Pages. What the hell, he thought. It wouldn't hurt to make a call.

It turned out that Gelb's mother was friends with Peltz's aunt. The two had never met each other, though. "We used to live two, three blocks from each other in Wynnefield," Peltz recalled. "He had called me one day—it must have been before my first fight card. We spoke for a few minutes. Then he hung up and called me back and said, 'Hey, we know each other!' He must have told his mother who he was talking to. He was thirty-two; I was twenty-two."

Gelb and Peltz. Peltz and Gelb. Despite the age gap, the pair would form one of the most fruitful partnerships on the Philadelphia boxing scene in the 1970s, a nexus in which the deficiencies in one would be shored up by the other. "Frank was much more savvy than me," Peltz said. "He didn't go to college, but Frank knew all the angles. I don't mean that in a derogatory way. I'm just a straight nuts and bolts guy, make good fights, ticket sales, you know. Frank knew how to schmooze people. Did you see the Godfather movies? Remember Moe Green—'I made my bones when you were going out with cheerleaders'—and then he got shot in the eye? We used to always say that was Frank—Moe Green."

"So, we made a good team," Peltz continued. "Because he was the front man of the masthead, the logo, the guy who went out making the deals, and I was the guy who went 'We'll fight that guy, we won't fight that guy.' Like, I remember he called me from Hawaii and Everett was over there fighting somebody. The original opponent fell out two, three days before the fight and Frank called me and said if it was OK to fight (the replacement). So those were our roles together. We never had a contract together between us. We just worked together because that's what you could do back then. Gelb was smart. He wasn't the nuts-and-bolts boxing guy. He couldn't tell you who won what, when, where, like the rest of us geeks could, but he was the businessman."

* * *

By the time J Russell Peltz, all of twenty-two years on a beanpole frame, strode into the office of the Pennsylvania State Athletic Commission in September 1969 to pick up his newly minted promoter's license, boxing in Philadelphia was on the downturn, if not in a full-blown decline. Historically, the Quaker town was regarded as a boxing powerhouse, a reputation it had held since the bare-knuckle days of the late 19th century. "Philadelphia" Jack O'Brien, as his moniker suggested, was among the best of the homegrown talents, and Jack Blackburn, a Kentuckian who made his name in Philadelphia, was a top attraction. There were plenty of non-natives who flocked to the city, too, lured mostly by the chance to fetch top dollar for their arduous craft. Joe Gans, Terry McGovern, Bob Fitzsimmons, Jack Johnson, Sam Langford, Harry Greb, and Benny Leonard were just a few of the top out-of-towners who regularly headlined in the city in the early decades of the 20th century.

In 1926, Philadelphia hosted the heavyweight title bout between feral Jack Dempsey and patrician Gene Tunney in front of a paying crowd of 120,000. In the summer of 1952, Herman Taylor, one of the most accomplished promoters of his day, delivered three ballyhooed title fights to the city, all in just a four-month span. More than 100,000 spectators passed through the turnstiles at the open-air Municipal Stadium to see Jersey Joe Walcott edge Ezzard Charles on points (albeit somewhat controversially) in the fourth and final matchup of their rivalry; the flashy veteran Kid Gavilan stop a young but otherwise game Gil Turner in the 11th round of a barnburner; and, most memorably, Rocky Marciano, "The Brockton Blockbuster," unhorse Walcott in the 13th round of a tight contest by landing perhaps the most famous right hand in all of pugilistica. It was boxing Arcadia in Philadelphia. Fat City ... or so it seemed.

Boxing had a pipeline problem, and the cracks were there for anyone to see. The rise of television in the late 1940s had permanently altered the landscape, creating a top-heavy imbalance in which small club shows, the linchpin of the fight game, were left to dry out. Small-time promoters found it increasingly difficult to attract and hold onto their stables, as more and more of their fighters were pulled away from their local ecosystems and fed into the rapacious programming machinery of the idiot box. The waning talent pool, however, was more than just a function of technological dynamics. The post-World War II economic boom and

the passing of the G.I. Bill meant men of the lower classes
had other opportunities—bricklaying, truck driving—they
could pursue that paid better and did not involve taking
left hooks to the chin. Boxing may have been on every
night, but as Arthur Daley of the *New York Times* noted,
the product had been cheapened. It was "give away" television that choked off the lower levels of the boxing food
chain, including the vital amateur scene. But soon enough,
the quality of televised fights also started to crater, thanks to
sponsors like Pabst Blue Ribbon and Gillette, who, in their
everlasting hopes of manufacturing a troupe of synthetic
Great White Hopes who could peddle their products, essentially dictated the matchmaking. In 1952, the year of Taylor's
trifecta, experts suggested that the number of professional
boxers had suffered a fifty-percent decrease. Philadelphia was
hardly alone in this regard. Popular venues in the city, like
the Alhambra and the Met, shuttered. The Cambria, another
well-established club that first opened in 1917, closed its
doors for good in 1963.

By this period, Philadelphia boxing was barren. Gone
were beloved draws such as Joey Giardello and light heavyweight Harold Johnson, both of whom won titles. As the
'60s drew to a close, even the decade's most noteworthy
and popular fighters in Bennie Brisco and Stanley "Kitten"
Hayward were starting to fade from relevance. (The lone
bright spot was the emergence of heavyweight Joe Frazier.)
This malaise extended beyond the fighters and their handlers
and seeped into the consumer base, casting a cynical pall
over its eyes. Even Briscoe, the crowd-friendly brawler, was

beginning to sense that he had outstayed his welcome—in his own hometown, no less. "It's hard for me to understand, but I get a better reception in New York than I do here," Briscoe told the *Philadelphia Daily News* in 1969. "I'm even more popular in Puerto Rico. Jimmy Iselin (his manager) wanted me to fight out of New York, but I just can't make myself do that. All my friends are here. This is my home. I don't want to be a New York City fighter, or a Rhinebeck, N.Y. fighter. I'm from Philadelphia."

Incredibly, the Philadelphia fans went so far as to shower Briscoe with jeers.

"I don't know why they boo," continued Briscoe. "Maybe the people here like boxers, and that's one thing I definitely am not. I hit anything I can see ... If they'd rather see a guy dance around and then hold, that's their choice. Let 'em boo."

Briscoe, of course, was not the first to get the cold shoulder from the "City of Brotherly Love." After he had blown out Floyd Patterson in one round at Comiskey Park in Chicago in 1962 to become the new world heavyweight champion, Sonny Liston, who had at that time made Philadelphia his adopted hometown, expected, or at least hoped for, a homecoming reception that befitted his accomplishment: a key to the city, a photo op with Mayor James H. Tate, the gaggle of fans and press, the whole megillah, short of a ticker-tape parade. But the moment he descended onto the runway at Philadelphia International Airport, Liston was greeted only with the image of an airline crew going about their workaday duties. This humiliating episode would prompt Liston to move to Denver, but not before dropping one of his more infamous lines: "I'd rather be a lamppost in Denver than mayor of Philadelphia."

It was tanking season in Philadelphia. In 1969, Tom Cushman, writing for the *Philadelphia Daily News*, decided to pen a three-part series examining the crumbling state of prizefighting in the city. Cushman solicited the opinion of Herman Taylor, the grand-père of Philadelphia boxing who had been promoting shows since 1912. Taylor, suffice it to say, was not optimistic.

"We used to have a half-dozen clubs in Philadelphia, and we don't have anymore," groused Taylor. "So the young boxer has to try and learn his trade fighting prelims on what cards we can put together. The opportunities aren't very many. Oh, there are a lot of boxers around, if you want to call them that. But most of them are of a very, very, very poor grade. And I, for one, refuse to run a show just for the sake of having a show. I do not believe in staging lopsided matches. I don't want the customers walking away disappointed."

The infrastructure of small club boxing was falling apart; the talent, uncared for, was withering away. And all Taylor, eighty-two years old and ensconced on the second floor of a prim office that sat right above the marquee of the Shubert Theatre (now the Merriam), surrounded by his secretary, matchmaker, and a gallery of vintage photographs of the championship fights that he once promoted—all Taylor could think of doing was to offer up a few Hail Marys.

"You see, it has come to this point," he said. "With everything that has happened to boxing, we're desperate for talent… even enough to keep us going along like we are. And then there are too many things that can happen to a young fighter before he is properly developed. We just have to pray when some good prospect comes along, that he falls into the right hands. We can't afford to lose even one anymore."

"It is a sad thing," Taylor added. "I can't think of a half-dozen young fighters who have excited me in the last two or three years. I don't really think that boxing will ever die completely. But we have to face it. We'll never again have the activity we had in the years gone by."

The prognosis Taylor had charted out was mostly on the dot. The annus mirabilis of 1952 was never coming back to Philadelphia. Underscoring his pessimism was the fact that there was not a single club show between May 19 and September 30 in 1969. Jaded managers and myopic promoters still ruled the land. But Taylor would be proven wrong, to an extent. Less than two months after Taylor caviled to the *Daily News*, Philadelphia boxing would be put on the path to its next boom in a way the octogenarian never believed was possible. And Taylor, along with the other hard-crusted curmudgeons of the reigning gerontocracy, would have a self-described nice little Jewish boy from the Main Line to thank for that.

* * *

As Peltz tells it, he was destined for boxing. By the time of his bar mitzvah, he had memorized all the boxing encyclopedias he could get his hands on. He saw his first live fight shortly before his fourteenth birthday, when his father took him to a card featuring local lightweight contender and crowd favorite Len Matthews in the main event against Douglas Vaillant. But the climax of the night occurred when two hometown middleweights with twenty-one losses between them, Jesse Smith and Jimmie Beacham, swapped leather in a donnybrook that ended with Smith knocking out Beacham in the 10th and final round. It was the sort of matchmaking for which Peltz would one day be known: down-market, perhaps, but rapturously violent. For better or worse, boxing would now inform every move of his waking life. "Very few people get into boxing today because they love boxing. They get into it for the business," Peltz recalled. "When I started out I never even thought about the money. All I wanted to do was be involved in boxing because I love boxing."

So it was that Peltz pursued a journalism degree at Temple University on the pretext that he could someday cover the fights at ringside. He was an ace student; as a senior, he was one of fifty-seven students nationwide honored for their academic achievement by Sigma Delta Chi, the oldest journalism fraternity in the United States. While attending school, he was hired by the *Philadelphia Bulletin*, landing a spot on the sports copy desk, where he worked the lobster shift. Peltz reasoned that the boxing gig, the beat he wanted the most, would fall into his lap sooner rather than later, considering that the retirement age was sixty-five and the senior boxing writer was fast approaching that milestone. Things appeared to be moving in the right direction, but one day his veteran colleague received an unexpected extension on his contract, effectively dashing any hopes Peltz had of covering fights for the paper, at least anytime soon. With his ambitions thwarted and already weary of his nine-to-five routine, Peltz reversed course and decided to throw his lot into promoting boxing. Peltz tendered a partial resignation, giving up his $7,500-a-year salary while agreeing to work as a stringer for the paper one night a week and full-time during the holidays, a contingency plan in case things did not work out. Of course, none of his colleagues took him seriously and viewed his initiative as nothing more than misguided ambition. Peltz recalled intercepting an office memo with the blunt shorthand "Russell B. Back." Boxing in Philadelphia, after all, was at its absolute nadir. "Herman Taylor only ran one show in 1969," Peltz said. "It was just a slow time."

Harebrained venture or not, Peltz was prepared to slog through some tough times. With his income from the *Bulletin* and his position as an editor at the Temple student newspaper, Peltz had quietly saved up around $5,000 (roughly $35,000 today). He had also spent days holed up at the State Athletic Commission office poring over statements of old fights, absorbing the obscurest of financial statistics, from gate receipts to purses to taxes, trying to get a sense of the economic feasibility of putting on a fight card. If Peltz was going to dip his feet into boxing, it would be on more than gut feeling and romance alone, and no one, not even his idols, was going to dissuade him otherwise. Indeed, in the summer before he got registered as a licensed promoter, Peltz sought out meetings with Herman Taylor and Teddy Brenner, the famed matchmaker of Madison Square Garden, to pick up a few pointers, to forge a relationship, to obtain, maybe, even their blessing. It was a pure courtesy call. But the moment Peltz revealed he was there not to speak with the paterfamiliases as a member of the press, but, in their eyes, as a potential competitor, an arriviste, a gatecrasher, cordiality went out the window.

"I went to see Taylor in the spring or summer of '69," Peltz recalled. "I just said, 'This is Russell Peltz from the *Bulletin*, I want to come and talk to you.' Around the same time, I went to see Teddy Brenner too. When they found out that I was just there to pick their brain they basically threw me out. Ignored me. I told Taylor that I'm going to be running fights, not to ask him for his permission but to get some (advice) and Taylor said, 'You'll never make it.' As did Brenner. To Taylor I said, 'Wait a second.' I started quoting figures to him and said, 'You did $4,900 at the gate with Henry Hank and Harold Johnson on national TV (in 1963).' 'No, I didn't,' Taylor said. I said, 'Yes, you did.' So he called Emily, his secretary, and she brought in the paper, and I was right. It was like going, facetiously, to a guy and asking for permission to marry his daughter. He was an old curmudgeon. I don't want to be like that … but I'm in Taylor's position today."

Still, Peltz remained unfazed. He was not immune to the pull of making a dollar, but he was not motivated by profit alone. Peltz was twenty-two. He was still a kid. He simply wanted to run his own small-scale operation of replicating the kinds of fights that had inspired him growing up. "I just like club fighters," Peltz once said. "I like the four-round guys.

I talk their language. Let somebody else have those $100,00 headaches. This is all I wanted."

* * *

IT WAS ONLY appropriate that the last hurrah for Philadelphia boxing would begin with the resurrection of a moribund auditorium. The Blue Horizon was a 1,300-seat fight club located at 1314 North Broad Street in North Philadelphia, and it was one of the premier sites for grassroots-level boxing. The big-ticket fights went to the Spectrum and the Arena, naturally, but the Blue Horizon, as everyone knew, was where the raw action was. It was paradise for the hardcore cultists and aptly nicknamed "The House of Pain." Though the building, a former Moose Lodge, was built in 1865, it was not until Jimmy Toppi, a prominent Philadelphia landlord who also owned local boxing venues such as the Alhambra, the Plaza, and the Toppi Stadium, that the Blue Horizon became a boxing arena. Toppi supposedly came up with the name after the Lou Christie song "Beyond the Blue Horizon."

From 1961 to 1963, Marty Kramer, the venue's flagship promoter in those years, staged roughly 30 shows. Between 1963 and 1964, Herman Taylor promoted three nationally televised fights at the venue, none more dramatic than the night native son Stanley "Kitten" Hayward rallied from an early knockdown to stop Dallas welterweight Curtis Cokes in the fourth. (A high-school-aged Peltz witnessed it from the balcony: "I consider it the greatest fight ever at the Blue

Horizon.") The venue would not host another fight until May 23, 1966, when Lou Lucchese, the main promoter during the lean years in Philadelphia boxing, hosted an excellent scrap between Gypsy Joe Harris and Johnny Knight. Thereafter it lay dormant, unused for boxing, for more than three years until Peltz arrived with his inaugural card on Tuesday, September 30, 1969.

"There were no real promoters there at the time," Gelb recalled. "The few good promoters that they had—they were falling off a bit. It's very interesting because of what boxing was. If you took away Madison Square Garden, there was not much boxing on the East Coast, except for small clubs that small promoters would run. Russell was the savior. He really was. He made the growth what it was. But the city was ready for it then. They had a big history when boxing was really on its top shelf of having the best boxers of all time. They had many gyms. Russell came to it at the right time, at the right place, and he'd rather see a boxing match than anything in his lifetime. So he fit in perfectly. If it wasn't for him they never would have reached where Philadelphia wound up in boxing with the greatest fighters of all because if you take a look at the history of it, when Russell got into it, he was the only one that was willing to take the risk and he shared the rewards for it."

"Russell was an enthusiastic and great promoter and at the same time he had this great talent that was just laying there," said Don Majeski, a longtime fight agent and close friend of Peltz. "You had Everett, Briscoe, Monroe, and Hart, Ritchie Kates, all these guys came up at the same period of time. The irony was that Frazier was the Philly boxer, but he rarely boxed there. So you had these middleweights that just clicked. Also, Perry Abner, Sammy Goss, Augie Pantellas. Just a wealth of talent of people willing to fight. They were fighting the matches that people wanted to see … The money was coming from the live gate, so you had to go where the money was. Then television came around and you could basically fight guys that were inferior so long as the television networks were willing to buy it. That was the last great era of the live gate. Synonymous with that, you had New York and Los Angeles, with George Parnassus. All of this was just a renaissance for boxing."

If Peltz had all the qualities that made up a good promoter—enterprising, industrious, and enthusiastic—he was not always beloved by his fighters. He had a reputation as a penny pincher and was notoriously stingy with comp tickets. At the same time, no one else in Philadelphia was putting up his own money to stage fights and giving fighters an opportunity to ply their trade. And the fighters, despite how many times they cursed Peltz under their breath, understood this.

"There were no fights happening then," said Mike Rossman, the light heavyweight champion who often fought for Peltz. "Russell kept boxing alive in Philadelphia. He don't like to pay. But he still kept boxing alive. It's the truth. He was the only guy doing it, and that's who you go with."

• • •

SCRANTON, PENNSYLVANIA. OCTOBER 30, 1971. It was a Tuesday night and Frank Gelb and his wife Elaine were ringside at the Catholic Youth Center, where they joined more than 3,200 paying customers to watch Bob Foster, the top light heavyweight of his generation, defend his world title against Tommy Hicks. The till whizzed all night, producing a gate of more than $25,000, no chump change in those days. The main event itself did not turn out to be much of a contest—Hicks was stopped in the eighth round—but it was a big night, nonetheless, as big as it got sporting-wise in the hardscrabble town of Scranton. It would take several years before Gelb would be prepared to give up his day job as a furniture dealer, but, in the meantime, here he was, in Scranton, of all places, moonlighting, like his newly revived pal Hurricane Roberts, in the boxing business.

Before it became known as the setting for the pop culture phenomenon of *The Office* or the birthplace of Joe Biden, Scranton was associated primarily with four things: coal, iron, steel, and locomotives. By the 1970s, much like what happened to Philadelphia, Scranton's industrial base—its anthracite economic identity—was slowly, but surely, coming apart, mirroring the nation-wide, post-World War II process of deindustrialization that afflicted Detroit, Cleveland, and scores of other once-proud blue-collar cities across the emerging Rust Belt. Nevertheless, it was in Scranton that Gelb formed one of the bases of his nascent boxing operations. Despite Gelb's serendipitous start, there was nothing slipshod or dilettantish about his new endeavor; he had real designs, hopes that went beyond being just the handler of a Norristown patrolman. "An avocation quickly became a vocation," Gelb later said. One of the first things he did was build relationships with local powerbrokers. From the management duo of William "Pinny"

Schafer and Pat Duffy, longtime fixtures on the Philadelphia boxing scene best known for handling the careers of Leotis Martin, Bennie Briscoe, and "Boogaloo" Watts among others, Gelb acquired a half-dozen fighters to form the core of his early stable. (A few years later, Gelb would purchase Matthew Saad Muhammad's contract from the same tandem.) In Scranton, Gelb paired up with local promoter Paul Ruddy to put on monthly fight cards at the Catholic Youth Center, a 4,000-seat arena that served as one of the primary athletic venues in the city. For several years, Gelb and Ruddy were practically the only game in town, promoting most of the boxing shows in northeastern Pennsylvania. It was, by most measures, a successful partnership, aided no less by the enthusiasm of the residents of Lackawanna County. As far as professional sports went, boxing was the most prominent attraction to hit Scranton, with the exception of college football. "When we did a fight there, it was a huge operation," Gelb recalled. "It was like a New Year's Eve party most of the time. Because people would go out to all the restaurants and eat before and go to the bars afterward and drink. They looked forward to boxing, and it was the biggest thing that happened for the city of Scranton at the time. Boxing was probably the most professional sport they had on a regular basis. We did that for many years. I was promoting, I was managing, I was handling a lot of boxers from that area that I tried to take to bigger heights."

One of those boxers was Ray Hall, a highly regarded featherweight prospect from nearby Wilkes-Barre. Gelb had slotted Hall into a four-rounder on the Foster-Hicks undercard. An accomplished amateur, Hall had already built up a name for himself in local circles. The thinking was that, in addition to becoming a top contender, he could also become a credible draw down the line. With a 5-0 record, he was on the right track.

But Hall was matched tough in his sixth fight that Tuesday night in October 1971, whether anyone on his side

Everett with his trademark hairstyle.

realized it or not. In the other corner was a wiry 18-year-old Black kid wearing pigtails from South Philadelphia with a 1-0 record. Unlike Hall, Tyrone Everett flew mostly under the radar as an amateur. Nothing was more indicative of his marginal status than the fact that local newspaper reports leading up to and after the fight referred to him as "Tyrone Edwards." Hall, for his part, was not under the same misconception, for it was Everett who had handed him his last loss as an amateur. By choosing to face him again, Hall and his brain trust clearly did not view Everett as much of a threat. Perhaps they were convinced that Hall's aggressive style would produce better results in the pro ranks. Stylistically, Everett was the complete antithesis to Hall and his headlong approach. But there was a simpler explanation for Hall's optimism in a second go-around. One month before, on September 25, Everett made his professional debut against fellow debutant Neil Hagel at the CYC on a card that had also featured Hall. In a four-round bout, Everett won a decision against Hagel—albeit controversially. While it was a close fight, most ringside observers believed Hagel had done enough to deserve the win, with one local newspaper describing how "heavy body blows had Everett reeling around the padded circle." The paper added, bluntly, that "Neil Hagel appeared to have been robbed of the decision in his debut as a prize-fighter."

So Hall was feeling bullish for all the right reasons. But Everett, bad debut notwithstanding, had good reason to feel confident in himself as well. Everett knew that two weeks earlier, in Philadelphia, Hall had picked up a relatively easy decision, but not without leaving with a large cut over his left eye, the result of a headbutt. Two weeks later, that gash was still tender, a fact that did not escape the guileful Everett. With the focus of an osprey scanning for trout, Everett made it a point to target the wound from the opening bell. As he would later say, "You look at a man's face to see if he's been cut. You check if there's a lot of scar tissue. I always look at the eyebrows." Before long, blood began drizzling down Hall's face from the same sore spot. The fight was resembling a beatdown.

Meanwhile, Gelb was looking on despondently, his heart in his throat, like one of those poor Las Vegas souls witnessing their life savings dry up on the slot machine. At one point, Gelb's wife Elaine turned to her blanched husband and cracked, "I think you're backing the wrong fighter." It was a shutout; Everett won every round on the scorecards. Gelb may have been a boxing neophyte, but he could sniff out a business opportunity as adroitly as a bloodhound sniffs for contraband. Heeding his wife's advice, Gelb moseyed up to the victor after the bout and floated the idea of working together. They struck a deal shortly thereafter. "Ray Hall was good, I mean real good," Gelb once told the *Philadelphia Tribune*. "I had visions of a championship fight(er). Everett ... destroyed my fighter. I couldn't believe it." When Gelb later spoke to Peltz, he gushed about his new signee and prodded the fledgling promoter to come to Everett's next fight to see for himself. The next fight would be on March 7, 1972, again in Scranton.

"So I went to the show and that was the night that Ray Hart—not to get confused with Ray Hall, and no relation to Cyclone Hart or any of the other Harts—was fighting Everett," Peltz recalled. "Ray Hart was a Joe Frazier with speed, and he came right after Everett. I mean Ray Hart really jumped on his ass. And he was a decent prospect at the time, Ray Hart, and he made Everett look like Sugar Ray Robinson. I saw that that night ... and when the fight was over I ran over to Gelb, and I said, 'Let's make a deal right here.' And then [Tyrone] fought for me exclusively. That night? Whew, he was good."

Of all the fighters to emerge from the Philadelphia renaissance of the 1970s, a hot crucible of competition that only waned with the emergence of Atlantic City as a destination for marquee boxing, none was as talented as Tyrone Everett. There were others, for sure, who were more thrilling inside the ring, others who were more accessible, and because they

**Briscoe, who typified the Philadelphia brand of
boxing, tees off on Jean Marais, Paris 1977.**
(Courtesy Peltz Boxing Promotions, Inc.)

were more accessible, more beloved: Bobby "Boogaloo" Watts,
Willie "The Worm" Monroe, Eugene "Cyclone" Hart, Billy
"Dynamite" Douglas, Stanley "Kitten" Hayward, Matthew
Saad Muhammad, and, of course, the doyen, "Bad" Bennie
Briscoe, the hard-nosed slugger often regarded as the quin-
tessence of the Philadelphia boxing spirit. As light heavy-
weight champion Eddie Mustafa Muhammad, who dropped
a decision to Briscoe early on in his career, once told *The
Ring*, "When you say Philadelphia, you right away think of
Bennie Briscoe. No nonsense, blue-collar worker. Bennie was
the greatest fighter to never win a world title." The Briscoe

Awards, the annual ceremony celebrating Philadelphia fighters past and present, are named after him for this reason. Unlike Everett, their names have continued to circulate today in the imagination of the boxing public. None of them ever won a title and a few of them, like Monroe, never received a title shot, but they nevertheless helped reinvent Philadelphia as the premier fight capital on the East Coast for a brief but bountiful spell.

And they all, crucially, fought as middleweights—a significant fact since almost all of them, at one point or another, faced the dominant middleweight of that era, Marvelous Marvin Hagler, who, from 1976 to 1978, made the long trek down from his home in Brockton, Massachusetts, to Philadelphia five times to face the city's top brass, going 3-2, dropping decisions to Monroe and Watts, both of whom he would later stop in rematches. Part of the reason why these Philadelphia middleweights have been assured a meaningful afterlife can be attributed to Hagler's enduring legacy.

That Everett was a diminutive fighter—he was a natural featherweight who found himself competing at junior lightweight for most of his career because of a dearth of opportunities at the lighter weight—was but one feature that distinguished him from the local orthodoxy. Where he stood out even more was in temperament and sensibility. With his smoldering good looks, his wind-flapping pigtails, and a swagger bordering on insolence, Everett assumed a style that was stridently opposed to the more rugged, workmanlike approach of his peers and predecessors. "Wily" and "cunning," after all, were not words often ascribed to the local fighters by the press, but they found their way to Everett. In this way, he was very much a cultural inheritor of a brand of brashness promulgated by Muhammad Ali. In a hard-bitten culture that, as Peltz puts it, was predicated on fighters "walking each other down and beating the shit out of each other," Everett was all silken polish and surface perfection. Stick and move, counter. Hit and not be hit. Critics called it hotdogging, boring, a time suck. For Everett, it was simply smart boxing. It was boxing, moreover, that preserved his face, which he always treated like a Romanov Fabergé egg.

His brilliance was also a source of repeated frustration. For all his technical astuteness, sangfroid, and whippet quickness, for all his ability to hit all the right notes inside the cordoned-off boundaries of a boxing ring, Everett rarely rose to that pitch of passion that exemplifies the prime appeal of a blood sport, that unhinged fervor which constituted nothing less than a natural state of being for fighters such as Roberto Duran and Aaron Pryor. His heavy reliance on finesse was often confused by his detractors as a sign of weakness. In fact, there was nothing in his background to suggest that he was any less resilient than the likes of Bennie Briscoe or Matthew Saad Muhammad. It is a truism that only the poorest and most marginalized in society end up choosing boxing as a pursuit, and, in this, Everett was no exception. His origins were as hardscrabble and harrowing as any of his more beloved peers.

CHAPTER TWO

*This Philly is a cold town. The people here are cold-
hearted. When I was fourteen I joined a gang. Had to
fight every member. Who needs it, man? I didn't want
to get shot up and wind up dead on the street. I got out
when I was fifteen. It wasn't for me.*

— "G Y P S Y" J O E H A R R I S
to *Boxing Illustrated*

TYRONE EVERETT WAS born on April 18, 1953,
in the predominately Black section of the blue-collar
stronghold of South Philadelphia. It might be said that
he came into the world with show business in his veins. His
mother, Doris Everett, named him after the debonair Tyrone
Power, one of the last male screen idols of the Hollywood star
system. According to family legend, Doris was in labor with
Everett while watching a Tyrone Power film. Like his
namesake, Everett was blessed with enviable looks, a fact that
may have contributed to the way he fought inside the ring.
"People say I don't like to get hit," Everett would later tell the
Philadelphia Inquirer. "That's true. They say I don't look like
a fighter, that I'm too pretty. I want to stay that way. Why

should I go in there and get all beat up, scar tissue over the right eye, scar tissue over the left eye, no teeth? Ask anyone. I attract more females to my fights than males. I want to keep that image."

Everett would live out the Hollywoodesque ethos in his small pocket of the universe in South Philadelphia, amid spiffed-up cars, the ceaseless blare of Dayton funk (Dazz Band was a favorite), and a rotating succession of doting girls. When his life abruptly ended at twenty-four, he left behind four children, all from different women. He lived his life to the hilt. But that was later. In the beginning, it was all hard living.

Everett was the oldest of five brothers. Mike and Eddie, the second and third oldest, would follow in their brother's footsteps and become boxers. Eddie fought no more than three times in the paid ranks

"The Mean Machine."
(Courtesy Peltz Boxing Promotions, Inc.)

before opting for a more stable career in civil service, but Mike would go so far as to vie for a junior welterweight world title. The trio was inseparable. As professionals, Eddie and Tyrone lived together in the same apartment, across the street from their mother.

Growing up in the Civil Rights era, Everett lived in a period of perpetual flux and tumult. But positive change rarely entered life in the asphalt underbelly of South Philadelphia. Segregation was still the de facto rule of the day. "There was a lot of racial tension down there," Eddie said of his life on 31st and Tasker Street. "There was a playground that only whites could use, and Blacks couldn't go in there. We would go in there anyway and there would be fights back and forth. That's how Tyrone got his arm broken, so that knocked him out of the Golden Gloves championships. The cops would come and they would protect the white kids. It was like we were fighting both. It was just the era that we came up there was a lot of racial tension back then in the '60s and '70s. We went through things today that kids don't experience now. By the time the '70s started, a lot of that started to go away."

Everett's maternal great-grandparents were originally from Virginia and arrived in Philadelphia in the early 20th century as part of the Great Migration that saw multitudes of southern Black families flock to the North to find employment opportunities denied to them by Jim Crow. But material prosperity was, in many ways, just as elusive as it was in the South. By the 1950s, the city was experiencing the first tremors of white flight, a response to the vast influx of Black migrants. Stoked by racial fears and harboring the belief that Black homeownership would slash property values, a view perpetuated by the real estate industry, middle-class white families began hightailing it out to the suburbs. Indeed, the total population from 1950–1960 in Philadelphia dropped by seventy thousand even as the Black population grew by six percent, from eighteen percent to twenty-four percent. And as white families moved out, so did their (white) employers, which, in turn, led Blacks and white working-class families in Philadelphia to fight over the same jobs in a diminishing market. The ultimate irony was that all of this happened under the watch of a liberal regime led by Mayor Joseph Clark and then his successor Richardson Dilworth. Both men recognized they were dealing with an urban crisis. In 1958, Dilworth, as mayor, famously told *Time* magazine that the suburbs were acting like a "white noose" around the neck of Philadelphia's urban center—white flight, he acknowledged, was choking the life out of the city. Dilworth's comment, however, was in response to a *Time* article critiquing the city's longstanding urban renewal project, a well-intentioned effort by the liberal coalition to erect more middle-class housing, a process, the bureaucrats crowed, that would coax the suburbanites to return. By doing so, the city would stanch its demographic hemorrhage and revitalize its tax base. *Time*, however, argued that the city was simply perpetuating segregation, that the construction of new housing, which involved razing down whole shantytowns, or "slum clearance," as the bigwigs called it, simply displaced and priced out impoverished families, who, of course, were mostly Black. This was class warfare at its most hypocritical, and it meant that as the Black population continued to grow to become the dominant demographic, there would be fewer resources made available to them, effectively ensuring their failure during a time generally associated with unfettered capitalism, when the so-called American Dream was manifesting itself in millions of sold laundry machines and vacuum cleaners.

To someone like Everett, this vision of America may as well have been agitprop from a foreign country. As the eldest male in the household, Everett did his bit to help the family stay afloat in those early lean years. He shined shoes, delivered groceries and newspapers, and stacked boxes for local stores while he kept a vigilant eye on his four brothers (there would be a fifth later on). Meanwhile, his mother Doris scraped by cleaning the homes of wealthy families. Her days were fraught with existential uncertainty. "My biggest worry with the three oldest was getting them lunch money and carfare for school for the week," Doris once told the *Philadelphia Bulletin*. "I lived in dread of Monday mornings. I had to wake up with $10 in my pocket, or else."

And yet, to the extent that Everett and his brothers were guaranteed clean clothes, carfare, fifty cents for lunch, and food on the table in the evenings, they were insulated from the most paralyzing effects of life in the Black underclass. Like Ma Joad, the steadfast matriarch in John Steinbeck's Depression-era novel *The Grapes of Wrath*, who helped guide her family of Oklahoma tenant farmers out of dustbowl penury to a better life in the West, Doris was a bulwark of security.

"We never felt like we lacked for anything, because somehow my mother provided everything," Eddie said. "To us, we never really understood at that time how difficult it was for her. We never knew because we always had clothes, food. We weren't rich, but we lived a happy life under her. We had fun growing up. She would go to work to clean houses and leave us to take care of each other. In those days you could play out in the neighborhood and your neighbors would look out for you also. So she would go to work and leave us a quarter or fifty cents—and that would go a long way back in the days. We never felt poor or needy or anything, but looking back now I realize what an amazing mother she was."

"I remember seeing kids going around with holes in their shoes," Everett once recalled. "We didn't. We didn't have to go out and steal and beat people up in order to get what we wanted. We had a bicycle, we shared it, we had lunch money, we had it pretty good. Deep down inside maybe my mother carried hurt for scuffling all the time, but she gave us what we needed, and she kept us out of trouble."

The brothers were generally well-behaved and stayed out of trouble. At least, this was the narrative that Everett offered over the years as his profile increased and journalists sought him out. "I've seen dope, I've seen reefer, I've seen all the drugs, it's all been put in front of me," Everett said. "I'm not going to say none of this is in my neighborhood. It's all out there, pills, pimps, prostitutes, all the temptations of life. You have to choose which way you go, I chose to go this way, you only go that other way if you're weak, if you can be easily led. If you have a strong mind, if you have a strong mother behind you, you do it this way."

"My mother never had to worry about coming to the police station to bail us out," Mike once told the *Philadelphia Inquirer.* "Other mothers'd stop by the house and tell her, 'My boy just got arrested, I'm going to get him out of jail.' My mother never had to do that. We saw her struggling for us, we saw her waiting at home for us, we saw her working to make it right for us. We didn't want to disappoint her. There was no way we could disappoint our mother."

Their father, on the other hand, was a different story. For one, he was seldom present. A day laborer who had difficulty holding down a steady job, Joseph Womack was a casualty of the wave of deindustrialization that swept through the country's urban capitals in the post-World War II era. Formerly a titan in shipbuilding and textiles, Philadelphia, the "Workshop of the World," was hit hard. By the 1950s, its skyline was dotted with derelict factories—from ice-cream makers to breweries—fossilized reminders of its once-robust manufacturing past. According to census data, from 1950 to 1960, Philadelphia lost a whopping 60,000 blue-collar jobs, a number that would skyrocket with each passing decade; the city would shed around 200,000 more blue-collar jobs by 1984. Male adults who were trained to make a living with their hands were becoming obsolete like so many pieces of scrap metal. Broken families were a common sight. Idleness abounded, resentment surged, and crime went up, a concatenation of events that the sociologist W.E.B. DuBois had already acutely observed take place in Philadelphia at the turn of the 20th century. And yet, if he was far from a model father, Womack, a former foster child, was not entirely absent from his sons' lives either. "One day, I asked my mother why she kept him around and she told me, 'You can't understand yourself unless you know your father. I wanted y'all to know him,'" Eddie recalled, describing the numerous conflicts his parents had with each other. "He didn't do much for us, but he was around and we had some relations with him. Like, early on, he never knew about us going to the gym and boxing. When we went to school he was never around. He never did homework with us. He never came to graduations. He was in and out. My mom was pretty much everything to us. But when our father was around, we loved him. We still loved him. Not only did we want to make our mother proud, but we wanted to make him proud. We never held it against him for not being in our lives. As Tyrone got bigger and bigger, he would come to the fights with all of his buddies from the bar."

Although Eddie never recalls his father bringing up the subject of boxing with his children, he says his father was a natural fighter whose street scuffles, at least on one occasion, left a notable impression on Tyrone. "My father got into a fight with somebody in Point Breeze [a neighborhood in South Philadelphia]," said Eddie. "Tyrone was a little kid then and he witnessed him fighting some guy. Whatever he did Tyrone must've been amazed by the fight. Years later, when I was twenty-four, I took my wife to see my father. He must've been in his fifties. When we got to his apartment he was wrestling with this guy who had a knife. And this guy was trying to stab him. When I got out of the car, I got the knife out of the guy's hand. My father said, 'I'm OK, move back,' and him and this guy started fighting. I had never seen someone beat someone that bad with that kind of precision. I'm a fighter, and I was totally amazed. My wife talks about it to this day."

Violence was unavoidable in South Philadelphia. For young, mostly fatherless inner-city kids like the Everett brothers, the lure of gang participation, in particular, posed a permanent threat. According to a 1969 report by the Philadelphia Police Department, there were over one hundred gangs in the city, a figure that would shoot up to two hundred three years later. Against the backdrop of a crumbling workforce and the rise of single-parent families, gangs, in a way, were a natural response to all the reigning aspects of legitimate society to which the underclass was not privy. Gangs, which held anywhere from twenty-five to two hundred and fifty members, offered easy kinship to wayward youth.

Throughout the 1950s, Philadelphia gangs mostly carried switchblades, although the more daring were able to procure pistols and develop improvised "zip guns" constructed out of rubber bands, tape, wood, a pipe, and a door bolt. That would all change in the late 1960s, with the emergence of the heroin boom. By 1969, the crime situation in Philadelphia was dire enough to compel Mayor James H.J. Tate to proclaim that "gang violence is giving Philadelphia a bad name." In 1962, there was one gang-related homicide; in 1969, there were forty-five, in addition to two hundred and sixty-seven gang-related injuries and countless incidents of burglary and purse snatching.

There was a gang holding court seemingly on every street block. Many of them took their names after the turfs they occupied: 19th and Carpenter Street, 20th and Carpenter Street, 8th and Diamond Street, Fifth Street, 15th and Oxford, 16th and Dauphin, 30th and Norris, 12th and Poplar, and so on. These complemented the more thematically oriented outfits, such as the Zulu Nation, who took special pride in their racial identity; the Moons, who believed they did their best work under crepuscular conditions; as well as Mongo Nation, the Empires, the Soul Diplomats, the T.G.Os, and the Moroccos. However misguided they were in their actions and intentions, gangs provided a sense of solidarity for the disenchanted and disenfranchised. Former Philadelphia gang member Salaam Muhsin described the appeal of gang life for young Black males in the 1960s. "My sister got a scholarship to Cornell," he told PBS. "I didn't! I didn't want to be like my sister. I wanted to be like the brothers in the neighborhood who were strolling real hard. Do you see how we dipped, man? With all that pride in our step? I wanted to be with them."

Drinking, not surprisingly, was a prevalent hobby among the ruffians. In the 1967 docu-fiction short film *The Jungle*, 12th and Oxford gang members are seen marching through a rubble-ridden street lined with abandoned cinder block buildings evoking the terrain of a war-torn country. The boys are dressed in long leather coats and pass around a brown paper-bagged hooch while chanting an ad-libbed invocation to their muse.

Up on the roof
Oh yeah
One hundred proof
Oh yeah
It's in my spine
Oh yeah
That's OJ wine
Oh yeah
Who drink the most?
Oh yeah
Them colored folks

Around the time when Everett was in the first grade, Doris decided to uproot the family and move to North Philadelphia. The reason, according to Eddie, was so that she could get away from her unhealthy relationship with Womack. Though Womack would eventually track her down, Doris continued to raise the family above South Street for several years and most likely would have continued doing so had Everett not arrived home one day with his new leather raincoat carved up. It turned out that earlier that afternoon, after attending classes at Stoddart–Fleischer Middle School, Everett had been delivering papers when he was suddenly accosted by "peewee" members of the Moroccos, one of the most notorious gangs of North Philadelphia. Everett had unwittingly crossed into their territory. As a result, he needed to pay the appropriate toll, which was basically everything he had in his pockets. When Everett refused, one of the Moroccos took a razor to his swanky threads. Doris decided it was time to head back to

South Philadelphia. "By the time he got to high school it was just impossible," Doris said to the *Inquirer*. "It was impossible to send him to school, impossible to send him to the store. It was really impossible to go anywhere unless you belonged to a gang." They re-settled in a clapboard row house along 20th and Tasker Street, by no means an oasis of calm, but free, at least, of the perilous influences that characterized life on the north side.

Still, gangland influences continued to trail the brothers wherever they went. At one point in high school, Everett had even formally joined the 20th and Carpenters, according to a profile published in the *Philadelphia Inquirer*. Everett, however, played it down as something he did on a lark, a short-lived experiment that only lasted a few months and in which his only benefit was that he was able to hone his schmoozing skills with the opposite sex. One day at school, Everett fell into bad favor with two members of rival gangs and ended up whipping both of them, one in the schoolyard and the other in the bathroom. That experience, ironically, ended up diminishing his appetite for street feuds. "After that, if I was going to fight, it was going to be against a whole gang," Tyrone said. "That made it better just to walk away."

Mike was not as lucky. One time, early in his youth, he was accosted by the scapegraces of 20th and Carpenter. The altercation left him with a long, gruesome lunar-shaped scar extending across his right ear and up to the hairline of his temple. "One cold day I got jumped by 20th and Carpenter," Mike described to the *Philadelphia Bulletin*. "They knocked me cold with a board. Me and my brothers retaliated a couple of days later. After that, the gangs didn't fool with the Everetts and the Everetts never did fool with the gangs."

Instead, the brothers responded by banding together and forming their own sort of congregation. Soon, the Everett home became a happening place in the neighborhood, where the brothers and their select buddies would shoot pool, listen to the latest funk records, draw up weekend plans, and, it goes without saying, mingle with the ladies. "Back then you were either from a gang, or you were in a club," Eddie recalled. "We had a social club, the Ecuador Club. We had other guys in it. We would have parties with other girl clubs. So we would meet up with girls around the city and party together. We were into having fun." Especially Tyrone, whose swoon-inducing good looks quickly became the talk of the neighborhood. Weekend after weekend, a dizzying gallery of girls turned up on the Tasker Street doorstep. "I was called a player," Everett once said. "This girl, that girl, I played a lot." As Mike once told the *Bulletin*, "The gangs didn't like [the social club] because they were never included."

For anyone else, bucking the gangs would have led to retribution in the form of, say, a crowbar. But Everett, of course, was not just another neighborhood schlub. "The gangs ended up respecting us because we could fight," Eddie said. "Back then you got your respect from gangs by fighting. Tyrone was respected by every gang in North Philly, South Philly, they knew who he was and his name and as he got bigger, they loved him even more. The people from the gangs that knew him loved him because they loved fighters. They loved guys that could fight. The best fighters were the ones that had their respect." Eddie would discover just how much clout his brother's name carried when he had his own blood-curdling encounter with the 20th and Carpenters. "One day I was sitting on the steps, and the 20th and Carpenter street gang came up and took out guns and knives and I knew they were going to kill me," Eddie once told *PhillySport* magazine. "My heart was down to my knees. Then the head of the gang said, 'That's Tyrone Everett's brother,' and they left me alone."

It was not only respect that the 20th and Carpenters imparted to Everett, but their total admiration. He was their guy. A few years later, when Everett was beginning to create buzz with his fists, they would be a regular sight at his fights at the Spectrum. At the height of his brief career, Everett would frequently tell reporters hankering after human interest angles that he had overcome the streets, that he had stayed above the fray. But given his proximity, and supposedly brief conscription, to one of the most cutthroat gangs in Philadelphia at the time, the idea that he maintained a lily-white lifestyle is a difficult one to swallow. As it would become clear later, one thing was for certain: Everett could quit the streets, but the streets would not quit him.

◆ ◆ ◆

WHEN HE WAS not busy delving into the intricacies of sheet metal manipulation at Edward Bok Vocational High School—the same alma mater shared by boxers Jeff Chandler, Matthew Saad Muhammad, Robert Adams, and Johnny Carter—Everett funneled all his energies into sports, if for no other reason than to score points with his female classmates. His brothers followed suit as well. For Doris, the extracurricular distraction was a godsend. "The boys can't sit very long," she told the *Bulletin*. "They love school because they were always doing something. They went out for every sport they had at Bok. And I thank the Lord. It kept them busy and probably kept them alive." Everett also had a knack for drawing, and several years later, when he was at the peak of his boxing career, he was in touch with a sponsor who offered to put up the money for him to attend classes at the Philadelphia College of Art (now the University of the Arts).

Everett tried out for swimming, soccer, and basketball in that order, achieving middling degrees of success. Although he was a natural athlete, Everett was only five foot, five inches tall, which meant that he had a decidedly limited future in basketball; in soccer, he was only able to score goals during practices; and in swimming, he usually finished last at the meets. Then one day, when he was seventeen, Everett ran into a neighborhood friend who happened to be carrying a shiny object in the crook of his arm. It was a trophy that he had just won from a boxing tournament. Everett was spellbound. For all anyone knew, it could have been nothing more than a gnarled, catchpenny piece of spray-painted plastic, but for Everett it was the equivalent of a Rolex. In other words, it was another trinket he could show off to the girls on Saturday nights. As Everett once stated to the *Inquirer*, "You know how a young man is. I got into this game just to collect myself a couple trophies."

He went down to the local gym off Passyunk Avenue and enrolled in a boxing class. A trainer named Jimmy Arthur happened to stop by one day when he noticed Everett whaling on the heavy bag alone. Arthur, a quiet family man who also worked as a butcher, was a mainstay at the Passyunk Gym and would go on to train future light heavyweight champion

Mike Rossman, Percy Manning, Alfonso Hayman, and Mike Rafferty, among others. A former fighter himself, Arthur had a feel for teaching, which may be attributable to the many years he spent working as an equestrian caretaker at the local tracks, according to Frank Gelb. Arthur liked what he saw in Everett and urged the scraggly youth to return. He would help him straighten out his jab and if he mastered that, he would teach him a few other things, like how to hook off of it. Everett had found his mentor. By boxing standards, Everett was certainly a late starter, but he proved to be a quick learner and soon Arthur had him competing in amateur bouts.

He may not have been a puncher like his Philadelphian confrères, but Everett was far from pillow-fisted. Here a straight left lifts his opponent into the air.
(Courtesy Peltz Boxing Promotions, Inc.)

Early on, however, Everett hit a roadblock in Jerome Artis and nearly quit boxing altogether. A brash and flashy fighter from North Philadelphia who trained out of Joe Frazier's gym, Artis was regarded as one of the premier amateur talents on the East Coast, a blue-chip prospect who, in the process of winning the 1972 national AAU featherweight championship, handed Sugar Ray Leonard his final loss as an amateur. The gabby Artis had a habit of dressing down his opponents before the fights by bragging about his vast amateur experience. "When we fought for the first time, he told me had seventy-four fights to my four," Everett once recalled to the *Daily News*. "It shook me up and I lost." Everett was crushed and six months into his new foray, he decided to hang up the gloves and go back to his prelapsarian lifestyle, back to the Ecuador Club, back to the girls, back to the welding grind. But thanks to the influence of his mother and Jimmy Arthur, Everett returned to the gym. The next time he faced Artis, he "whipped him" in a technical decision. (One of the ironies of this half-baked rivalry is that it was Everett who would go on to have the far better professional career. Artis, who flamed out in the paid ranks, repeatedly hounded after Everett like a jilted lover, presumably to drum up attention for a fight that would never materialize. Once, during a press conference for a fight card in which both were featured on separate bouts, Artis lashed out at Everett. "So you graduated high school. What did you do? Buy yourself out? Is that a speech impediment you have, or is it just your South Philadelphia upbringing? You like to talk about your investments. Why don't you take some of that money and enroll yourself in a public speaking course?")

Indeed, as talented as he was, Everett was not considered a hot commodity in the amateurs. His brother Mike, a three-time Philadelphia Golden Gloves champion, had more buzz going into the professional ranks. Everett also had confidence issues, unthinkable for someone later considered to have an ego the size of the Liberty Bell. After building up a 22-3 amateur record, Everett, once more, thought of leaving the sport behind for good. There was always welding to fall back on, he figured. But Arthur, who saw his potential writ large across the lean frame of his charge, offered some timely encouragement. "Don't give up now," he told him. "You're just getting good." Arthur—fight whisperer and surrogate father rolled into one—went a step further and even suggested that Everett turn professional instead of puttering around in the thankless amateur system. By doing so, he could steadily sharpen his craft and earn some coin at the same time. It was either that or going back to making air conditioning ducts for the rest of his life. What was there to lose? Everett took the bait. "Art doesn't have a big name like [fellow Philadelphian trainers] Yank Durham or Sam Solomon or Quenzell McCall, but he's just as good," Everett would later tell the *Daily News*. "He's younger and he hasn't had a big fighter yet. He's the only trainer who runs with his fighters. And he knows what to look for during a fight. When I boxed Ray Hart it was my third fight. Hart had knocked just about everyone out and he was giving me trouble. After the second round I told Art that the pressure was hard on me, and I was having trouble. He told me Hart was leg-weary and finished for the night. When I went out for the third, Hart was out of gas. I stopped him in the next round." Under Arthur's watchful eyes, Everett would not lose again in the ring for another five years, by which point he would have cemented himself as a leading man in the burgeoning theater of Philadelphia boxing.

CHAPTER THREE

Time is a dancing fire at twenty-one.

—DELMORE SCHWARTZ

FOR ALL HIS enthusiasm for his newfound charge, Russell Peltz was in no rush to put Everett into the teeth of competition. Everett, after all, was still a work in progress. After his dominant victory over Ray Hart in March of 1973, Everett spent the next two years pocketing wins like so many smooth pebbles along a shoreline. As Jimmy Arthur had expected, he was making it look easy in the ring. With the exception of the unusually durable Jose Resto, whom he decisioned twice, Everett stopped most of his challengers, a clear indication that, unlike the typical southpaw cutie, Everett had legitimate pop in his punches. No wonder Arthur was so eager to turn him professional. Granted, some of his opponents were downright risible, like the maladroit Ahmet Tosci, who had a record of one win against eight losses and one draw and who would go on to finish his career with twenty-eight losses. After that fight, a season ticket holder went up to Peltz to lodge a complaint. "'You know, I have all the respect for you,'" Peltz recalled the fan saying. "'You're a terrific matchmaker, but you should be ashamed to have made that.'" But there was no denying that with each win, Everett was building a case for himself as the most promising featherweight in the city.

Of course, early on, there were legitimate questions about how far Everett could go as a local attraction. While the talent was not in doubt, Everett was not exactly a public relations dream. Peltz, who always had his fingers to the winds of commerce, understood there was limited appeal for the sort of boxing that Everett espoused, which is to say that southpaws, in the understanding at the time, were viewed as a commercial liability. Southpaws disrupted the natural symbiosis in a fight, that flow and interchange of punches thought to be integral to boxing, what Norman Mailer called the dialogue of bodies. Few right-handed fighters were ever in a mood to willingly go up against southpaws. Hence, most trainers generally tried to convert lefties into the orthodox stance. It was better for business. "It is the general opinion of most boxing managers that southpaws should be drowned at birth," wrote Gene Courtney of the *Inquirer*. "They are avoided like patients with contagious diseases. To the average manager, an opponent with halitosis has a better chance of coming close to his fighter than a lefthander." If southpaws found it difficult enough to convince their fellow stablemates to participate in something as humdrum as a sparring session, how were they going to be any more appealing to a promoter? Or, as Peltz put it more bluntly, "Where were you going to make money with a Black, left-handed featherweight on the East Coast?"

But Jimmy Arthur apparently resisted the temptation to turn Everett around, thinking his charge's seeming youthfulness would garner him fights with overconfident opponents. "We knew we were taking a chance," Arthur told Sports Illustrated. "But we figured Tyrone was so young-looking, people would think they could beat him." For Everett, his lefty stance was of a piece with his other heterodox qualities, such as his flowing patch of cornrow braids, an uncommon sight in those days and which irked the older members of the boxing establishment. But more importantly, in what was another blow to public approbation, the stance dovetailed with his naturally defensive-minded sensibilities. The idea of taking a punch to land one himself was never a calculus Everett ever cared to entertain, despite the fact that he operated in a prizefighting climate that cherished only brawlers. Not to mention that Arthur also preached the principles of safeguard above all else. "Inside a ring, Everett was quicksilver," Tom Cushman once observed. "He was so nimble and skilled he could flit inside an opponent's defenses, leaving his calling cards, and be back at the periphery, beyond range, before any kind of counter possible."

By the start of 1973, *The Ring* had selected Everett as one of its Prospects of the Month. The local papers were calling him the "hottest prospect in Philadelphia." Talk of Everett facing Trenton's Sammy Goss, the North American Boxing Federation super featherweight champion, was starting to mount. As both fighters shared the same promoter, it was only a matter of time before the two would collide in the ring someday. With his exclusive new deal with the Spectrum, the biggest indoor fight venue in town, Peltz was keen on establishing new names to make up for sluggish ticket sales on fight cards that did not have the Bennie Briscoe imprimatur. "Listen, things were rough years ago over at the Spectrum,"

Peltz recalled. "When I started there in '73, they were coming up with all kinds of gimmicks. We were going to have the Persuasions sing—they were an a cappella group. Maybe people would come in and listen to them. We had—and this is a true story—we had a guy named Komer, 'The Hindu Fakir,' who would lay on a bed of nails, and this was supposed to attract people to come to the fights. This isn't going to work. What we need is good fights. People want to see good fights. They don't want to see some guy laying on a bed of nails. You go to the circus to see that."

On April 16, 1973, on the undercard of a Sammy Goss main event, Everett notched his thirteenth straight win with an eighth-round stoppage over New York journeyman Danny Figueroa. Despite a record of 10-14-5, Figueroa was considered to be Everett's stiffest test at that point. A month later, Everett appeared in his first co-feature role—and first 10-rounder— against Azael Curet on a tripleheader that included stable-mates Alfonso Hayman and Perry "Li'l" Abner. It was another breezy outing. With a few seconds remaining in the third round, Everett dug a crisp left hand into the solar plexus, causing Curet to freeze, spit out his mouthpiece, and then stagger back to his corner with his hands raised in capit-ulation. In what would become a pattern, Everett was less than conciliatory about his fallen foe. "[Curet] looked pretty smart out there," Everett told the *Daily News* afterward. "But Spanish boys can't take the body shots. They eat a lot of peppers. It weakens their stomachs." Still, as long as Everett was stopping his opponents, few were going to begrudge him for a salty put-down here and there.

• • •

A WEEK BEFORE Tyrone Everett went head-to-head against Azael Curet, Mike Everett drove up to New York City to face palooka Ronald Whyms at the Felt Forum in Madison Square Garden. What was supposed to be a routine outing for Mike quickly devolved into a nightmare. He was stopped, on the ropes, in the second round. Mike would blame his performance on his legs, claiming he had left them behind on the dance floor in Atlantic City during a weekend bender after his high school prom. He was the first of the Everetts to record a professional loss.

• • •

"I WASN'T SURPRISED when Mike got knocked out last week in New York," Tyrone remarked. "Mike didn't train for that one. He had his school prom three nights before and he wasn't in the gym all weekend. Mike has to learn that you can't knock everyone out in the first or second round. You've got to be in shape to go the distance. When I lose, at least I want to be in shape." Tyrone himself would spend many an occasion boogying away his nights, but unlike Mike, when it came to fight-time, he never failed to prepare. "You never had to ask him if he trained," Gelb would later say.

On June 25, Everett, now ranked the No. 7 feather-weight on the East Coast, faced battle-tested Eliud Garces of Brooklyn. Philadelphia fight fans were well acquainted with

Garces; he had faced local favorite Luis Lopez—the pride of North Philadelphia's Puerto Rican community—three times, winning once, a mild upset, in 1972. That same year, Garces went up against Goss, only to get mowed down in two rounds. If nothing else, Garces was a decent indicator of where Everett stood in the pecking order of the lower weight classes. Yet just as soon as the fight was made, Everett began to wonder if he was being pushed too quickly in facing a tough journeyman such as Garces. He also had his doubts about facing Goss, telling the *Daily News* point-blank that he felt he was "at least a year or more away" from facing the veteran, fearing that he was "not physically strong enough now to stand up under Goss's body punches." Once again, Arthur played the part of consoler and told him not to worry. Garces was the right fight at this point in his career. Everett, as always, listened.

The fight took place at the Spectrum. More than 9,000 fans poured in from the streets to witness what figured to be a barnburner main event between Bennie Briscoe and Billy "Dynamite" Douglas, two of the deadliest punchers in the middleweight division. It was the biggest matchup in Philadelphia that year, and Briscoe would stop Douglas in the eighth round. But if Everett was still undercard material, a supporting role for the redoubtable Briscoe, he made it clear to everyone that night that his days as a prelim fighter were numbered. Barely a minute-and-a-half into the opening round of their fight, Everett and Garces traded left hooks. Both landed, but it was Garces who crashed to the canvas, sparking an uproar in the stands. A dazed and rheumy-eyed Garces fumbled around on all fours and was counted out. It was bedlam inside the Spectrum. "Promoter J Russell Peltz's eyeballs spun like two cash register tapes," Tom Cushman observed. "Tyrone Everett was in business." Bruce Trampler, the manager of Douglas and future matchmaker for the promotional firm Top Rank, walked over to Peltz and told him, "Congratulations, a fighter just made himself in front of this crowd tonight."

The Spectrum, the nerve center of Philadelphia boxing in the 1970s, and home to the Flyers and 76ers. The arena was demolished in 2011.
(Courtesy Peltz Boxing Promotions, Inc.)

Afterward, Jimmy Arthur was all smiles, if somewhat circumspect in his praise. "Tyrone is a small boy, but he's strong and I think he is convinced now that he can go the longer distances," he said. "He was a little scared the first time he went eight [rounds] and he was worried about Garces, but he's acting all right this time. The one thing I worry about now is that he'll get to thinking that everybody is going to go out the way Garces did."

But there was no mistaking the buzz. Suddenly, it appeared that the Black, left-handed East Coast fighter may not be box office poison after all, and Peltz was licking his chops in anticipation of the receipts to come. "I've heard people talking about Tyrone in the gyms, in the streets," Peltz told Cushman. "There is enough flamboyance in his style, just enough controversy in his appearance and the way he handles himself to bring the people in. They're either gonna love him or they'll come to see him get beat."

In a show of faith, Peltz picked Everett to headline his own card the next time out, and anyone who followed the Philadelphia boxing scene closely would not have missed the symbolic significance of this decision. Relegated to the undercard was none other than Eugene "Cyclone" Hart, the hard-hitting middleweight prospect adored by the city's most fervent boxing fans. Like Briscoe, he was molded in the image of his city: a two-fisted bruiser whose toil in the ring reflected the workaday toil of his fellow hard-luck denizens. Under Peltz, Hart had steamrolled twenty-one of his first twenty-two opponents and was steadily working his way up the rankings when a barrage of legal and managerial hiccups and two straight knockout losses stymied his momentum. Hart was now fighting for his promotional life on the undercard of another upstart.

The occasion of Everett's main event bid also called for a more carny approach to matchmaking. Now was hardly the time, after all, to try and test Everett's chin. So Peltz brought

over a ham-and-egger from Mexico named Jose Valdez, who
had nearly sixty fights to his name, twenty-six of them losses,
fourteen of which were by knockout. Valdez was a bowling pin
waiting to topple over. Peltz laid it on thick in the newspaper
ads: "Monday Night Fights! at the Spectrum presents THE
FATAL FEATHERWEIGHT! It's Tyrone Everett, unbeaten
and unbeatable, in a volatile, anything-can-happen 10-round
featherweight fight against Jose Valdez. Everett is an explosive
fighter who goes straight for the kill ... a real K.O. artist.
And he's the brightest young featherweight on the boxing
scene. So come ... see Tyrone Everett in action where boxing
is happening ... at the Spectrum!"

The public lapped it up. More than 4,000 ticket buyers
descended on the Spectrum on fight night, August 6,
harboring deep reserves of curiosity and high expectations. It
was a stellar turnout, given that most of the other headliners
that year, with the exception of Briscoe, had failed to crack
3,500. But there would be no dazzling encore that evening.
Everett proceeded to prat around for ten rounds en route to a
pedestrian unanimous decision. It was a lost opportunity, to
say the least. "It was really nothing," Peltz said of the fight.
"He [Tyrone] was content to go the limit and beat him by
decision. Valdez only wound up being knocked out seventeen
times. But you know Everett didn't put out. You see the scores.
Look at all the [lopsided] scores."

Even Everett could not hide his disappointment, though
he pinned the aesthetic failure of the bout on the reluctance
of his opponent. "I wasn't pleased with my performance,
but I couldn't get the shots I wanted," Everett told reporters

afterward. "He was leading with his right, then laying back and waiting to counter with a right. I didn't think he was that strong. If he had been, he would have worked inside. Instead, every time we tied up he was the one yelling to 'break.'"

North Philadelphia's Cyclone Hart, a fighter made in the image of his own city.
(Courtesy Peltz Boxing Promotions, Inc).

As always, his tutor came to his defense. "I kept telling him to not pay any attention [to the crowd], to keep his mind on his business," Jimmy Arthur said. "There was no sense taking chances against an opponent who is strong enough to hurt you if you get careless. The guy was just sitting back, waiting to drop a right hand."

The local boxing writers, perhaps unconvinced by Everett's main event status, made sure to give the majority of their column inches to Hart, technically a preliminary fighter on that night but who ended up stealing the show by bludgeoning Doc Holliday, who had previously only been knocked down once in his career. In the second round, Hart connected with a single left hook that sent Holliday into a deep slumber and the crowd into a tizzy. "I'm back on top!" Hart blustered to the crowd as he prowled around the ring while his foe remained stretched out. "They could have held a Watergate hearing while they were reviving Doc Holliday last night," observed Tom Cushman.

Nobody was more pleased than Hart's new handler Cus D'Amato, the obsessive and garrulous fight molder of Floyd Patterson and Jose Torres and, later, Mike Tyson. D'Amato, not the most genial personality, was uncharacteristically praiseworthy of his charge after the fight. "Gene is the hardest punching guy I've ever seen," he told reporters. That was Philadelphia boxing in a nutshell. Hard, brain-cell-scattering punching.

. . .

FROM THE HIGH of the Garces stoppage to the low
of the Valdez waltz, from a spirited knockout to a soporific
decision, inconsistency would become a central motif in
the career of Tyrone Everett. It was not an inconsistency
of style so much as it was an inconsistency of temperament, an absence of a recognizable will to power. One night
Everett would be hot, leaving his opponent senseless on the
canvas; the next night, cold, settling for a dreary decision.
This whiplash effect may not have affected the allegiance
of his key support base—the South Philadelphia set in the
Superfly getups, many of whom were not necessarily up
to snuff on their boxing and could care less about distin-
guishing between, as the saying goes, a left hook from a fish
hook—but it certainly alienated the hardcore base, the fight
cognoscenti who expected their native talents to behave as
decreed by tradition: to slug, to brawl, to fight in a state of
manic self-abandon. That is what a boxing ticket signified in
Philadelphia, and Everett ran afoul of the time-honored silent
contract repeatedly with all his flitting and jigging. It made a
mockery of the blue-collar ethos that dominated the culture.
Caution was not a respected quality in a fighter. Everett was,
in short, for the traditionalists, boring, an assessment that,
according to Cushman, often found its clearest expression in
jeremiads like, "He fights like a fag."

Ironically, one of Everett's biggest detractors was his own
promoter. Part of this was a matter of preference. Peltz, after
all, was nothing if not a representative member of that rarefied

class of Philadelphia fight enthusiast nourished on a diet of a good old-fashioned donnybrook. Peltz grew up worshipping punchers like Dick Tiger and come-forward types like Gaspar Ortega while deploring stylists like Ralph Dupas and Willie Pastrano. Consequently, as a promoter, Peltz regarded no one in his stable as highly as Briscoe. Everyone knew Briscoe, the consummate puncher, was his guy, "the love of my boxing life." Everett? Everett drove Peltz up the wall, mainly because he believed that his charge, with his superlative boxing ability, could have afforded to fight more often with Briscoe's verve. "I thought he could've been better than he was," Peltz said. "That's what frustrated me. He wouldn't lose a round, but it got monotonous because he wouldn't take chances a lot of times. These guys were not in his league, but he was just a safety-first guy."

The disconnect was understandable. Everett did not grow up idolizing the Tigers and Ortegas, so he did not share Peltz's romanticism for the sport. Where Peltz was prone to blandishments in his encounters with the greats of yesteryear, Everett simply responded with a shrug. He looked at their faces, at the way they walked, listened to their speech and found nothing inspiring in their pelted-down brows and floppy eyes, shuffling gait, and tongue-tied garbling. For Everett, they were nothing more than walking memento mori, reminders of the possible debilitating fate that awaited him in his chosen profession. "When I quit, I want to be able to walk down the street and say, 'I'm Tyrone Everett.' And not have people hear me mumble and not know who I am," he would later say.

For obvious reasons, there were dire economic consequences for boxing stylists, as the skillful but light-hitting Richie Kates,

one of the top 175-pounders during the 1970s and who frequently fought in Philadelphia, could attest. "Philadelphia is
the type of place that doesn't appreciate boxers … If I had to
depend on fighting there, I'd starve," Kates once mentioned to
the *Daily News*. What distinguished Everett from Kates, or,
say, the equally elusive heavyweight Jimmy Young, was that
Everett was a genuine draw; at his peak, he was bringing in
$60,000 gates, which only made his reticent performances all
the more maddening to Peltz. "Everett had his faction from
South Philly," Peltz said. "Later, it turned out that a lot of them
were in illegal businesses. But he drew his crowd. He was a big
drawing card. I just thought he could have been bigger. It was
just frustrating because that was the kind of town Philly was,
a walking-slugger-like-Bennie Briscoe kind of town." Wasted
potential—it is one of the oldest tropes in boxing.

It was no secret that Peltz and Everett rarely saw eye-to-
eye on most matters. Peltz wanted more aggression inside the
ropes from Everett; Everett wanted more money from Peltz.
Peltz felt Everett was a bad sport in the way he derided his
opponents after beating them; Everett felt Peltz was full of
himself, that he operated too much like a fan and did not have
his fighters' interests at heart. And so on. "Everett and I, we
never really got along," admitted Peltz. "There are newspaper
articles where he says, 'I'm so tight my pants squeak,' and
things like that.' In fact, Peltz rarely gave out comp tickets to
his fighters and once even refused to give Everett's mother a
freebie. "One time," continued Peltz, "when we were sitting
around a table in a luncheon and Gelb was between us, and
I'd say, 'Frank, tell Tyrone this,' and he'd [Tyrone] say, 'Tell

Russell this,' because we wouldn't talk to each other. It's funny because the Everett brothers have this annual awards affair in Philly and they honored me two years ago, and in my speech I said, 'Well, this is ironic.'"

Their acrimony at times spilled out into the public arena. In September 1975, at the Spectrum, Everett was getting the works from a tough Puerto Rican gatekeeper named Benjamin Ortiz. At one point in the seventh round, Ortiz nailed Everett with a punch that sent him sailing into the ropes (today the punch would have been counted as a knockdown). His spine abuzz with a tingling shiver, Peltz launched into the air from his ringside seat and yelled, with undisguised glee, "Yeah, c'mon!" thinking that "it was about time Everett dealt with some adversity," and that "finally, maybe we'll find out what kind of fighter we have here." But just at that moment, Mike Everett, who was patrolling the perimeter of the ring barking words of encouragement to his brother, happened to pass by Peltz. Mike turned around and, with his head cocked and eyebrows raised, locked eyes with Peltz. "Oh yeah?" he seemed to say. Everett would recover to win a clear decision. Crisis averted.

"I never wanted him to lose," Peltz said. "Why would I want him to lose? I just wanted better fights. That's what promoters used to want. They used to want better fights. They weren't just in there for their guy to get the 'W.' Because promoters were promoters back then."

But if Everett was not exactly keen on Peltz's tough love treatment, he was not above coveting adulation, be it from his promoter or from the city's hardened boxing fans. He saw too clearly the awe that was heaped on Bennie Briscoe, that great unwobbling pivot of Philadelphia boxing, and Everett was deeply envious of that reception. Philadelphia was still Briscoe's town, and anything that Everett did in the ring tended to fall under that broad, unrelenting shadow. "Acceptance, validation—he always wanted to be loved," Peltz said. "He was just dying for me to give it to him." Professional envy, at times, warped into full-blooded resentment. "Everett knew Briscoe was my fighter," Peltz recalled. "So when Briscoe fought Emile Griffith in October of '74, it looked like it was over for Briscoe—he looked like a horse's ass, like he didn't care anymore—and Everett had bet money on him. So, after the fight, Everett came over and said to me, 'That fuckin' Briscoe, he's shot.' You know, just to stick it up my ass. Just because that was our relationship. He's trying to dig me. And I'm digging him back."

One memorable exchange occurred in 1975, during a press conference ahead of one of Everett's fights. Everett promised a roomful of reporters a first-round knockout. Peltz rolled his eyes and retorted, "Tyrone is not the bravest fighter in the world."

"That's Peltz, talking like a promoter, talking like a fan," Everett volleyed back. "If I'm not the bravest, how have I gotten to where I am? Peltz has never had a pair of gloves on. One day, I'd like him to climb inside a ring. How come there's so many fighters scared to fight me?"

"You have to understand that during the time of Everett's career, I was less than seven years older than he was," Peltz recalled. "I was in my late twenties; he was in his early twenties. I was as immature as he was. Had I been the person

I hope I evolved into, I would have sat down with him and worked out our differences. Instead, I fed into his childish games and countered.

"I remember being at some kind of dinner or reception at Palumbo's in South Philly, and I was dancing with my wife Linda, about eight months before we got married. Tyrone was dancing with someone, and he saw us and said he was surprised I was with such a good-looking woman. He shook his head. Another time at the Spectrum—he was not fighting that night—he feigned surprise at the new three-piece suit I was wearing. We were children."

◆ ◆ ◆

AUGUST 1973. EVERETT informs Gene Courtney of the *Philadelphia Inquirer* about his retirement plans. He has no intention to become a boxing lifer, traipsing for paydays past his prime. In fact, he envisions a rather quaint afterlife to his boxing travails. In two years, when he is no longer a local prospect but a prime mover with a fast lifestyle, these words will seem unrecognizable. "I only expect to stay in boxing five more years, and I don't want to come out of it punchy," he says. "I like boxing, but I don't love it. Of course, I'd like to be a champion. But what I really want to do is to be a gym teacher. I'd like to open my own gym and work with little kids. I think that would be very satisfying for me."

* * *

IN HIS NEXT fight, Everett would return to top form, dropping veteran Natalio Jiménez twice and wobbling him several more times before stopping him for good with a right hand in the ninth round. It was win number seventeen. Perhaps the Valdez fight really was just a fluke. In any case, demand for Tyrone Everett continued to ratchet up, and it was not about to recede any time soon.

For the final Spectrum card of the year, Peltz decided to offer Everett as the headliner against Richie Villanueva. It was a hardy recognition of Everett's budding drawing power and a sign of how far he had come since his days as an anonymous whippersnapper. Once again, however, Everett would have to vie for the attention of the boxing public. Slotted on the undercard was the re-emergence of Stanley "Kitten" Hayward, a celebrated Philadelphia middleweight. Hayward was the real highlight of the night, at least to those in the know.

Stanley Hayward was a man about town, a smooth-talking hepcat with a penchant for pretty women, horse betting, and convertibles. He was tight with all the nightclub players and celebrities in Philadelphia and was something of a trans-Atlantic personage as well, having spent some time in Europe making B-movies with Yul Brynner and partying with star Omar Sharif. Hayward was an unrepentant believer in the High Life, but he approached his laborious métier seriously and managed, for the most part, to stave off the more dissolute temptations associated with his lifestyle. During the 1960s, a fertile decade for middleweights and welterweights, Hayward notched wins over Bennie Briscoe, Emile Griffith, and Curtis Cokes. He suffered a string of losses later in his career, none more devastating than a one-minute demolition by "Cyclone" Hart in 1971. Hayward called it quits after that bout. Now, two-and-a-half years later, he was priming himself for a comeback. Those chinchilla furs and Cadillacs, after all, were not going to pay for themselves. Naturally, all the publicity in Philadelphia went to Hayward and his impending return. Everett may have received top billing, but for most boxing fans, Hayward was the real attraction. Although he had never been much of a draw during his prime, Hayward was instant feel-good material for the nostalgists. A scion of the old guard, he reminded gimlet-eyed fans of a superior, bygone boxing era. Meanwhile, the media snub had Everett seething between rounds on the heavy bag. Where was Gene Courtney? Tom Cushman? Each day at the Passyunk Gym where he trained, Everett expected the beat reporters to waltz through the doors. None showed.

* * *

MONDAY, DECEMBER 3, 1973. Hayward delivered as promised. After feeling his way through a shaky first round—a right hand momentarily buzzed him—and most of the second, Hayward showed his superior class against Jose Anglada of New York, dropping him twice before the end of the round. After a brief kerfuffle between the referee Hank Cisco and Zach Clayton, the chairman of the State Athletic Commission, Hayward would finish off Anglada in the third. "I've dedicated myself to living clean for two years," Hayward crooned afterward, "and by then I'll be champion."

Next up was Everett. Heeding his trainer's instructions, Everett took his time with Villanueva, henpecking him with stiff right jabs and following up with hard left counters. In the eighth round, Everett kicked into a new gear, scoring two knockdowns. By the ninth round, Villanueva's face was jetting blood from the left eye and mouth like a faulty fountain, forcing referee Pete Tomasco to stop the bout at the 1:20 mark. "It may have been the kind of night that unleashed the tiger in Everett," Cushman observed, "a youngster of unquestioned skill who had been working, for the most part, with uninterrupted caution." Win number eighteen was in the bag.

But Everett was in no mood to savor the win, due to the general absence of press coverage leading up to the fight. He did not hide his irritation from the reporters who were now huddled around him in the locker room after the night was over.

"Just think, I was the main event fighter, and I didn't get one writeup in the newspapers," Everett groused. "I've won eighteen fights and everybody was talking about the other guy. My man [Villanueva] came into town telling about how he was gonna walk over me and then have a bout with Sammy Goss. He hardly mentioned my name. I think he'll remember me, now."

"Everett was pissed," Peltz recalled. "Here's a guy [Hayward] who hadn't fought and they're not writing about me. I think one of the [newspaper] headlines was, 'It's Write On with Everett' in one of the papers. And he was pissed about that."

Peltz was pissed, too, although for different reasons. Hayward and Everett had turned in a pair of solid performances, but the turnout was dismal. It was yet another night in the red for Peltz in what had frankly been a year chockful of box office flops. Peltz put on twenty shows at the Spectrum in 1973, but only three were profitable, and all three featured Bennie Briscoe, whose presence, like a hunk of reinforced concrete, was just about the only sure thing in Philadelphia boxing. Nevertheless, Peltz was $50,000 in the hole, a fact that greatly distressed Louis Scheinfeld, the Spectrum president who had hired Peltz to be the arena's marquee boxing man and was less than enthused about the noticeable lack of return on his investment. "We took [boxing] on for a year and threw everything into it, and I'm not satisfied with the result," Scheinfeld told Bob Davis of the *Times-Tribune*. "If there is no pickup early in 1974, we'll be pretty much out of the boxing business […] It costs us $10,000 a day to open our doors. We need $20,000 to break even on a show. We have trimmed to the bare (ushers, security, ticket takers, etc.), but our expenses are very high. Some of the fights which were put on could do $10,000 at smaller arenas and make money." The alarms had been sounded.

But Peltz was not about to panic, even if he was, at best, cautiously optimistic. He pointed out that most of the financial hits that the Spectrum incurred that year were sustained over the final five fights, a result of being in direct competition with *Monday Night Football* telecasts. Peltz promised to move his fights to Tuesdays starting the following fall, and their flagging attendance rates would improve accordingly. But Peltz drew his confidence from more than just a technical adjustment. There was nothing mystifying about the depressed gate numbers, after all. The fight had been mostly one-sided routs. Peltz was the first to admit that many of the cards he produced in 1973 were not up to snuff. But he also argued that the loss leaders of that year had been a necessary experience because nobody in the boxing community of Philadelphia had spent much time cultivating the soil of the local talent base. In short, the plowing and hoeing were left to Peltz. His labor would eventually produce plenty of healthy shoots. Hart, Watts, Monroe, Goss, and Everett would all thrive under Peltz's watch. Now Peltz reckoned that his fighters were on the verge of taking on the next logical assignment of their maturation, that the inroads he had made over the past five years stretching back to 1969, when he was an untried twenty-two-year-old novitiate, could begin to pay off. "There wasn't much around in the way of headline talent, so we had to develop some," Peltz told the *Daily News*. "We're at the point now where we have the fighters, so all we have to do is get them to fight. Each other, I mean."

Fighting each other. That was the Philadelphia fighting philosophy. It had been neglected in previous years, but the city was now ready to harness that ethos once more. Peltz now commanded a bevy of top middleweights and perhaps two of the best small fighters on the Eastern seaboard, all of them puffed up and ripe for public consumption. For the first quarter of 1974, Peltz had penciled in a pair of compelling bouts: Willie Monroe against Eugene Hart, and Stanley Hayward against Perry "Lil" Abner. The future, that of Peltz and of Philadelphia boxing at large, was coming together. As far as Everett was concerned, it could not arrive any quicker. He brightened up before leaving the dressing room on the night of his final fight of 1973. "I'm ready for anyone they want to match me with," he said with a smile. Everett had Goss in his crosshairs. Peltz was less sure about the timing, but he was pleased by Everett's sudden willingness to entertain that matchup straight away.

"I want to match Everett with a couple of good Mexicans first to see how he stands up," Peltz cautioned. "But, as for Tyrone's willingness to take the Goss fight, he has changed completely. He had been saying he was a year away. Now he says he'll fight him tomorrow."

* * *

By the end of March 1974, the Goss-Everett fight was set. At stake: Goss's North American featherweight title and intracity bragging rights. Everett, just shy of twenty-one, was the top featherweight on the East Coast; Goss, twenty-seven, was the top junior lightweight on the East Coast. They would meet on April 29, the date Peltz had reserved. There was one last obligation. Both fighters needed to come away victorious in their respective tune-ups on the same March 11 card at the Spectrum.

Goss—who was coming off a seven-month layoff after experiencing signs of brain damage sustained in his over Edwin Viruet the previous August but which were later diagnosed as a "frontal virus"—fought gingerly against Clemente Mucino, like a busser holding up a tray of highballs, on his way to a clear decision. Otherwise, it was a disappointing outing from someone who made a name for himself as a frenetic pressure fighter. Indeed, Goss looked downright sluggish at times. The crowd voiced their disapproval by showering him all night with boos.

Everett was hardly better in the entertainment department, pitching a drowsy 10-round shutout against crosstown cohort Luis Lopez. Once again, the clinical performance left hardcores shaking their heads. But if the stalwart Philadelphia boxing fans were heckling the decision, no one could really tell. Most of the nearly 5,000 customers who showed up that night were Everett partisans from South Philadelphia. Each punch he landed— or seemed to land—was greeted with a reception resembling a Mardi Gras celebration on Bourbon Street. Afterward, Everett was in high spirits. As he settled in the dressing room, Everett took up his favorite post-fight pastime: denigrating his opponents. This time, he saved up his invective for his co-head-liner. "When I was coming up, people used to tell me I'd never be able to beat Goss," Everett said. "Now people tell me Goss would never be able to beat me. And they're right. Sammy Goss isn't even in my class." "He's not as strong as Lopez," Everett continued, "and I believe I can knock him out."

When this remark was relayed to Goss, an easy-going man who probably never uttered a profanity in his life, he simply uttered, "Look, all he does is jab and run. I didn't see his bout, but I bet that is all he was: stick and run. He's not a fighter." When reporters continued to press him on his lack-luster showing, Goss became irritated. "I don't want to talk about Everett anymore; just be there April 29th. I'll do my talking in the ring with my fists."

* * *

Goss, born in Newark but made in Philly; one of boxing's sadder tales.
(Courtesy Peltz Boxing Promotions, Inc.)

SAMMY GOSS WAS not a born-and-bred Philadelphian, but it was in Philadelphia that he discovered himself as a prizefighter. A native of nearby Trenton, New Jersey, Goss was an elite amateur, winning five Golden Gloves titles and a berth in the 1968 Olympics in Mexico City, where he lost in a preliminary round. In the punch-to-pay ranks, Goss quickly made a name for himself as one of the premier lower-weight-class fighters on the East Coast, climbing all the way up to number seven among junior lightweights on the rankings system of the World Boxing Council. By shunting back and forth between headlining acts at Madison Square Garden in New York and the Spectrum in Philadelphia, Goss built himself into a known quantity, drawing the particular admiration of the Tri-State boxing fans, a not insignificant feat considering all the attention was hardwired into the heavyweight scene in those days.

Goss was a model fighter. He went on two six-mile runs each day and spent at least two hours in the gym honing his skills on the bag and sparring. He was workmanlike in every sense of the word. "People sometimes expect Sammy Goss to carry a lunch pail and container of milk when he walks to work—into the ring," wrote Lee Samuels of the *Courier-Post*. Goss went about his business like a career civil servant. He always showed up to press engagements on time, made weight, and took his paycheck without grumbling. The less said, the better was the kind of age-old code of conduct to which Goss subscribed. Indeed, Goss came up in an era in which the brazen behavior of Muhammad Ali was still a threatening novelty.

So imagine the shock on the faces of the reporters who had gathered at a press conference in downtown Philadelphia five days before the showdown to witness Goss spew out a diatribe worthy of *Glengarry Glen Ross*.

"I just don't want to knock [Tyrone] out," said Goss, his voice quivering as he stared icily behind his horn-rimmed glasses at his adversary across the room. "I want to beat him up, whup him, break him, wreck him. I want to send him to the hospital ... I'm looking to beat him to death. I want to hurt him."

Then again, given how Everett had spent the better part of the past year disparaging Goss in the press, this should not have been a surprising reaction. In fact, it went beyond mere ribbing. Everett liked to point out how Goss lacked firepower in his punches, which, in boxing terms, is somewhat tantamount to questioning a fighter's manhood. Goss compensated for this deficiency with a frenetic work rate. Because of how he bobbed and weaved on the inside, Goss often drew comparisons to Joe Frazier. Still, punching power was a touchy subject for Goss, whose own trainer once said, "A fighter has to know how to punch. Sammy doesn't, but he'll learn." That was back in 1969.

The tipping point came a week before their fight, when Everett went on another rant, swearing he would "knock [Goss] out in about six rounds. I'll take it to him and make him fight my fight." There was no end to the denigration. Initially, it appeared that Goss had batted away those earlier jibes like they were so many shuttlecocks, but that was far from the case. Goss had finally cracked.

"I'm sick of Everett's talk," Goss snarled. "He's been telling everybody I can't punch, I cut easy, I'm over the hill and he's going to retire me. What kind of talk is that from a punk kid who hasn't fought anybody? If I fought the guys he fought, I'd have all knockouts. He told my trainer [Percy Richardson] I couldn't punch anymore. He said I was through as a fighter, washed up, and that kind of talk hurt me. Now, I'm going to hurt him for saying it [...] I guess he thought he was putting the fear in me because I wasn't answering. Well, now I'm answering and I'm telling Everett exactly what to expect."

Richardson, Goss's new trainer, was also among the astonished, and he suddenly found himself facing the reality that his charge might have been better off spending the remaining days before the fight mentally recuperating on a psychoanalyst's couch than exerting himself in the gym. "I've never heard Sammy talk about any opponent the way he's been talking about Everett," Richardson told the *Daily News*. "He really wants to hurt the kid, and I know he has the tools to do it. But I don't want Sammy coming in a foot off the ground. My biggest job is to make him keep his cool. If the kid runs like a thief, which I expect he will, I don't want Sammy to lose his patience. He's coming too far to flip out over some kid's mouth."

There were other matters to tend to during the luncheon, but everyone seemed to be in a bickering mood. Pinny Schafer, Goss's manager and one of the longtime stalwarts on the Philadelphia boxing scene, raised the vexing issue of their opponent's choice of hairstyle. "I don't care what you call them," Schafer started. "I don't want those corncobs flying in my fighter's eyes. They tape the laces on boxing gloves to keep them from damaging a fighter's eyes, don't they? Well, this kid, Everett, has a headful of laces when he fights. If he wants to have his own hairdresser working the corner, that's all right with me, just as long as there's nothing flying around loose on his head. But the way Sammy's been talking, I think Everett would be better off with a good cut man in his corner."

Was Schafer really concerned? Or was he looking to get a rise out of Everett? His subtext, in any case, was self-evident: Real fighters—hard-hat Philadelphia fighters—do not wear pigtails.

Meanwhile, across the room, the "kid" continued to stir the pot—slowly, with two hands on the ladle and a gleeful smirk on his face. "[Goss is] going to need more than a 10-round tune-up to prepare for me," Everett quipped. "He looked slow, and the fans booed the decision. I'm going to use speed, punch and power and beat him real bad [...] He doesn't have the power to hurt me. In fact, he may not even hit me."

It was not exactly on the level of the animosity between Ali and Frazier, but the Goss-Everett discord was far from just harmless joshing. Everett promised to perform a sanguinary dissection on fight night. This time, Everett did not need Jimmy Arthur to prop his ego up. It was in full flower. "He has some facial scars and I'm going to work on them," Everett said. "I'm going to cut him good ... slice up his face, to make him bleed."

Comments like these were becoming much more frequent from someone generally considered tight-lipped and reserved coming out of the amateurs. In fact, Everett's ability to interface with the public was so poor that he spent time with Gelb rehearsing what he was going to say to the press. Which is to say that part of his maliciousness was clearly informed by a desire, however warped or misguided, to create theatrical flair, as he would admit years later.

"This game is one of the lowest-regarded sports," Everett told Gene Courtney. "People don't talk about it, don't write about it unless it's the heavyweights fighting. We in the other classes have to start selling ourselves. Writers are used to coming around, asking, 'What kind of shape you in?' The boxer goes, 'Duh, OK.' 'How you going to do?' 'Duh, OK.'

That's what you're used to hearing, cats mumble. But we have to make people realize that not only low-class people are in boxing. The public thinks only people who can't read or write are in it. I want to prove that image wrong. I'll boast about myself a little bit, maybe a lot."

⁕ ⁕ ⁕

"YEAH!" EXCLAIMED MIKE Everett, as he entered the locker room to find his brother cooling off on the rubbing table before a horde of reporters. "All he does is slap. I thought you was in the ring with a girl."

Tyrone Everett flashed a haughty smile. He had just spent twelve rounds creating a patchwork of gory incisions in the face that belonged to a proud man, just as he had promised. The girls he knew from his neighborhood block would have put up a stiffer fight. More importantly, his own face remained unmarked. There would be no bandage dangling from his brow when he hit the dance floor later that night. "My sparring partner, Baby Kid Chocolate, hits harder than Goss," Everett cawed. "Goss didn't hurt me at all. He couldn't hurt a egg with his punch."

The biggest "little man" fight to land in Philadelphia in years, a fight regarded as a pick-'em affair, had turned out to be little more than a vehicle for carrying out the sadistic fantasies of Tyrone Everett. Round in and round out, Everett made good on his prefight comments that he would "slice up" Goss, whom oddsmakers had pinned as the slight favorite. Goss had been sliced up, all right. By the end of the third round,

Goss's left eye was already puffed up. In the sixth round, a one-inch gash formed over his right eye. By the ninth, he was swallowing his own blood between gulps of oxygen, courtesy of a half-inch cut on the inside of his bottom lip. The score-cards were as stark as they were uniform. Earl Vann and Dave Beloff scored the bout 59-49 (on the five-point must system), while referee Hank Cisco had it a shutout, 60-49, all for the Philadelphian. Jab, circle right, counter left: Everett was a broken record repeating the same riff over and over again to masterful effect. He may have drawn his tactics from a familiar source. In the weeks leading up to the fight, Everett binge-watched footage of Willie Pep, arguably the greatest featherweight and defensive mind to ever cross the threshold of a boxing ring, internalizing the pinpoint counterpunching and nimble footwork of the "Will o' the Wisp."

The only complaint—and this would become a familiar one—was that the fight may have dragged on longer than it should have. Everett certainly had his chance to pursue an early stoppage when he dropped Goss with a heat-seek-ing left early in the second round. Then again, Everett was brought up to fight only one way. "You'll notice I didn't get big-headed" after the knockdown, Everett told the *Daily News*. "If a knockout comes, it comes. I've learned how to coast, not take chances." Later, Goss, who had brief, isolated moments of success connecting to the body in the middle rounds, admitted that that punch was "a great one … it really got me good." Instead, Everett let the fight go on as it steadily morphed into a vaudeville act in the late rounds. By the 10th round, Goss was in complete shambles, lurching forward, swiping at air, looking every bit like a man clinging onto a tree trunk during a hurricane.

"It was so lopsided. It was almost sickening," wrote Lee Samuels of the *Courier-Post*. In the 11th round, some ringside observers were begging for the fight to be called off. With each punch he delivered, Everett followed up with a verbal joust. A dejected Goss, the man who vowed to send Everett to the ICU, offered up only the feeblest of retorts. "He didn't say nothing," Everett said. "Except when I hit him, he said, 'Good punch, that was a good punch.' I kept hitting, and he kept saying how good the hits were." Everett had made Goss into a yes-man, had emasculated him on the most transparent of sporting stages.

"It was not the outcome that was surprising because Tyrone is an excellent young fighter, it was the enormity of it," Tom Cushman wrote in the *Daily News*. "Not the fact that the torch had been passed, but that it was done so conclusively. Sammy's long, carefully constructed career suddenly is shattered. Scrambled eggs."

"I think he was scared the whole fight," Everett said. "When we went out for the introductions he wouldn't even look at me. He was looking at the floor. He kept talking about the guys I've fought. The truth is, the only two guys he fought that were any good stopped him. I tell you, Luis Lopez gave me a harder fight than I had tonight."

Then he added, with a touch of melancholy, "I can't understand how [Goss] got up as far up there in the ratings as he did."

It had been a successful night on most levels. Of the 8,628 fans in attendance, which translated to $60,000 in ticket receipts (more than $360,000 in 2023 dollars), the vast majority of them came from South Philadelphia. It was clear Everett had a reliable constituency that was less concerned about the clinical nature of his boxing ability than with the swaggering force of his personality, the charm in his smile. There was no denying it anymore. Everett was a legitimate local attraction. Still, for others involved, it was far from a perfect night. Although Peltz was elated with the box office tallies, he nearly blew a fuse listening to Everett trample over Goss in front of the media after the fight. Once again, Peltz felt it was another lost opportunity for Everett to endear himself to a larger swath of the fan base. Once again, promoter and fighter were at loggerheads.

"Why come back into the dressing room after the biggest win of your career and say, and I quote exactly, 'He can't break a egg?'" Peltz recalled. "That was the first thing he said when he sat on the rubbing table. Listen, he was arrogant and he would say, 'That Goss, he slaps like a girl.' [I'd say] 'You know, you're putting a guy down that you just beat and it's only going to detract from what you just did. So you're hurting your own accomplishments.'"

There were no open complaints from Jimmy Arthur. The trainer stood in the back of the locker room, quietly basking in the ambiance of the victory.

"The main thing I was worried about was pace," Arthur told the *Daily News*. "I figured Goss would try to make Tyrone work hard in the early rounds, so that he could come on late. I kept emphasizing this in the corner. I'd have to say Tyrone listened very well. I can't think of anything we'd really change."

Meanwhile, Goss sat slumped in the other dressing room and struck a rueful note. "I fought the wrong kind of fight for him," he said. "I should have let him come to me. I should not have pursued him. I knew he could counter, but I thought if I pressed it would tire him, but it didn't. He's fast [...] He punched really good. He'll make a good champion."

Goss was a gentleman in defeat, but he was still in a state of shock, unable to process the extent of the denuding that had occurred. A year later, he would tell the *Courier-Post* that he was "sick with tonsillitis" heading into the fight and that the medication he was on threw him off his usual rhythm.

"All that talk, I never heard talk like that," Goss muttered. "When he said I was through as a fighter, I wanted to beat him so badly, to put him in the hospital."

Goss promised a swift rebound. Three months later, he was back in the ring—only to lose again. The truth was Goss was never the same after Everett. His record stood at 39-3 before their encounter. Afterward, he was a ghastly 4-11-3, an alarming drop-off. Never again would he be able to string together consecutive wins. His paltry four victories came against dilettantes with single digits in their win columns. In the blink of an eye, he became a steppingstone for rising contenders such as Jerome Artis, Alfonso Hayman, Ronnie McGarvey, Ray Lunny III, Anthony Fletcher, and Rocky Lockridge. In a cruel instance of symmetry, he would even drop a decision to Augie Pantellas, the man he beat so easily early on in his career to become the top little man on the East

Coast. His final fight was a knockout loss to prospect Brian Baronet in South Africa. In his twelve-year career as a professional, Goss never received a title shot, something that still irks Peltz to this day.

"Goss was a tragedy in and of himself," Peltz said recently. "Boxing really fucked him over. There was not a lot of power on the East Coast for little guys. I was still feeling my way around. When you look at his record, when he went to fight Everett, he was like 39-3, something like that. And he had beaten some really good guys, guys who went to get title fights, like Jose Fernandez and Viruet, and he never got one. He should've.

"In recent years I feel bad for Goss because I knew Everett was going to beat him. You couldn't make that fight today because Goss' people would've said, 'What do we need this for?' It was a tough undefeated lefthander. But it was probably one of Goss' biggest purses."

As for Everett, the good times were about to begin rolling.

"Now I'd like to try a title shot," he said. "I'm going to the top."

CHAPTER FOUR

He's a beautiful kid to work with. He's got all the tools, power, speed, good reflexes, and most of all he listens. He's going to be the next champion. I can't see anybody in the junior lightweight division that can beat this kid.

— GEORGE BENTON
to the *Philadelphia Tribune*

DORIS EVERETT HAD to be the happiest mother in all of Philadelphia. Life, once impossibly grueling, had improved immeasurably for her since the daily hand-to-mouth travails that characterized her existence in the 1960s. She found herself on better financial footing and no longer had to rely on a welfare check, a not unremarkable fact given that the country was deep in the throes of economic stagnation. More importantly, she still had her sons by her side—five healthy and devoted boys. Perhaps the ultimate testimony to her resilience was the fact that her three oldest sons, all prizefighters, were going to be participating on the same card on August 19, 1974, at the Spectrum. Tyrone, Mike, and Eddie. Surely that was a first for Philadelphia boxing. Doris would be there, albeit in the cheap seats. She never enjoyed going to the fights for obvious reasons, but she would make an exception this time. "One of my boys gets clubbed, you know who the first one up there in that ring?" she told the *Bulletin*. "Me. Now can you imagine how that would look?" The week leading up to the fight should have been an extended champagne jamboree for the Everett clan, an occasion to reflect on how far the family had come. But the oldest was not inclined to join in on the spirit of celebration. He was in a foul mood.

It all started a week before the card when Everett, something of a publicity hound, was scouring the local papers and spotted his name in an advertisement announcing his match against Blakeney Matthews, a tough South African veteran with a supposedly gritty 39-7-3 record (Matthews' trainer claimed his record was actually 54-8-2) and who claimed to never have touched the canvas in his career as a professional. On paper Matthews, who grew up in an orphanage during the height of apartheid, appeared to be an even more formidable challenger than Goss. On that front, Everett had no issues. It was the fact that there was a name above his own in the billing that had him reaching for the phone quicker than an Old West gunslinger unholstering his Colt.

WILLIE (THE WORM) MONROE VS. DYNAMITE DOUGLAS: A BRUTAL SLUGGER AND A SUPER BOXER GO ROUND & ROUND!

Accompanying the text was a portrait of each fighter. Then, below, in smaller letters, "Tyrone Everett vs. Blakeney

Matthews." Everett was livid. Peltz had assured him main event status after beating Goss. He was the NABF super featherweight champion, after all, and the toast of the town. Sure, there were bigger fighters than him in Philadelphia, but in his mind, they did not include Monroe or some mid-western carpetbagger in Douglas.

"Look at the advertisements in the paper," Everett groused to the *Inquirer*. "There's Monroe's picture. There's Monroe and Douglas in big black letters. There's me in the small print. Look at the fight posters. This is a Monroe card … and I don't want to talk about it."

But Everett was never one to stop talking.

"I don't understand why I'm not on top (of the bill)," he continued. "I'm ranked No.4 in the world's top contenders and I'm fighting the semi-windup. And I'm the only one on the card with a title. It doesn't make sense for me not to be on top."

Peltz was put on the defensive. It was true. Everett deserved to be the main event. But Monroe-Douglas was a vintage Philadelphia fight, another manifestation of the middleweight round-robin Peltz had been trying so desperately to enact over the past few years. Monroe-Douglas was a fight after his own heart, and it deserved to be the headliner, too. "I tried to give them equal billing," Peltz moaned. "I really don't know what I'll do about it. I haven't made up my mind yet." But Everett did not see what was so perplexing. From a meritocratic standpoint, there was no argument. He had a title, albeit a regional one, whereas Monroe had none. For Everett, who could care less about middleweight slugfests, Peltz was acting like a fan again instead of a promoter.

"The impression I got from the start was that I would be the main event," Everett told the *Daily News*. "I've got two titles [Pennsylvania State and North America] and Monroe's got none. They tried for two years to get some of these guys like Monroe to fight each other and they wouldn't. I've only been fightin' for two years and in that time I never heard any talk about me pulling out on anybody [...] They came to me and asked me to fight Sammy Goss, who was a champion and I said, 'Fine.' I could have said, 'Let me have two more years' experience,' but I didn't. They keep saying that Monroe and Douglas have more experience than me, like they're old-timers. Well, I tell them that I'm a young-timer and that I fight anybody."

Everett was trying to send a message, to Peltz, to Philadelphia. He was the goods, and he demanded to be treated as such. "It seems like such a petty thing," Peltz sighed.

Eventually, they reached a compromise. Peltz decided that the Tyrone-Matthews bout would be scheduled last on the card, thereby giving it the appearance of a main event. Eddie Futch, the legendary trainer and Monroe's manager, was fine with that arrangement so long as the Monroe-Douglas tilt continued to be billed, and hence regarded, as the top attraction. Of course, such matters were completely frivolous to Futch and his charge. "I ain't got time to be worrying about things like that," Monroe snarled. "He's spending his time worrying about fighting the main event. I'm more concerned with beating Douglas." Once again, Everett was litigating the divide between the old culture and the new, of which he was its most prominent exponent. "I mentioned to Eddie Futch that Everett IS a champion and Eddie laughed and said that with the North American title and ten cents Tyrone could get a cup of coffee," Peltz told the *Daily News*, no doubt, with a grin on his face. But no one could deny Everett now, not with the way he was performing inside the ropes.

On August 19, a crowd of 7,122 convened at the Spectrum. There were a few boxing luminaries in the building. Frazier was seated ringside to cheer on Monroe, his Cloverlay stablemate. Angelo Dundee, the trainer of Muhammad Ali, was also there, but strictly for business, as he had a prospect on the undercard. (At the time, Dundee was based in Deer Lake, Ali's private training compound an hour-and-a-half north of Philadelphia, where he was busy prepping the garrulous heavyweight for his cross-cultural extravaganza with George Foreman in the Democratic Republic of the Congo.) A last-minute commotion in the Matthews camp had them scrambling to find a cut man. Dundee kindly stepped in, although it was not one of those nights where his dexterity would be required.

Channeling the built-up tetchiness of the past couple of weeks, compounded by the fact that he had to shed two pounds earlier in the day after coming in slightly overweight at the weigh-in, Everett wasted no time stripping apart the supposedly heavy-duty Matthews. After staggering Matthews with a trio of left hands in the first round, Everett dropped the discombobulated visitor with a crisp right fifteen seconds into the second. A minute later he followed up with a ramrod straight left that deposited Matthews to the mat once again, and this time the referee waved off the carnage. The Spectrum

_____

blew up. There was still a chunk of spectators milling out in the hallways next to the concession stand who rushed back to their seats to see what the hoopla was about. It was precisely the kind of violence Peltz expected from Everett each time he ducked through the ropes. The thinking was that with a few more explosive finishes like this and even some of the most unyielding of doubters would have to reassess their convictions. There was no second-guessing from Dundee, though. A native of South Philadelphia himself, Dundee seemingly converted on the spot. Immediately he put Everett in the same class as some of the best southpaws he had seen in his more than three decades in the sport. Dundee reckoned his beloved city would soon have another champion. "Anytime you get a southpaw that hits you with both hands, moves in-and-out, moves from side-to-side, then you got a great fighter," Dundee gushed to the *Daily News*. "If I'm not mistaken, this kid is the next featherweight champion of the world. The kid is only sensational."

A shell-shocked Matthews joined Dundee in the rapture. "He's the best I've fought," Matthews told the *Bulletin*. "Most young fighters when they hurt you, rush in, but this Tyrone is very calm. He timed me. Norman Salter, Matthews' manager, was just as shaken. "I still find it hard to believe that I saw what I saw," Salter muttered. "A lot of people around here told us Everett couldn't punch, but one good shot and my fighter was through. He is also one of the slipperiest blokes I've ever seen."

As for Matthews, the chastened veteran had not only hopped on the Everett bandwagon, but he was also practically driving it. "Since I have been here, I have heard many people talk as though they don't like Tyrone Everett and I don't understand this," Matthews told the *Daily News*. "If the people of Philadelphia stand behind him, they will have a champion. This Tyrone is going to bring their name up, like Joe Frazier did for Philadelphia. They should get behind him, because he is going to be their champion, very soon."

Meanwhile, Everett was kvetching as usual in the locker room after the fight. "I'm tired of these guys coming into Philadelphia saying they're not worried about Tyrone Everett," Everett sneered. "Today all they did was fuss about me being overweight—made me take off two pounds—and then all they did was fight two rounds."

Crankiness aside, Everett knew he had arrived at a new station in his career. He now turned his attention toward a title shot, putting WBA featherweight champion Ruben Olivares in his crosshairs, as well as the winner of the upcoming WBC featherweight title fight between Bobby Chacon and Alfredo Marcano. "What I want now is a couple more bouts, and then the champion," Everett said. "I want Ruben Olivares early next year. I keep hearing him called 'Mr. Knockout,' but I've seen him on TV, and he don't look like nothing to me."

By defeating Goss so effortlessly four months ago, Everett had accelerated the pace of his development. Practically overnight, he had outgrown the strictures of East Coast boxing. That much was obvious. By calling out Olivares, one of the top "little men" in the sport, Everett was signaling to his handlers and confrères that he was primed for the world stage. Of course, calling out Olivares and actually fighting him were two distinct propositions. Everett would not simply be able to leapfrog the rest of the competition for a shot at the champion. He would have to observe the pecking order, however ad hoc and informal. He would need to build up his name into a recognizable commodity, as it pertained to the West Coast, the unofficial seat of power for the lower-weight classes. This was the rationale that Rafael Mendoza, the top fight agent of Mexican talent, laid out to Everett's handlers. Mendoza was a familiar figure in Philadelphia circles since he was the man indirectly responsible for throwing a wrench in the once-promising careers of Augie Pantellas and Goss by booking Ricardo Arredondo and Jose Luis Lopez as B-sides; the former stopped Pantellas, and the latter kayoed Goss, well before Everett ever laid his own hands on him. Now, Mendoza, with an upset on his mind, had another fighter of Mexican stock that he planned to bring to Philadelphia, the southpaw Jose Luis Madrid, whom Everett was scheduled to face on September 10 at the Spectrum, a date that became available to Everett after the original headlining act, the Benny Briscoe-Emile Griffith title fight, got pushed back to October.

"Tyrone Everett can never get a title fight or make a name for himself until he starts fighting and beating the top Mexican featherweights in the world," Mendoza pontificated to the *Tribune*. "If Everett would fight and beat six or seven good Mexicans, then the Mexican people would say, 'Let's see this Everett. Who is he? Why doesn't he box for the title?' Mexicans are very proud. They want revenge. When an outsider beats a good Mexican, the fans want revenge. This is the only way Everett will get a title fight with someone like Ruben Olivares. Who cares if he beats Blakeney Matthews?

What does that mean to the Mexicans? They could not care less. But if Everett beats a good Mexican, then the people take notice [...] The people have much to say in the matter."

But, like clockwork, Everett was once again fuming over the circumstances of his scheduled bout. This time the point of contention concerned Madrid's ledger. As was the case with many Mexican fighters in those days, their records could often be as reliable as the mortality rates supplied by *Pravda* or *Rodong Sinmun*. Combing through ten years' worth of *Ring* magazines, Peltz concluded that Madrid had a 10-4 record and, from that figure, determined that Madrid would be a serviceable tune-up for Everett to take on at the last minute. Later, after Everett had signed the bout contract, Peltz learned that Madrid's record was closer to 39-10 with thirty-four knockouts. Suddenly, Madrid was looking a bit more like Lopez or Arredondo, an upset specialist, not some Jalisco clod. It was not the end of the world, but Everett, as well as his handlers Jimmy Arthur and Frank Gelb, were plenty peeved by the revelation since it disrupted the risk-reward calculus that they were now beginning to carefully heed. Madrid was a sideshow, not a steppingstone, thus, as the thinking went, a contender like Everett had little to gain in victory. If he lost, he may as well say goodbye to his championship aspirations. "I've got to stop fighting people like this—I've got to stick with the top 10 contenders from now on," Everett told the *Courier-Post.* "If I lose to someone like him, it would be a disaster for me—I can't afford to take those kind of chances."

Still, Everett was not about to lose any sleep over his challenger, whom he viewed with typical derision. His confidence swelled twofold when he sized up Madrid for the first time at the pre-fight press conference and noticed the outcrop of scar tissue on the visitor's mug. As if by primal urge, his eyes lit up with anticipation. "I will use a strong jab and slice him open," Everett said, echoing his previous claims. "As soon as I saw his face, I knew exactly where I was about to attack. His face told the whole story."

But there would be no time for opening old wounds. For the second straight outing, Everett put away his man in a pair of rounds. "It was pure viciousness," observed Lee Samuels of the *Courier-Post*. "Suddenly, Tyrone Everett is not only an undefeated fighter, but possibly a world-class boxer, too." The end began halfway through the second, when Everett landed an unsuspecting body punch that caused Madrid to splay out on the ropes—that was payback for a body punch that Madrid landed in the opening round that briefly froze Everett in his tracks. He followed it up with a laser right hand to the chin that dropped Madrid to his knees for an eight-count. Madrid managed to pull himself up, only to have the rapier-quick Everett send him spiraling down into the whiteness of the canvas once more. This time Madrid did not get up. Immediately, in a move that was to become a prominent part of his repertoire, Everett aimed his glove at his prostrate foe, raised his arms in the air, and, finally, sashayed back to his corner, as 4,425 roared from the stands, all before the referee had a chance to call off the bout. It was straight out of the Muhammad Ali Playbook of Extracurricular Theatrics. Everett was bringing a new culture of razzmatazz to Philadelphia boxing, and depending on one's leanings and allegiances, it was either going to elate or alienate fans. With Everett, it was always either/or. When asked about his vindictive behavior in the ring, a hyped-up Everett responded with his usual acid brio: "I build up a hate for everyone. His trainer did all his talking for him. Said I'd never met a puncher like Madrid. Said he had more knockouts than I had fights. People come in here, thinking I'm a nobody. I'm not Sammy Goss. I can punch."

The gospel of Tyrone Everett was spreading fast, and like Angelo Dundee, Blakeney Matthews, and Norman Salter before him, Mendoza, the fight agent, became another adherent. "He can go anywhere in the world and win a fight," a humbled Mendoza told the *Courier-Post*. "I don't care what country he is in. He doesn't have to worry about a hometown decision because the result will be a knockout. He is so quick, and he has speed and timing—he can go against anyone, even Bobby Chacon. That would be a terrific fight." (A few days earlier, in Los Angeles, Chacon steamrolled Alfredo Marcano to win the WBC featherweight title. As soon as the results reached Frank Gelb, he mailed a $25,000 check to Dewey Fragetta, the international booker, to try and entice either Chacon or the WBA featherweight champion Olivares to come defend their respective titles in Philadelphia.)

Emboldened by his sudden string of short nights in the ring, Everett found his bellicose approach to be highly becoming and vowed that he had turned over a new stylistic leaf. Henceforth he would fight coming forward, baying for blood, ready to throttle the other man into oblivion. He was, in other words, ready to embrace the fighting spirit of a true

Philadelphia pugilist. "I wanted to bang it out. I don't want to go the distance no more—just go out there and destroy, real quick," Everett said. "From now on I'm gonna take all my power to these guys. I don't want any long fights"

It was music to Peltz's ears, even if they were just words. Jimmy Arthur, Everett's caution-first trainer, was pleased as well and even approved of the showboating.

"He realized he had finished the guy, so he pointed at him as he went down," Arthur told Stan Hochman of the *Daily News*. "He knew he had knocked him out. That's good because some fighters don't know when they've got a guy in trouble. Ty's learning. He's learning how to finish a guy."

"I think I'm ready for a championship bout," Everett told Gene Courtney of the *Inquirer*. I don't want to wait until I'm an old man. If I have to lose, I'd rather lose now to a champ or a high contender so that I can come back."

He would never know the irony of those words.

CHAPTER FIVE

*My dad took me to that one fight that was at the old
Spectrum. I was still in high school. My dad told me
we had to go see this guy. He's just a beautiful thing to
watch. He had that hand speed, athletic ability. He was
the full package. He just wasn't the prototypical Philly
fighter. A Philly fighter walks you down and bangs with
you. He wasn't a big puncher, he wasn't that type of guy,
but he was just a beautiful guy to watch. My dad said,
'This is what you want to do when you want to fight.' If
my dad was going to drive seven hours to Philadelphia
just to see him fight, he must've made an impression on
him somewhere. He must've been special.*

— GREGORY SIRB,
Executive Director of the Pennsylvania
State Athletic Commission

TOWARD THE END of 1974, as the country
continued to reel from the disastrous anti-inflation
policies implemented by President Richard Nixon,
it was clear that Peltz's de facto middleweight tourney was

approaching a dry spell. All the participants had fought each other. A simple solution would have been to invite elite foreign fighters to Philadelphia, but given the limited bankroll Peltz was working with, that was not a viable possibility. Why, for instance, would Jean-Claude Bouttier, one of the top middleweights in the world, ever leave Paris, where he could make as much as $60,000 in one fight (more than the total revenue of some of Peltz's shows), just to fight Bennie Briscoe in his backyard for a pittance? In any case, Peltz was running out of ideas.

Moreover, despite the inroads made in matchmaking and the increase in general turnout, the year was a financial disappointment. Fighter pay had gone up, and even on seemingly successful shows like the Griffith-Briscoe fight, Peltz wound up losing money because of the relatively steep purses that the two fighters commanded. Peltz blamed himself for not thinking enough like a businessman. It also did not help that in many of the matchups that Peltz staged in the past year that featured a boxer against a puncher, the boxer usually won, not exactly a formula for success in a city that loved its punchers.

Still, despite these hiccups, there was a lot to admire about the past year. Altogether the shows at the Spectrum had attracted more than 60,000 fans and generated more than $400,000 in gate revenue. It was also a far cry from 1973, when the Spectrum registered a $50,000 loss on boxing. Things were trending in the right direction. To that end, Peltz inked a new two-year extension with the Spectrum. There was a palpable sense in the air that boxing was once more a big deal in Philadelphia. It was not enough to say that Peltz, barely twenty-eight, had rehabilitated boxing in the city. He had turned it into a powerhouse. Philadelphia was back on the map, a bustling fight capital on par with New York City, Miami (South Beach), and Los Angeles. (Actually, there was a real argument to be made that Philadelphia had succeeded New York as the premier pipeline for up-and-coming talent. On New Year's Eve 1974, Madison Square Garden announced it would suspend its boxing club show program indefinitely at its sister arena, the Felt Forum, citing economic reasons and a desire to focus on big bouts, meaning if you wanted to catch a decent club show on the East Coast, you needed to trek over to Philadelphia. Lester Bromberg, the veteran boxing writer for the *New York Post*, did precisely that, hopping on an Amtrak to catch the first Spectrum card of the new year.)

Peltz was feeling frisky about the next year and believed that the solid crop of featherweights under his wing, led by Tyrone Everett, the No. 5 ranked junior lightweight in the world, were ready to take center stage. "I think that 1975 will be the year of the featherweights," Peltz predicted. "We've got about ten good talented featherweights around here—like Tyrone Everett, Baby Kid Chocolate, Jerome Artis, Goss, Al Evans, Lynwood Snowden, Carlos Dupree and that new kid from Trenton, William Berry. I guess that will be the next group that will make some money now that the middleweight elimination has been settled."

Peltz had a clear directive from Everett: Top-ten fighters only from here on out. That meant no local fighters, like heel-nipping Jerome Artis, against whom Everett had nothing to gain and everything to lose. "I'm not scared of local fighters but none of them are in the Top 10 and they all look like they're at least a year away," Everett said. "So they can talk all they want. I won't fight them." Everett was, in a way, haunted by how quickly Goss had become irrelevant after the beatdown he himself had administered. Goss was a cautionary tale. "Goss might have gotten a title shot if he didn't lose to me," Everett told Gene Courtney of the *Inquirer.* "He had nothing to gain by fighting me and I'm not going to make the same mistake of fighting nobodies." So Peltz needed to look far and wide for top opponents, just as he did in luring Blakeney Matthews from South Africa. Unlike with the middleweight division, the financial demands of the lower weight classes were far less onerous, making it more feasible for Peltz to consummate deals. It also helped that Everett had legitimate drawing power; challengers may not necessarily be in the mood for facing a slickster of his caliber, but they would get paid adequately for their troubles. Over the next two years, Everett would take on no less than six rated junior lightweights, many from different corners of the world.

His next fight would land on the first Spectrum show of 1975, against twenty-four-year-old Bert Nabalatan, a Filipino residing in Hawaii and the ninth-ranked junior lightweight. In a move laden with symbolic significance, Everett received the main event nod over Bennie Briscoe, who was scheduled to face Lenny Harden on the semi-windup in what was regarded as a comeback fight. Briscoe had suffered back-to-back losses the previous year, dropping a decision to Emile Griffith at the Spectrum and suffering a shocking knockout to Rodrigo Valdes in Monaco—shocking since that was the one and only time in his more than two-decade, ninety-five-fight career that he had ever been stopped—and the thinking was that Briscoe, thirty-two, was now on the decline. In other words, if Everett was planning on making a statement, now was the time.

Nabalatan was no stiff. A southpaw with a granite chin, he had never been knocked out before in more than forty-four fights, thirty-four of them wins. He could punch a bit, too, as Everett would discover for himself on the night of January 14.

Everett dominated Nabalatan but rarely pressed the action.
(Courtesy Peltz Boxing Promotions, Inc.)

Heeding his new gung-ho philosophy, Everett sprang out of his corner at the opening bell, like a mountain lion pouncing on a hiker from behind a boulder. A left briefly stopped the Filipino challenger in his tracks, but he took it well. In fact, it only emboldened him. Unlike Goss and Matthews, Nabalatan was an educated pressure fighter, and soon he was the one doing the stalking. Indeed, once Everett tasted a few punches and realized that Nabalatan was not going to collapse like Matthews and Madrid, he quickly reverted to his old habits: sidestepping, backpedaling, jabbing, counterpunching. So much for all the talk about standing and trading. In the 10th round, when things started to heat up in the middle of the ring, Everett began running his mouth, informing his adversary, in so many words, that he was going to be the next champion. It was the kind of performance that had his detractors frothing at the mouth. In the end, Everett won a comfortable decision (49-41, 47-44, 49-44). But there were few among the 8,215 in attendance that night, outside of his usual faithful, that went home thinking he was must-see material. "The other guy was on a Honda," Nabalatan scoffed to the *Inquirer*. "I pressed all the way. If I had backed off like he did, it would have been a dance contest. He fought only in the last round and if he didn't run, the fight would have been a knockout. If he has any idea of becoming a champion, he better change his style and fight."

Pol Tiglao, Nabalatan's manager, doubled down on those comments, pointing out that while Everett had genuine ability, his killjoy style was not a winning formula on the world stage. "If he was in another country and got on his bicycle and went away from the other fighter, he'd be thrown out of the ring," Tiglao told the *Courier-Post*. "If Everett wants to be a world champion, he has to show more than this. My fighter wanted to make exchanges, and, except for the 10th round, there was none to speak about. Everett has potential—but he has to be polished before he can go out of Philadelphia."

Tiglao added, "To be big box office a fighter must show a fighting heart."

There was little sass from Everett afterward. He gave Nabalatan credit, admitted that fighting a southpaw was difficult, but also tried to steer the conversation away from the insipid conditions of his victory and instead to the quality of his chin. A fighter never knows what kind of chin he has until he gets clobbered with a consequential shot and Everett admitted that Nabalatan had clocked him harder than anybody else in twenty-two professional fights.

"I've never been hit like this, ever," a subdued Everett said. "But I proved I could take the punches, right on the chin. I wasn't hurt. I heard the punches crack and crunch on me, but I didn't feel any pain. Really, it even kind of surprised me, too. I didn't hurt when he hit me. That has to prove something. I tried to take him out but couldn't."

Jimmy Arthur, never one to throw his fighter under the bus, pointed out that Everett had damaged his left hand sparring a middleweight during training camp, which explained why he had it holstered for most of the fight. Overall, Arthur viewed the subpar showing as a meaningful teaching moment. "People ask, can he take a punch? Well, he got hit pretty good. And he didn't show no fear," he said.

In any case, Everett could cross off Nabalatan from his list. The goal remained the same: to make a beeline for a title shot, either against Ben Villaflor of the Philippines, the WBA junior lightweight champion, or Kuniaki Shibata of Japan, the WBC champion. But the Nabalatan fight left a taste of tea dregs in his mouth. "Couldn't sleep worrying about that fight," Everett later told the *Courier-Post*. "I knew I disappointed all of the people. I won, but I didn't do it the way I wanted to—by a KO. I want to demolish other fighters. A knockout artist. Hit and hurt 'em. People like that."

* * *

EARLIER ON THE card, Briscoe shook off a rough start to drop Harden four times en route to a 10th-round stoppage. It was a savage fight, another Briscoe specialty. After the night was over and the janitors were sweeping up empty beer cups from the floor, Peltz ran into Everett.

"Well, I beat that guy pretty easy," Everett quipped.

Peltz felt something shoot up in his head, a choleric flash. Slowly, enunciating each word, he sneered back, "Yeah, but Briscoe stole the show."

And Everett knew that Peltz was right. Briscoe had stolen the show. Philadelphia was still Briscoe's town.

* * *

A SENSE OF urgency was forming in the Everett camp. Frank Gelb planned to take his charge on a business trip to Los Angeles to watch Bobby Chacon defend his WBC title against Jesus Estrada. It would be Everett's first exposure to the fervid climes of West Coast boxing. It would also count as a kind of proactive PR exercise, getting Everett in front of some of his potential opponents and hopefully stirring up some intrigue. "I hope to be able to arrange something for Everett when we get there, but I'd rather see the Spectrum try to promote a title fight for Tyrone," Gelb said. But talks went nowhere fast. Gelb made it clear to the handlers of the champions that they were more than open to traveling to Asia to face either Shibata or Villaflor. But for the same reasons that Everett did not want to face anyone who was unranked, the other top-rated contenders and titlehold-ers saw no reason to fight Everett, who essentially brought nothing to the table. As Eddie Futch had put it, the North American title was worth the cost of a cup of coffee.

In the meantime, Team Everett needed to keep the ball rolling, so Peltz brought in a familiar face for Everett's twen-ty-fourth fight: Jose Luis Lopez, the veteran Mexican with a bazooka right hand who had stymied Sammy Goss years ago in Philadelphia. After coming up short against the world-class likes of Hugo Barraza, Alfredo Escalera, and Ben Villaflor, "The Durango Kid" had seemingly reinvented himself with a knockout over Hubert Kang, a rugged South Korean who had once stopped Kuniaki Shibata, who at that point was still the WBC junior lightweight titleholder. The win over Kang pushed Lopez up to the No. 6 spot on the rankings, right behind Everett. His record stood at 55-20-3 with thir-ty-one knockouts. Going in, many of the local beat writers considered Lopez to be the toughest opponent that Everett ever faced, second to Nabalatan.

* * *

MARCH 3, 1975. The money he had been making up until this point was nothing to brag about—not nearly enough, anyway, to keep him from cursing Peltz under his breath—but after more than twenty professional fights, Everett was beginning to form a decent nest egg. Showing it off, then, was only a natural corollary. So it was that Everett strutted into the Spectrum ring on Tuesday night with an enhanced sartorial consciousness. He wore a spiffy, custom-made, lime-colored velvet robe with matching trunks, a far cry from the homespun terrycloth that Briscoe typically donned, and a seemingly surefire way to rile up his puritanical critics who disapproved of the slightest iota of glitz. But with his latest fashion statement, Everett tried to extend an olive branch to his detractors, not inflame them. Stitched conspicuously on the lower left front of his trunks was the Star of David— and, no, Everett had not suddenly found Jehovah. "I heard it brings you good luck," Everett later said. "Besides, lots of fans like to see the Star of David. And it shows I'm not prejudiced. Besides, no matter what sign I wear, I'm for the people. All the people." All the people—It was a sign that Everett wanted to temper his polarizing persona. Recall the bewilderment of Blakeney Matthews, who was shocked upon finding out that Everett seemed to have as many naysayers as supporters in his hometown.

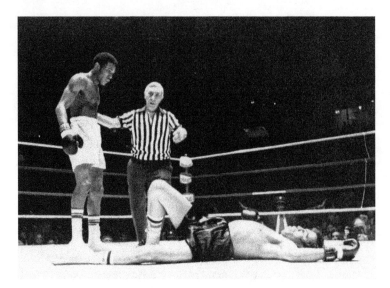

Everett admires his work.
(Courtesy Peltz Boxing Promotions, Inc.)

So what exactly was going on with this act of cultural appropriation? One explanation is that Everett believed a large faction of the Philadelphia fanbase was Jewish and that by sporting such an evocative emblem he could, in effect, garner their allegiance. But there is a far simpler, more probable explanation. According to Peltz, Everett was most likely attempting to imitate Briscoe. As a Black fighter, Briscoe was notable for embossing the Star of David on his trunks, not as a schmaltzy publicity stunt, but as a tribute to his former Jewish manager Jimmy Iselin. Since no one was more popular in Philadelphia than Briscoe, Everett, who was always lusting for the limelight, took advantage of the trope. It was a gesture of one-upmanship. After all, he was not about to pick up the Torah anytime soon. He was imitating Briscoe in a bid to overtake him. The message was abundantly clear: On a night in which Briscoe, the marquee man in town, was subordinated to the semi-windup, Everett aimed to capture the hearts of Philadelphia fight fans. The only question was which version in his nonstop Jekyll-and-Hyde routine was going to show up? This time, it turned out to be Hyde.

Everett fired on all cylinders that night, rip-snorting his way to a fourth-round stoppage. He played both stalker and counterpuncher and flitted between both roles seamlessly. It was another reminder of how dangerous Everett could be when he was inspired, when he did not retreat into his shell. "We did not expect that kind of style," Lopez said later. Lopez began to rally in the third round, briefly rattling Everett with a body shot followed by a pinpoint right hand to the chin. It was a purely Pyrrhic moment for Lopez, however, as the punch only unwittingly accelerated his own demise. Instead of taking a step back to reset, Everett immediately barreled forward and fired back with a fusillade of combinations that had Lopez tottering back to his own corner at the bell. Lopez was a dead man walking. With a minute left in the fourth round, Everett lifted Lopez's chin into the air with a sweeping right hook, cueing it up perfectly for a booming overhand left. Lopez flailed backward, landing spatchcocked on the canvas. As Lopez struggled to sit up, Everett went on a victory lap around the ring, his hands raised as a crowd of 6,413 blew the roof off the Spectrum. It was the only time he "ran" that night.

"I've never punched better, or harder," Everett crooned afterward. "It was short and sweet. That's the way I like 'em. This was the best I've ever fought. I picked my shots perfectly. He was a tough dude. You saw him demolish Sammy Goss. Well, I'm different from Sammy Goss. He was laying for right-hand shots. They said he knocked lots of southpaws out. Well, I'm the best southpaw that ever lived. I can do it all. Those were dumb southpaws he fought. I'm a thinking southpaw."

Even more, this time, there was nobody who had upstaged him. Not even Bennie Briscoe. For once, it was all Tyrone Everett. "The last time I was on the card with Bennie Briscoe, and I was doubtful if they came to see me or him," Everett reflected. "This time the card was me."

◆ ◆ ◆

MAY 5, 1975, the *Inquirer*: "For years Philadelphia fighters were easy to recognize. They all had two things in common—a powerful left hook and a reputation of being unable to win the big ones. Then along comes unbeaten Tyrone Everett and the old standards no longer apply. The tall, lanky junior lightweight from South Philadelphia is a lefty so he has a right hook instead of a left and, in compiling his 24-0 record, he has won all of the big ones."

◆ ◆ ◆

ALL SPRING FRANK Gelb had been at his wit's end trying to procure a title shot for his restless charge, who was now positioned as the No. 3 junior lightweight in the ratings of the World Boxing Association. It was as if Gelb needed to create a bonfire to get the attention of the belt holders but only had two twigs to rub together. No matter how many calls he made to opposing camps and genuflections he made to the sanctioning bodies, he always got the same runaround. "We'll get back to you." Maybe Peltz was right: There was simply no market for a tricky Black southpaw. At one point, Gelb, thinking a title shot was moot, went to Peltz to tell him that Everett had received an offer to face the feared Panamanian Roberto Duran at Temple Stadium, an outdoor football venue in the northeast part of the city. Peltz shot it down. "You're out of your fucking mind," Peltz recalled telling Gelb. "Tyrone wasn't ready. Looking back now, I don't know."

But, finally, in early May, there was a minor breakthrough. Gelb had received a cryptically worded telegram from the WBA informing him that Everett could be in the running to challenging its 130-pound champion, Ben Villaflor, within six months but only if he got past his next assignment, Pedro Aguero of Argentina. The fight was set for May 5 at the Spectrum. As with Everett's last few opponents, Aguero, the No. 5 ranked junior lightweight, was a credible contender. Once again, Everett showed he was willing to run the gantlet. "We're not going to fight any stick-in-the-muds," Gelb said. "Ty will only face world-class fighters."

But the situation was not so cut and dry. Villaflor, a Filipino who, like Bert Nabalatan, made his home in Hawaii, had sustained a detached retina, one of the great career killers in the sport, during his title defense against South Korea's

Hyun Chi Kim back in March. There was a real possibility that Villaflor would have to hang up the gloves for good, pending the results of his surgery. If that turned out to be the case, Everett would have to duke it out in an elimination match with one of the other top contenders, either against No. 2-ranked Victor Echegaray of Argentina or No. 1-ranked Kuniaki Shibata of Japan. That was the plan, at least, by the WBA.

After the first five rounds, it was obvious that Aguero, the Argentine junior lightweight champion whose record stood at 34-4-3 and included a victory over countryman Echegaray, was limited. Everyone knew it. Peltz knew it, Gelb knew it, and most of all, the crowd of 6,711—the biggest gathering at the Spectrum up at that point in the year—knew it. Only Everett, it seemed, did not know it, boxing at range for most of the fight, until he finally decided to stand and trade in the final round, by which point it was all too late. He did a number on Aguero, however, jolting him all fight long with every punch in his arsenal and opening up slits above each brow. "I couldn't fight his style," Aguero said afterward. "I have no excuse. He is definitely the next champion in the junior lightweights. It's no disgrace to lose to him." In the end, Everett pitched a dominant 10-round shutout, but it lacked the verve and urgency of his previous outings. It was one of his low-energy Jekyll performances, a disappointing development for those on the Everett bandwagon. "I should have caught on sooner, but I didn't know how strong he was," Everett later said.

Everett boxed the ears off an overmatched Aguero—but
he was more hammy than bloodthirsty in doing so.
(Courtesy Peltz Boxing Promotions, Inc.)

But if the match was mostly forgettable, one of those
nights that was meant to be swept away under the rug, it was
memorable in at least one regard: an ill-advised action that
Everett took in the eighth round, after he dropped Aguero

with a left uppercut. The custom after a knockdown is for the referee to tell the standing fighter to go to the neutral corner. But in this case, instead of heeding those time-honored instructions from referee Hank Cisco, Everett merely sidled right behind Cisco as he was administering the automatic eight-count. As soon as Cisco finished the count and a woolly-eyed Aguero had propped himself back on his legs, Everett emerged from under Cisco's shadow and bore into his opponent, like a militiaman ambushing a Redcoat. Boos cascaded from the stands. Everett, once again, had riled up the "old heads." Gene Courtney, already unimpressed with the performance, wrote the next day that "what [Tyrone] had in talent, he lacked in sportsmanship."

Everett shrugged. "This is a rough game," he said. "I am after my opponent. I want to kill him. Sportsmanship is later."

• • •

BY THE END of 1976, Everett was still trapped in title shot purgatory, auditioning for a role that seemed to grow more elusive by the day. Frustration was setting in. Everett envisioned being a two-division champion before his twenty-third birthday, with titles in both the featherweight and junior lightweight classes. Had he plateaued out?

"If Villaflor does not fight (because of the eye injury) in September, his title could be stripped from him because he has to put his title on the line at least once every six months," Gelb said. "However, Villaflor can protest a decision to strip him of his title and that process could take six weeks. So we're taking an elimination fight for the crown somewhere around November. Involving Tyrone. Those are the ifs."

Everett also contemplated dropping back down to 126 to face either Alexis Arguello, the WBC champion, or Bobby Chacon, the WBC junior lightweight champion. Contingencies abounded.

Still, Gelb, never one to mill around, had already lined up the next fight for Everett on June 10. This time Everett was going to the land of alohas, leis, and mai tais—Hawaii. It would be the first time he left the state of Pennsylvania for a prizefight. Though he was only given two weeks to prepare, Everett knew the large implications of a victory there. If Villaflor's handlers could not get their act together and agree to a matchup, he would force their hand by whipping up Hawaiian support for it.

"I took the fight for two reasons," Everett told the *Tribune*. "No one in that part of the world has ever seen me, and Ben Villaflor's people will be there at the fight."

He would be fighting Rolando Pastor from the Philippines, unbeaten through twenty-seven fights, in what was understood as a showcase bout for Everett. Beat Pastor, look good, and come September, he may be staring across at the WBA champion.

"Tyrone is going to beat Pastor, and Villaflor's people and his fight fans will see it," Gelb said. "The win should mean a title fight either in Honolulu or here at the Spectrum. I would say most likely the fight would be in Honolulu and the fans will know all about Tyrone after the Pastor fight."

The fight lasted two minutes and fifty-seven seconds, giving Everett his twenty-sixth straight win. As Gelb sat down with Villaflor's handlers to hammer out the terms of the fight, he noticed the goals posts were starting to move again.

"After the quick knockout, Villaflor's people began finding fault with the terms of the tentative agreement," Gelb groused. "I hope they might be embarrassed into going through with the fight."

• • •

MEANWHILE, RUSSELL PELTZ was busy at home trying to pull strings to bring Everett—and Philadelphia—a world championship. He was feeling the heat. This was the era, after all, when there was still a certain ad hoc quality to making fights, before promoters started locking in fighters with stifling, multi-bout contracts. Like most everybody in the business at the time, Peltz worked on a fight-per-fight basis with his group of fighters, which meant if Everett decided to fight for the title in, say, Hawaii, Peltz would be effectively shut out of the promotion—and out of a payday. It had already happened once before, much to Peltz's displeasure, with Sammy Goss, when Goss fought Augie Pantellas for the North American title. The last thing he wanted was to have a fighter that grew up under his wing get his biggest opportunity outside of Philadelphia. So, with the dog days of summer setting in and a lull emerging in the Spectrum fight schedule, Peltz decided to head out west, to Los Angeles, and try his luck with the power brokers there.

He picked the right weekend. Ruben Olivares and Bobby Chacon, two of the most popular fighters in Southern California, were set to put on a donnybrook at the Forum, the home of the Los Angeles Lakers and, more appropriately, the site of some of the best prizefighting in America. Here, featherweights roamed about the town like heavyweights. The turnout, the presentation, the buzz—Peltz, green with envy, was brought to his bony knees.

"The crowd was 18,770 and the gate was $410,000," Peltz told Tom Cushman. "It's outrageous how the little guys draw in that city."

If Peltz was ever going to come close to reproducing those numbers for his "little guys" back home, he knew it would have to start with Everett. At least there, he knew he had the right thoroughbred for the job. So Peltz spent all weekend consorting with the managers of title-holding featherweights and junior lightweights, pitching them on the merits of a big-ticket fight in Philadelphia. Right away, however, Peltz could tell few of them wanted anything to do with his proposals. It came back down to the age-old question: Why should they— anyone—care about a Black, left-handed spoilsport from the East Coast? Case in point was Peltz's meeting with the handlers of the WBA Nicaraguan featherweight champion Alexis Arguello, a rail-thin but murderous puncher whose name is often evoked in conversations about the greatest featherweights in boxing history. Arguello was just coming into his own, having only wrested the title from Olivares the year before. But Peltz did not get the sense that Arguello's people were enthusiastic about Everett. Still, they decided to hear what Peltz had to offer. "I could tell they were anxious," Peltz told Cushman. "I had an appointment to meet them at 6:30 [p.m.], and they showed up six and a half hours later." The meeting was a washout. The Arguello side effectively priced itself out, asking for a purse of $130,000 before taxes and options on Everett's first two title defenses, in the event that he won, in addition to a staggering raft of other concessions and perks. Peltz countered with an offer of a non-title fight in Philadelphia against Everett in late September, for which Arguello's handlers would dramatically lower their asking price to $20,000. It was all too obvious to Peltz: the Arguello camp viewed Everett as a real threat, and the reward did not quite offset the perceived risk.

Nevertheless, the Tyrone Everett Show had to go on. To that end, Peltz was able to entice another top-ranked contender to come to Philadelphia: South Korea's Hyun Chi Kim, the No. 4 junior lightweight in the world, as decreed by the WBA. The fight would take place on July 24 at the Spectrum (it was originally scheduled a week-and-a-half earlier but postponed because Kim had issues with his travel visa), and once again, the stakes were consequential. With both the No.1 ranked Kuniaki Shibata and No. 2 ranked Victor Echegary suffering recent defeats, the winner of Everett-Kim would, in theory, get to face Ben Villaflor, provided his doctors gave him the green light to continue his career. Then again, for all anyone knew, the WBA's byzantine rules could have been written on a palimpsest. That was why Kim, eager for a rematch against Villaflor, decided to take the fight with Everett, even though he would be foregoing the $10,000 he could make back home for Peltz's $3,500 peanuts. "I just want to get this fight over with," Everett gloated. "Then I can get my shot at the title."

"Cultural exchange."
(Courtesy Peltz Boxing Promotions, Inc.)

Not everyone was as giddy as Everett. In fact, Frank Gelb had not even given his blessing before Everett went ahead and signed the bout contract with Peltz. Gelb had a right to be nervous about the fight. Kim, after all, was the one who had damaged Villaflor's left retina in a fight that the South Korean wound up losing narrowly by split decision in Villaflor's backyard in the Philippines. For Gelb, taking on a man who nearly defeated the man they had been gunning for all these months just seemed like bad math, pure foolishness.

He opposed the fight. But the potential payoff in a win was too tempting for Everett to ignore.

"I know I'm taking a big risk with this fight," Everett admitted to the *Courier-Post*, "but I figure if I beat Kim badly, I'll be in position where the champ will have to respect me. If I lose, I'll still be in the Top 10, and I'm young enough to come back."

"He made me wait ten days, and I'm gonna take my anger out on him," he added. "He's thick in the face. The best I can do is try and cut him up. Around the eyes."

• • •

"PHILADELPHIA IS #1 In Pro Boxing," reads a headline in the May 25, 1976, issue of the *Philadelphia Tribune*: "In the last three years, professional boxing in Philadelphia has vacated the cellar and moved into the penthouse in the pugilistic sport. As far as box office receipts, patronage and putting bread on the tables of pro boxers, Philadelphia takes a seat to no one in this country."

CHAPTER SIX

Until now, I've been more popular overseas than I've been around here. Now since I signed for this fight, I've been in the papers. I've been on TV. Little kids are saying, 'There goes Tyrone Everett.' Before, you say Tyrone Everett to them, and they thought it was some kind of cookie.

—TYRONE EVERETT
to the *Associated Press*

JACK MCKINNEY WAS a man of the Philadelphia zeitgeist, a hard-drinking radio personality and newspaperman who approached life with swashbuckling aplomb. One time he entered a lion's cage with nothing more than a bullwhip and topee. Another time, he flung himself out of an airplane. He always flocked to areas in the throes of perpetual conflict: Latin America, Northern Ireland. An eclectic culture vulture with an unremitting love for opera, McKinney could recite, from memory, arias from Verdi, lines from Shakespeare, and whole passages from James Joyce. After having had a few, he was prone to burst into an obscure Irish ditty or two. He was to Philadelphia what Pete

Hamill and Jimmy Breslin were to New York City: a tabloid champion of the down-and-out underdog who kept his ear to the ground and distilled the secrets of the streets to thousands upon thousands of readers and listeners for whom he was a vital conduit to the outside world. It all started in the 1950s when a twenty-year-old McKinney was whisked away from his insurance gig by the *Philadelphia Daily News* to write music criticism. Later he moved over to the sports department. (In the mid-1970s, he transitioned into a columnist, a post he would hold down for another three decades.) One of his favorite sports to cover was boxing. He struck up a friendship with Sonny Liston, sparred with him on one of his many misadventures, and had even participated in a sanctioned prizefight against a palooka, which he wound up winning by first-round knockout.

McKinney was assigned to cover the Tyrone Everett-Hyun Chi Kim fight for the *Daily News*, so he found himself within the bowels of the Spectrum on July 24. What he saw that night was perhaps the single most egregious example of unsportsmanlike behavior that he had ever witnessed in a boxing ring in Philadelphia. It was as though he was watching a conman trim his mark in real-time but was helpless to do anything about it. McKinney penned a scathing recap the next day, some of which is worth reproducing here at length:

"After 27 straight victories as a pro, it's beyond Tyrone Everett's comprehension that anyone should doubt he is the class of the junior lightweight division. The undefeated southpaw from South Philadelphia might very well be the best 130-pounder in the world today, for whatever that's worth.

He certainly deserves an immediate shot at the junior light-weight championship of the world, for whatever that's worth. But class? Only for people who prefer hot dogs to sirloin. Everett displayed his perverted sense of class last night by needlessly taunting a beaten, half-blind, bewildered opponent who might have jumped out of the ring if his handlers hadn't responded to his pleas to throw the towel into it. [...] So, after 27 wins, Tyrone Everett still leaves a lot of people with the distinct impression that he is a front runner whose courage is directly related to his recognition of his opponent's ineptness. And from what local fans have seen of the barely warm bodies that have been imported for him, Everett's division must be the most abundantly inept in all of boxing."

It was the second time in a week that someone had called into question Everett's character. For McKinney, frontline defender of the underdog, Everett had breached a moral line, his ire reflecting the years-long antipathy of the portion of the local fanbase that had never been sold on the South Philadelphian. Showboating was one thing, but this was a shameful prat-out. The unspoken rule in boxing is that a hapless foe deserves pity, not humiliation.

Everett had no intentions of extending this courtesy to Kim, whose limitations were quickly apparent. The Korean challenger was as primitive as an art brut painting, molasses-slow, technically unsound, and feather-fisted. With each jab and hook he pistol-whipped across Kim's gaunt cheekbones, Everett would growl, "I'm mean, man, I'm mean." And if that was not grating enough to the sensibilities of the diehard constituency, Everett began to contort his face into

"I'm mean, man, I'm mean."

a hundred different Kabuki expressions, as though he were Marcel Marceau. Nursing a cut over his right eye, a battered Kim was ready to call it quits at the conclusion of the fifth round. His handlers, however, practically pushed their charge back into the ring, only to find themselves frantically waving their white towels midway through the sixth round and prompting the referee to halt the bout. A crowd of 8,104 was whipped into a rabid frenzy. There was not a single nick on Everett's face, only the luster of sweat and a preening smile. "I was just using psychology on him," Everett quipped afterward. "The people know I'm good. It's me they come to see. Not these bums I fight."

Later, Everett would double down on his burlesque actions. "It's an art to be able to fight that way. People call it hot-dogging, but the only reason they do that is because I'm not getting beat and they want to see me knocked on my ass. They come to see that, but that's OK, that's just more money for me. And it is an art, I can do those things because I've learned my art. It's a talent to be able to spin your man around and spank him like a baby. It's showmanship."

* * *

WITH HIS UNBLEMISHED record intact, Everett continued to maintain a tenuous balance on his tightrope trot to the title, but there was an inconvenient truth obvious to everyone on his team. The longer he had to wait for a championship opportunity, the more likely he was to lose his footing at some point, if only due to a freak occurrence.

Indeed, the dominoes nearly came toppling down in his next fight, against a top contender named Benjamin Ortiz of Puerto Rico on September 16 at the Spectrum. After a few uneventful rounds, Everett ran into a right hand he never saw coming late in the seventh. His legs instantly slackened, and he dropped back into the ropes as the crowd collectively gasped. Had it not been for the lowest strand on the ropes, Everett would have certainly hit the canvas. Luckily for him, there were only a few seconds left in the round. In the end, Everett was able to regroup and notch a fairly wide unanimous decision.

The brief flirtation with catastrophe turned out to be something of a godsend for Everett. Ortiz was handled by Filiberto Lebron, a prominent front man for many Puerto Rican fighters and whose clientele included Alfredo Escalera, who had won the WBC junior-welterweight title after knocking out Kuniaki Shibata earlier in the summer. At best, Lebron thought the fight against Ortiz should have been declared a draw. Still, aware of how desperate Everett was for a title shot and spotting what he felt was a clear defensive weakness in his craft, the manager was more than happy to entertain the notion of bringing Escalera to Philadelphia next year, the year of the American bicentennial. Of course, the money had to be right and Escalera had to win a few scheduled mandatory defenses, but Lebron was sufficiently intrigued. Plus, the way Lebron saw it, there was little risk on their part. It was clear to him that Escalera, a lethal puncher, would have his way with Everett, an opinion that was also backed by Ortiz. "Two rounds," Ortiz said through an interpreter when asked how an Escalera-Everett fight would shake out. "Escalera grande, hits with either hand."

In a rare faux pas, Everett is clipped hard by an Ortiz right.
(Courtesy Peltz Boxing Promotions, Inc.)

Because of the Ortiz fiasco, Everett had to field concerns about his ring ambitions for the first time in his career. True, he was always something of a lightning rod, but while his critics might gripe about his sometimes-tedious style or his haughty attitude, no one had really questioned his seriousness about boxing—until now. "My pride was hurt," Everett told Gary Smith of the *Daily News*. "The crowd told me I wasn't training, that I was messing with girls." But the crowd had a point. A lot was going on in his life, and little of it was related to boxing. For one, Everett was looking to diversify his financial portfolio and now found himself juggling a variety of different business ventures. Most significantly, earlier in the year, he took out a loan and purchased an old dive near his home on 31st and Tasker Street and renamed it Ty's and Mike's Golden Gloves. He also took out mortgages on the apartment above the bar and the home adjacent to it and began subletting both. Everett estimated he would have everything paid off by the time he was twenty-five. It was a humble but nonetheless promising start to what Everett envisioned would become his own personal empire. He was considering buying more real estate, running a laundromat, managing his own stable of blue-chip fighters and, hell, he even had ambitions of acting in the movies someday. He saw himself as a poster child for local businesses. "If I were white I'd be known all over the world. I'd be doing advertisements, I'd be driving a car for a dealer who wants to use my name," Everett told Smith. Everett was also busy tending to his civic-minded ventures. At one point, he was gearing up to raise money for his former high school by participating in an exhibition match at the nearby Graterford prison (the same correctional facility that would one day house middleweight champion Bernard Hopkins). And, of course, there were always the girls to tend to.

The person who most likely encouraged Everett to think more entrepreneurially about his future was Frank Gelb. "Tyrone was a smooth-talking, good-looking, and what I thought was a fairly bright man," recalled Gelb. "I tried to show him through my own family, to try and find a route for himself (outside of boxing)." While he was always butting heads with Peltz, Everett got along with Gelb and, in some ways, looked up to him as a father figure. Frequently Everett would spend a weekend out on Gelb's beach-front summer home in Atlantic City. Like Leroy Roberts, Everett was part of the well-adjusted Gelb family. Early on in their collaboration, Gelb even taught Everett how to comb through the language of his own bout contracts. When it was time to close a deal with Alfredo Escalera for a shot at the title, Gelb would remark, "He has gotten to the stage where he can negotiate his own contracts. In this upcoming title fight, he's the one that laid the groundwork and I just followed up with the trimming. He'll squeeze a nickel. He's invested most of his earnings. He's not a big spender." Whatever the veracity of that statement, the business know-how was yet another example of the chasmic differences between Everett and his Philadelphia cohorts. Could anyone imagine Bennie Briscoe poring over legalese or traveling to New York alone to start negotiations with the other fighter's managers, as Everett once did with the Escalera side?

"Maybe in the old days, the 1930s, maybe boxers blew [their money]," Everett once recalled. "Someone would tell them they had to fight for $300 and they'd have to say, 'Sure, boss, anything you say.' But now I have a chance to read a contract, to say what I think I'm worth. Now if a promoter wants me, he can't squeeze me. I can fight for what I want. Because I talk this way people say I'm getting cocky. I'm not cocky. A promoter's going to be around for a long time. A fighter's not around that long. Maybe a year from now it'll be someone else in my position. When I was coming up, Bennie Briscoe was the star, then Gene Hart, now it's just my time to be the star in Philadelphia. There's been a lot of stars. They come. They go. I'll go, too."

Naturally, there was a unique bond between Everett and Gelb, even if, in the opinion of many, they had no business trusting each other. Gelb, a Jew staunchly ensconced in the tax bracket of the upper-middle class, resided in the suburban idylls of Wynnefield, and Everett was a Black kid from the inner-city who grew up dodging razor blades and watching heroin bags get passed from hand to hand. On the surface, they were hardly the ideal tandem. But Everett did not perceive the world through such reductive, black-and-white filters.

"Some of my so-called friends still say to me that I shouldn't be with Gelb," Everett would later say. "He's a white man, they say, and I tell them, 'Does that mean we have to try and kill each other?' He's out hustling for me, making money for me, which means I'm all for him. I've heard them say, 'He's a Jew, so all he's interested in is making money.' And I say, 'Good for him, because if he's making it for himself, he's making it for me.' Look, one thing I've already learned is that this world is run by money. You can forget that black-white bullshit. There's only one color that matters, and that's green."

• • •

A U G U S T   2 ,   1 9 7 6 ,   Caracas, Venezuela. The rain had been lashing down hard on the ramshackle open-air amphitheater all night as in a Kurosawa epic, turning the sand into porridge. The weather had been fine earlier in the day, when the same arena had hosted a bullfight that saw several matadors gored, an appropriate start to what was supposed to be an evening of delirious entertainment, one macho spectacle after another: bullfighting, then boxing. But boxing got the short shrift. Still, the card proceeded, and now, with the downpour showing no signs of slowing and the crowd virtually all emptied out, Tyrone Everett and Hugo Barraza, shadows on a rickety ring, were swapping punches in front of a few measly judges and organizers. Frank Gelb and Jimmy Arthur were both stripped down to their waists, using their shirts to mop up the runoff in their corner. If there was any night on which Everett could use a quick knockout, it was this one. Aside from the obvious desire to get under a roof, his team knew that foreigners typically had a poor track record of eking out decisions in Latin America, where skullduggery seemed to be standard procedure. In addition, this was a fork-in-the-road moment for them. Win, and Everett, after months, years even, of being strung along by one fighter's faction after another, would finally get his coveted title shot against Escalera, or at least that was the latest dictate offered by the WBC. In any case, it was abundantly clear that a defeat would send him hurtling down the rankings, losing the credibility he had meticulously built up for the past two years.

In the end, the fight, which, according to most accounts, was not very competitive, went to the cards. The referee, a Mexican, scored it a draw, 116-116. Fortunately for Everett, the other judges had it 118-114 in his favor.

"We'll never forget this one," Gelb later said. "I never saw it rain so hard."

To add to the brouhaha, Gelb, Everett, and Arthur were waylaid by the Venezuelan authorities at the airport and had their passports confiscated. Two days later, they were given the green light to get back to Philadelphia. It was a hell of a way to earn a title shot, but Everett was not one to lack confidence.

If Gelb had left his poncho at home, he had nevertheless insured himself in other areas. In the blurring deluge, he could count on a friend. According to the international rules of the WBC, each side had the right to choose a judge from the fighter's hometown. In a slick move, Gelb brought along Hank Cisco, a veteran referee of the Pennsylvania boxing scene and fellow Norristown denizen who worked a day job as a juvenile police officer. It was all done in wink-wink fashion, but Gelb, who prided himself on being the savviest man in a roomful of sharks, knew he could depend on Cisco. "Anytime you go away, you're behind the eight-ball," Gelb recalled. "You're at the mercy of the people who tried to trick you into a fight without any kind of formula on your part to make sure that it would be, on your part, fair and square. I guess I was a little smarter by being on top of it more than most other managers would have because I went to gyms all over the city where the boxers trained."

Cisco may have been more instrumental than even Gelb had let on. According to Peltz, he had heard that the score-cards were soaked to the point that they were illegible. "The rest of that is what Gelb may or may not tell you," Peltz said. "It's obvious from what I heard that Everett definitely won the fight but that didn't mean he was going to get [a decision]."

There was too much at stake, after all. Hugo Barraza was the No. 1 junior lightweight contender of the WBC, and Everett was No. 2. But with a decision in hand, he had finally secured his place in line to fight Escalera for the championship. Per the WBC rules, both sides now had sixty days to negotiate terms for the fight, and this time, the sanctioning body did not come up with inane last-minute diversions.

After two years of nonstop politicking and passport-stamping, Everett's moment had conceivably arrived. Feeling hamstrung at home, Everett had taken his act on the road and, unlike many of his Philadelphian peers, had fared well. "He could go away from home and win," Jimmy Arthur would tell *PhillySport* years later. "Most of our Philadelphia fighters can't go away from home and win." In his last fight, Everett had returned to Hawaii and won a decision against another humdrum Filipino, in the hopes of pressuring Villaflor into giving him a title shot that, once again, never materialized. He had also made his way over to San Francisco the previous

December and fought Ray Lunny III, a highly regarded contender and popular local attraction, on a card that also featured a post-Zaire George Foreman in an exhibition bout. It was precisely the kind of high-risk-low reward type of match that managers do their mightiest to avoid. Everett ended up beating Lunny by a wide margin, albeit one judge scored it for the hometown favorite.

"Tyrone fought Ray Lunny in San Francisco, in his backyard, in Barraza's backyard," Peltz said recently. "Who does that today? It's just a different business."

It seemed only fitting, then, that Everett's globetrotting would end in a Latin American country 2,000 miles away from home during a monsoon at a site used routinely for ritualized sport slaughter.

◆ ◆ ◆

AFTER WEEKS OF frazzling, down-to-the-wire negotiations between the two sides, Everett and Escalera finally came to an agreement on October 20. They signed contracts in front of a crush of media during a hastily arranged news conference at the Spectrum. Escalera's junior lightweight championship would go up for grabs on November 30, in Philadelphia, in the year of the American bicentennial, making it the first world title fight to take place in the city since Joey Giardello defended his middleweight crown against Rubin "Hurricane" Carter in 1964. A win for Everett would make him the second active U.S.-born fighter at the time to hold a world title, joining Muhammad

Ali. To think that it was only seven years earlier that he jostled the chains on his first heavy bag.

To encourage turnout, the backers at the Spectrum decided to scale down ticket prices from the usual $25 to $7. They needed, at the very least, 11,000 (of a 19,300-capacity arena) to show up in order to break even. But given the momentous occasion, few were worried about the attendance, not even the perpetually angst-ridden Peltz. After eight years of grinding through the fight game, Peltz was on the cusp of realizing his childhood dream of staging a world title fight in his hometown. Gelb, too, felt the significance of the moment. In another life, he would have still been greeting customers at his furniture store. "To me this is what it's really all about," said Gelb. "Being in a championship fight is like being in the World Series."

The terms of the fight left no doubts as to who the A-side was. Escalera was set to receive the lion's share of the purse, with a guarantee of $90,000 against forty percent of the net gate. Escalera would also have exclusive rights to the revenue drawn from Puerto Rican television. Everett, on the other hand, was guaranteed a purse of $15,000 against fifteen percent of the net receipts; it was chump change compared to Escalera's end, admittedly, but Everett had the long view in mind. He knew that a win against Escalera would guarantee him monstrous earnings down the line. Plus, it was a career-high payday for him, anyway. In fact, Everett was originally set to earn $27,500, but that was when the fight was scheduled to take place in Puerto Rico on November 19. Escalera's team eventually backtracked on that prospect because the rainy season was entering high gear there, and they had already seen up close the month before how inclement weather had nearly derailed the attendance for a junior welterweight title bout between Wilfred Benitez and Tony Petronelli.

There were a few riders attached to the contract, naturally. Joining the fray was bigwig promoter Top Rank and its founder Bob Arum. In those days, virtually the entire television landscape in boxing was controlled by either Arum or his nemesis, the rabble-rousing kleptocrat Don King. Without Arum, there would be too much money left on the table. If Everett won, Top Rank would have options on the next four title defenses, all of which would have some kind of television or closed-circuit support in place. Even Escalera was in on the act; in the event that he lost, he would become a fifty percent partner in the promotions of Everett's first two title defenses. It was the price of doing business in the championship game.

* * *

INCREDIBLY, AFTER HAVING accounted for every nickel, dime, and penny in the financial pot for the past three months, both sides had yet to properly sort out the matter of the judges. Per custom, there was a tentative understanding that they would be selected by the athletic commission of Pennsylvania. But it was not long before Filiberto Lebron and Pedro Aponte, the chief handlers for Escalera, started angling for a more neutral process. Unbeknownst to Peltz at the time, Lebron and Aponte were

counting on a piece of fine print to back them up. As this
was a WBC-sanctioned title fight, the WBC rules were in
play, which, in brief, called for one official from the champion's hometown, one from the challenger's, and one from
neutral territory handpicked by the WBC. There was one
problem: Pennsylvania was not a state that fell under the
purview of the WBC; instead, it was part of the WBA
constellation. With a few weeks to go before the big fight,
Lebron and Pedro threatened to pull their man out of the
fight. The commission held their ground, citing that the
WBC's supposedly "neutral" judge would most likely be
biased toward Escalera.

"The biggest problem was the judges," Peltz recalled.
"[Initially] the managers said, 'We don't care who the judges
are,' so, being naive, I said, 'Hey, this is great. They don't
care who the judges are.' Not that we were going to load it up
with three Philly guys, but at least it wouldn't be the usual
shenanigans, not even realizing that they knew all along
that Sulaimán [the WBC president] was going to appoint
them. They left that part out of the equation. Remember,
this is 1976 and I'm 29 years old. I thought I knew everything there was to know."

The standoff came down to the wire. But with a few
days to go before the fight, the commission eventually caved
in to the WBC's demands, thanks to a timely and no less
forceful entreaty. Fearing that a cancellation would deprive
Philadelphia of future world title fights, the Spectrum, led
by Peltz, bypassed the commission and instead leaned on the
state governor to intervene. Their appeal worked. In the end,

there would be one judge appointed by the Pennsylvania State Athletic Commission, another judge by the Puerto Rican Boxing Commission, and a "neutral" referee, Ray Solis from Mexico, whom Peltz and Gelb had investigated for weeks and had deemed was fit for the job. (Referees at the time were still called on to judge bouts.) The implications of this arrangement were clear enough. With each regional judge supposedly looking out for the interests of their countryman, the decision would come down to a single vote by the supposedly neutral judge, Solis. In any case, the Escalera camp was appeased, and the fight could move forward. As for the Everett camp, they felt that they had done their due diligence in ensuring that their man would not get shafted on fight night. At the time, the controversial third fight between Muhammad Ali and Ken Norton, in which Ali won by unanimous decision, was still fresh in the public's mind.

"I'm going to make sure Everett doesn't get robbed like Ken Norton did," Gelb averred.

• • •

FEW COULD BE said to exhibit as much *joie de vivre* as Alfredo Escalera. They called him "El Salsero" for his love of dancing. But it was not necessarily his chronic shimmying that people thought of whenever his name was brought up in conversations. Twenty-four and carefree, Escalera had a curious pre-fight shtick: He would walk into the ring with his seven-and-a-half-foot pet boa constrictor draped around his neck.

The pre-fight hoopla was a contrast of personalities:
Everett's surliness against Escalera's goofy charm.
(Courtesy Peltz Boxing Promotions, Inc.)

But Escalera's naturally frothy spirits belied the hard-bitten years of his youth spent in the backwaters of Puerto Rico. Like Everett, he was a child of the streets. In some ways, his was the starker childhood. One of nineteen brothers, several of whom grew up malnourished, Escalera was seven years old when he had his first "fight." His father had a sadistic sense of spending his downtime. After a few drinks, he would routinely drag his youngest sons into the street and square them off against anybody who happened to be walking by. Fighting, then, was hardwired into Escalera. Later, he moved to New York City and lived there briefly as an adolescent. While his English cannot be said to have improved, he grew fluent with his fists by pounding away at sandbags in the city's grimiest gyms. In 1970, he won the New York Golden Gloves 135-pound novice title. Although Escalera did not exactly possess the polished skill set of, say, his countryman Wilfred Benitez, he compensated for his somewhat janky fundamentals and coltish mobility with his natural brawn and a howitzer of a right hand.

It was thanks to this power that Escalera was able to dethrone WBC champion Kuniaki Shibata of Japan—indeed, left him counting stars on his back—inside two rounds in their 1975 title fight. Escalera followed up with six successful defenses of his title and developed something of a fondness for fighting on foreign soil. Four of his defenses took place outside of his native Puerto Rico. Philadelphia would make it five. It was easier to fight on the road when you expected to knock out all of your opponents. His record, which stood at 35-7-2, with twenty-four knockouts, was proof of that.

"There is not one among us who does not believe that Alfredo will knock out Tyrone within seven or eight rounds," his manager Aponte huffed at the pre-fight physical during the week leading up to the fight.

"The day is coming when we will send you to the hospital," Lebron chimed in, glaring at Everett. Escalera, no trash-talker, simply grinned from ear to ear. "Always happy, I'm always happy," he said.

The tale of the tape favored Escalera. At five-foot-nine, he was nearly four inches taller than Everett and boasted a longer reach by two inches. Escalera was a strapping junior light-weight who had trouble in the past making the 130-pound limit. Everett, on the other hand, usually made it with a pound or two to spare. (Ironically, this fight was the exception; Everett ended up needing to shave off one pound at the weigh-in.) They shared common opponents in Jose Luis Lopez and Ray Lunny, who believed Everett would beat Escalera based on his superior speed. Size helps, sure, but speed kills. Not that Escalera was much concerned.

"All I really know of Tyrone Everett is that he is good at track and field," Escalera said. "I prefer runners, though. The fighters who have given me the most trouble are the ones who come straight into you. Runners I chase until I get tired. Then I stop and watch them for a while then resume the chase. Eventually I catch them."

But Everett had come too far to get enmeshed in Escalera's rabbit trap. Yes, there was the glinty green WBC strap, the career-high purse, the recognition, the women, and, perhaps, a new Cadillac that he stood to gain. But material riches not-withstanding, Everett also hoped to change a few minds. His doubters, after all, were legion. But maybe a conversion was simply beyond the pale with this stiff-necked crowd. In that case, he would have to make do with spite.

"Angelo Dundee told me two years ago I could beat this guy [Escalera]," Everett told the *Daily News*. "The people in the business I talk to, they all tell me the same. But down on the street they still don't believe in me. Some of them don't want to … I know that I've always had those who came to see me win and those who came to see me lose, but that's the way you want it. You have to talk with an attitude that's gonna make some people hate you. Those people buy tickets, too.

"The thing of it is with me, I sign for a big fight and even after all this time it doesn't seem like many believe. I remember when I fought Sammy Goss, they were talking behind my back. The same dudes came up later—their pockets empty—and said, 'Hey boss, we knew you'd do it.' I've been working for weeks for this fight, but I walk down the street and a dude will stop me and ask, 'You started training, yet?' Know what I tell them? I say, 'No, I'm only gonna train the last week. I've got a lot of parties to go to, lot of girls to take care of.' Then they run off and make their bets. One reason I've been able to work so hard for so long is that I want to see the expression on their faces the night I win the championship. It'll be a hard fight, but I'm gonna disappoint all of them by winning."

Still, whatever enmity he might have harbored against his detractors, deep inside, Everett yearned to be someone the city could advocate. Besides, Bennie Briscoe was fading fast. Boxing in Philadelphia needed a new face. Why not him?

"There are some things about this town I don't understand," Everett told Tom Cushman. "I was watching one of those talk shows on television the other day and they had the owners, or managers, of all our teams on ... the Eagles, the Flyers, the Phillies, the 76ers ... and it was mentioned that none of them will bring a championship to Philadelphia in 1976. Nobody seemed to remember that we still have one chance ... that there is in this city a young man—one of their own—who very definitely plans to bring a world championship to this city this year."

Peltz was right. Everett "always wanted to be loved." As the preliminary introductions were being made inside the ring on fight night, the ever-surly Peltz walked over to his fighter and, for the first time, told him what he had wanted to hear all along. "When the fight was over the next day," recalled Peltz, "I don't know if Tyrone said it to Frank, or somebody else, but he said, 'I can't believe Russell told me he loved me.'"

All Ladies With Escorts

Will Be Admitted

Free

To The

Win Or Lose Party

For

Tyrone Everett

At The

Marriott Hotel Ballroom

(City Line Ave)

Tues., Nov. 30, 1976 – 11 P.m.

Immediately

Following The Fight

A Complete Buffet Will Be Served Plus

All The Champagne You Can Drink

Donation $10.00

Everyone Will Be There, Including

Tyrone Everett

For Tickets And Information Call

925–3788

PART TWO

CHAPTER SEVEN

*This was just highway robbery. By far the worst decision
I ever saw.*

— HAROLD LEDERMAN

November 30, 1976.

I N ONE CORNER, the champion wears crushed velvet
maroon trunks with white trim and a grin as wide as the
Schuylkill. In the other, the challenger sports a somewhat
more contradictory ensemble: shocking hot-pink trunks and
matching gloves to go with a glowering mug of a West Point
drillmaster. In their own ways, they ooze sangfroid. The
arena is shrouded in darkness as wisps of cigarette smoke
curl toward the hot lights bearing down on the ring. A loud
hum of nervous chatter unsettles the air. It is a packed house.
The official attendance is 16,019, a record for an indoor fight
in Pennsylvania that stands untouched to this day. That is one
less worry for Everett, at least. The city had turned out for him.

Referee Ray Solis motions the two fighters and their
seconds to come to the center of the ring where they huddle
up for the customary instructions, delivered in Solis' broken
English. Everett is accompanied by three members of his

team, which includes his trusted head trainer Jimmy Arthur, assistant Jimmy Hayes, and veteran cut man Eddie Aliano. A girthy, amiable boxing lifer, Aliano brought a pharmaceutical rigor to a profession filled with slapdash practitioners accustomed to using their white towels to wipe down everything from spilled water on the canvas to the blood on a fighter's open wound. Aliano routinely spent his own money to procure the best in sterilized pads and latest in cutting-edge coagulates, a commodity to which he had easy access thanks to a sister who worked at a hospital. Aliano would look back on this night as the toughest repair job of his career.

**Team Everett: the fighter flanked by Arthur to his left
and Aliano to his right with Hayes behind him.**
(Courtesy Peltz Boxing Promotions, Inc.)

The bell rings and the fighters begin pawing at each other with their lead hands. The southpaw Philadelphian glides around the ring on feet as nimble as those of Philippe Petit, continually changing up his direction, fluttering in and out, shifting to the left, then right, then left again. He targets the body early on with the jab. Halfway through the round, he scores with a shoveling left hand to the body and pulls back to avoid the Puerto Rican's response, which looks comparatively sluggish. The difference in speed is painfully obvious. In one motion, Everett follows up with a counter right hook while circling away to his right, a move he will repeat over and over again on this night. Escalera has yet to land a decent punch, but he soldiers forward with the long game in mind. There is a brief exchange at the end of the round that favors Everett. Escalera, unimpressed, scowls at his adversary as he walks back to his corner.

Everett starts going to work in the second round. Escalera throws a lazy jab that Everett counters with his own over the top, a ramrod right that lands flush. A beat later, he connects on a one-two. The punches are flowing now. Escalera, who has been hitting air so far, responds by bull-rushing Everett, who simply wheels away to his right, causing Escalera to crash into the ropes. Everett lands a blinding straight left before the bell that briefly stops Escalera in his tracks. Once again, Escalera fires off another cold Basilisk glare in Everett's direction.

With a few seconds left before the start of round three, Everett is already bouncing on the balls of his feet, looking straight ahead at a still-seated Escalera, his shoulders slumped, legs spread wide, relaxing as if he were on a Carolina beach sipping a mojito. At the bell, Escalera recovers his animal urges and leaps from his stool. He uncorks a right hand that narrowly whistles over Everett's head. Another miss, but Escalera remains unruffled. A left hand connects for Everett, who is five feet away by the time Escalera has unfurled another punch. Everett follows up with a right hook, then a jab, and suddenly a dribble of blood appears over Escalera's right eye—a cut. For weeks, Everett had fantasized about drawing first blood. "I was looking at the scar tissue over both of his eyes," he said. "If I can split them open, then I'm going to jump on him like a vampire."

Fight night program.

Escalera, emboldened, charges after Everett, but he eats a booming straight left instead. Escalera takes it well, like a sponge to water, smiles and starts yapping at Everett. Seconds later, there is a brief skirmish, and this time Escalera prevails. He gets in a stiff right hand that puts Everett on his heels. Everett looks genuinely startled; he never saw the punch coming, and now there is a small nick over his left eye that begins to bleed. For the first time in his career, the skin on his immaculate face has split open. That is enough to disabuse him of fighting in the pocket on this night. So much for those pre-fight declarations.

Escalera tries to mount another offensive, but the Philadelphian pivots away and, for good measure, performs the Ali shuffle. The fans roar. Escalera spews out a few more angry words in Spanish like a street hawker in Times Square.

Everett finishes the round out with a hook and left to the body. Escalera raises his right hand in the air at the bell, as if to signal the change in the fight's tenor.

A look of concern dawns on Everett. He is blinking hard, the lids of his eyes shifting as quickly as a split-flap display. Aliano hovers over him and presses down hard on the cut with a cotton swab. "People forget about that [cut], but I got it stopped pretty easily," Aliano would say years later.

Round four. The fight slows down for Everett. He lands jabs and hooks, like rapier thrusts, in between Escalera's tortured wind-ups. A minute in, Everett staggers Escalera with a right hook along the ropes. Escalera swings with his right and misses badly. Everett takes a few baby steps backward and lures Escalera into missing with another sloppy right. This time, Everett punishes him with a counter right hook-straight left combination. Escalera stumbles; the skin on his face erupts again.

The jab to the body was open in the early going for Everett.
(Courtesy Peltz Boxing Promotions, Inc.)

But the cuts are relatively innocuous. He has incurred far more gruesome lacerations on the streets of San Juan. Finally, in the fifth round, Escalera extracts his pound of flesh. He lands two whiz-bang right hands on the challenger that draws a sharp gasp from the partisan spectators. But Everett has an A-grade chin, as well—how else would he have been able to withstand the punches of his middleweight stablemates from all those sparring sessions?—and he gets back on track with his jab. Late in the round, Everett redeems himself with a straight left, but Escalera simply grins in response, flashing the white of his gumshield.

Southpaws are told to move counterclockwise when they go up against orthodox opponents. Circle right, so you can cut off the angle right-handers typically require for their cross. But in the second half of the fight, Everett abandons this conventional wisdom. He repeatedly steps to his left, instead, in an effort to bait Escalera into throwing more careless right hands. Everett has no intention of mixing it up on the inside, but he will counter, stymie, and flummox his bird-dogging foe from afar before the latter has a chance of closing the gap between them. The punches for Everett come in ones: a jab here, a hook there, potshots. Somewhere at ringside, Russell Peltz is scrunching up his fight program, praying silently for Everett to stand and trade.

Meanwhile, Escalera continues to swipe at air.

Everett stuns him again in the eighth. A right-left combo jostles his synapses, and Escalera quickly latches onto the rail-thin waist of Everett, giving him the few seconds that he needs to clear his head. Everett continues to spiral around Escalera, smacking his head with jabs and straight-down-the-pipe left hands. But Escalera remains undaunted. There is not a neurotic bone in his body. He is pure id. Pavlovian. He never sulks or loses poise but simply presses forward. In the ninth, Escalera charges at Everett again with his right cocked from behind his shoulder, but Everett darts away. This time, instead of skating out to the center of the ring as he usually does, Everett anchors his right arm around the torso of Escalera and spins himself around until he is facing Escalera's back. As Solis steps in to break them up, Everett gives his hips a riggish shake. And then another. Who's the dancer, now? Squeals burst from the stands.

Everett follows up with a one-two, then two straight rights, and then punctuates the round with a counter right hook along the ropes. With the histrionics emptied out from both men, the fight settles into a lull. The legato pace favors the challenger, who continues to operate in perpetual motion, eating up as many miles on the ring as a Bugatti on the Autobahn. He keeps Escalera at arm's length at all times, touching him up with the occasional jab. Escalera is the bigger and stronger man, but he is, at heart, a ham-handed fighter with few ideas of how to cut off the ring or set up his power punches behind a jab. He is losing this fight.

The crowd gets a pick-me-up in the twelfth round, courtesy of a few flurries in the middle of the ring. Everett puts together his first three-punch combination of the night; Escalera continues to heave right crosses that sail over their target. The Spectrum swells to a crescendo. Left and rights bounce off of Escalera's steel helmet of a head like a shower of rock-hail, and it seems as if the momentum is firmly siding with Everett.

Then, in the thirteenth round, Escalera lunges in with another crude right that whooshes over his quarry. Nevertheless, he manages to land his most meaningful blow of the fight— that is, with his head. Suddenly, the right half of Everett's face— the face that had never so much as suffered a razor scratch—is shrouded in a sheet of morbid crimson. A noticeable crosshatch has formed underneath his hairline. After the fight, Escalera, pointing to his mouth, would reveal that one of his teeth had been responsible for causing the rupture.

Escalera's seconds urge their man to seize this opportunity. They had underestimated the hometown opponent, had chewed away their fingernails waiting for the knockout that never came. But here was their chance, their deus ex machina. It was now or never, headbutt be damned.

Everett and Escalera trade heads blows.
(Courtesy Peltz Boxing Promotions, Inc.)

Even in the fuzzy half-light of a lamentable VHS transfer, the red pasted across Everett's face is shockingly pronounced, almost Fauvist. Escalera surges forward, arms churning about like windmill turbines. Although his vision is now obscured by a bloody film with the most perilous moment of his career before him, Everett neither falters nor retreats. A monastic calm falls over him. With punches fizzing past him, Everett bites down on his gumshield and lands three consecutive counter one-twos, some of the cleanest punches he has landed all fight. It is as if the blood serves as a catalytic agent. Flecks of it land on the judges' scorecards and the commentator's stat sheets at ringside. The crowd shrieks and howls like banshees.

For years he was criticized for lacking the heart of a true Philadelphia fighter. Over the next three rounds, Everett lays waste to this school of thought that has hounded him since he turned professional in 1972.

Aliano is able to stanch the blood flow. The gash looks like a crack in a piece of china. With ten seconds remaining before the start of the fifteenth and final round, Everett springs from his stool at the bell. He shakes his head and smiles, looking as though he could go ten more rounds. He continues to find a home for his straight left.

Midway through the final round, a rare right lands for Escalera, and blood spurts from Everett's raw wound once more. But Everett answers back straightaway, clocks him with a hook. He lands another that freezes Escalera in his tracks and causes blood to leak from a different orifice, his nostrils.

The noise inside the Spectrum is so deafening that the fighters continue trading punches for several seconds after the final bell until Solis finally intervenes. Then, as if a switch went off, the adversaries embrace each other like long-lost friends. Their teams flood into the ring. Mike, who is set to fight in the walkout bout, bops over to his brother.

After Aliano finishes tending to the cut, Everett pumps his fists in the air as adoring onlookers voice their approval. They are itching to beat a path to the afterparty. After an unusually long lag, veteran announcer Ed Derian takes the center of the ring and bellows into the microphone.

"Ladies and Gentlemen, the scoring as follows: Judge Lou Tress has scored it ... 145 Escalera, 143 Everett."

Everett, gored up.
(PhillySport)

A ghastly chorus of boos rains down on the ring. Everett starts pacing nervously. Peltz, standing by the ring, slaps his hands on the canvas. In his mind, Derian flubbed the score-cards. "Eddie, you're such a fucking putz," Peltz recalled thinking. "You just embarrassed yourself here in front of 16,000 people by reading the score wrong."

Derian continues. "Judge Ismael Fernandez of Puerto Rico has scored it ... Escalera 146, Everett 143."

More boos. Hearts start to plummet. The fight is sealed. There was no point in reading the last scorecard. Escalera's team knows this as they lift their man into the air. Everett dashes off to the changing room.

"Ladies and Gentlemen, Ray Solis has scored it 148 Everett, 146 Escalera," Derian recites, his voice barely audible amid the growing cacophony. "And so, the junior lightweight champion of the world ... Alfredo Escalera!"

* * *

THE SPECTRUM HAD all the powder keg it needed to kindle a riot on the night of November 30. That the "backlash" consisted of no more than some spilled beer and heartache seemed like a minor miracle. But thanks to a few serendipitous reasons, the situation did not escalate into a calamity. The first had to do with the fact that by reading the two Escalera scorecards right off the bat, announcer Ed Derian had deprived the proceedings of the kind of pent-up suspense that could spark an out-and-out melee. Typically, in the case of split decisions, announcers arrange the order of the scorecards so that the verdict is not revealed until the third and final score is read. This way, dramatic tension is maximized. For whatever reason, whether intentional or not, Derian declined to do that in this instance, thereby sapping some of the drama from an already volatile situation involving a heavily partisan crowd. And yet, ironically, the other reason why the Spectrum avoided an uproar was that while Everett was a popular fighter, he was not exactly, say, Bennie Briscoe popular. "I say to this day that if that had been Briscoe in there that night, they would have torn the place down," Peltz recalled. To be sure, the idea that a riot had been staved off may have just been a coping mechanism for Peltz. Who could blame him? In the face of such a travesty, the human impulse is to glean some sort of silver lining, imagined or otherwise. Nevertheless, thousands walked back home that miserable, absurd night with heavy hearts and demands for justice.

But Peltz was hardly the only one sweating bullets. A few minutes after he read the decision, Derian returned to the microphone to announce that the verdict was not final and that it would be subject to a hearing among the officials. His directive came from Howard McCall, the chairman of the State Athletic Commission but who, in reality, had no intention of changing the verdict or launching an investigation. But he sensed the growing turmoil of the moment and figured that telling the crowd that the decision was being suspended would defuse tensions. Of course, that left the bettors irate. The "revised" results would not be announced until the next day.

To what extent did the official decision diverge from the general consensus? A look at the media results paints a lopsided picture. Every news outlet had it overwhelmingly for Everett by a margin of at least five rounds, including the *Associated Press* (146-139), *United Press International* (146-141), the *Philadelphia Daily News* (148-139), the *Philadelphia Inquirer*

(145-140), the *Bulletin* (148-140), and the *Courier-Post* (147-138). Pat Duffy, the prominent Philadelphia manager, told the *Inquirer* that he had "never seen anything like this in my 50 years of boxing. That kid won it easily."

Both Gene Courtney of the *Inquirer* and Tom Cushman of the *Daily News* referenced the Great Brink's Robbery of 1950, then the biggest heist job in American history, in their recaps. Here is Cushman, who did not temper his disgust in describing the indignity and bewilderment of that night:

"The only really logical place to begin this story is with a full report of the felony. I mean, I realize that thievery at prizefights is an accepted part of the rich history of this community and that until last night we did not have an entry adequate for our Bicentennial celebration. Well, compared to this latest robbery, the Brink's job was two kids ripping off the candy counter at the corner grocery [...] Tyrone Everett won the junior lightweight championship of the world last night. Won it with a whirling, artistic, courageous performance that brushed against all edges of brilliance. Everett was standing tall, proud, bleeding in his corner after the fifteen rounds, waiting for the championship belt to be draped around his waist, when they snatched it from him. Picked him so clean it's a wonder they didn't take his shoe and trunks along with everything else. There is no way to explain how this kind of thing happens in Philadelphia."

Longtime HBO analyst and boxing judge Harold Lederman, who had an enviable view of the fight, also had difficulty accepting such a flagrant disavowal of reality. "Tyrone won that fight," Lederman recalled 40 years later to Doveed

Linder. "I was sitting ringside, maybe five rows back. In giving every break in the world to Alfredo Escalera, I still scored it ten rounds to five for Tyrone Everett. He just beat up Escalera."

Although Everett had a reputation for being a poor sport, he took the loss in stride and sounded even a bit gracious. "[Escalera] said, 'Everett's got no guts, I was a chicken,'" Everett told a group of stunned reporters. "Well, that was a bloody battle out there. I think I proved I had heart. That's what people have said about me all along, that I had no heart. Well, I figure if nothing else, I proved different. I got butted. I couldn't see the guy because there was so much blood. And I didn't let it excite me. I didn't freeze."

But as the adrenaline receded, Everett found himself gripped by a painful comedown. Like most everyone in the arena that night, he struggled to find an adequate rationale for such a distortion of reality. "The thing that hurts is that I handled him so easy," Everett muttered. "He was off-balance all night. Anybody up close could see his punches were not hitting me. Honestly, I didn't think he'd be that easy."

Meanwhile, in the other dressing room, a hyped-up Escalera, with his arm snugly wrapped around his wife, rattled off the ways in which he deserved to win the fight while berating the journalists who questioned his assessment. "Of course, I won," Escalera snapped. "He is a chicken; he kept backing about. He didn't want to fight me." Then he added, "I'm ready to fight him again. I need the money. I don't care when. Any day, any day. Anywhere. Yes, I come back to Philly." His manager Filiberto Lebron was leerier. "We don't come back to Philly no more," he said. "No, no, I don't think we fight Everett again."

"The only reason I'm not lying down, screaming, beating my fists on the floor is because of the pride I feel in the way Tyrone handled himself," Gelb later said. "Not only in the ring, but afterwards. I think he proved himself champion in every way even though they decided not to recognize him. I was the one running around kicking things afterward. He was the guy talking quietly to the writers, to people who were telling him how he'd been robbed. He was the guy with the class."

The loss had significant repercussions for Everett, especially from a financial standpoint. In the event that he won, his contract stipulated a $50,000 title defense at the Spectrum against a mid-level top-10 contender. After that, assuming he was successful, his guarantee would have shot up to $90,000 for his second defense in Puerto Rico.

The fiasco, of course, centered on an intolerable irony: that the hometown judge had rubber-stamped his scorecard for the out-of-towner. In favoring his countryman, the Puerto Rican judge, Ismael Fernandez, merely acted as everyone had anticipated. But Lou Tress—the man handpicked by the Pennsylvania Commission and who was, by most accounts, one of the most credible scorekeepers on the Philadelphia fight circuit, the man who received many of the city's top assignments and had been judging fights since at least the early 1930s—had somehow lost the memo. He had failed to observe the code: Be fair, by all means, but don't screw over one of your own.

McCall, along with three other local commissioners, all believed that Everett should have been crowned the champion, and when they went to question Tress after the announcement of the decision, McCall recalled that Tress "seemed surprised that we didn't agree with his scoring." A day later, McCall followed up with the veteran judge again only to get the same incredulous response. "Lou was upset about the whole thing," said McCall. "He said he scored the fight as he saw it. He went over his scorecard trying to see if he had done anything wrong. He said that he would score the fight the same way again."

But the scores were shady across the board, including the card of referee Ray Solis. Although he gave Everett a two-point win, he also put down nine evenly scored 10-10 rounds, including the critical 13th round. Tress had that round even as well, and Fernandez, somehow, had it for Escalera, despite the fact that Everett strung together some of his best combinations in the fight—through a mask of streaming blood, no less. "The blood did it," Everett reasoned post fight. "The judges scored the blood instead of the punches in the last three rounds."

It was reported at the time that Tress scored the fight for Escalera because he thought he was the more aggressive fighter, which, even then, was considered a bit rich. If stepping forward is synonymous with aggression, then, yes, Escalera was the clear aggressor; no debate there. But even a layperson, uneducated in the finer details of the sport, would have realized that the fighter who landed the far more blistering punches was also the one who was on the backfoot the entire night. That should have been obvious to a seasoned professional like Tress, no matter how disinclined he was to vote for defensive boxers, a mentality, no doubt, widely shared by those in Tress' generation. Matthew Franklin (later

Matthew Saad Muhammad), a stablemate of Everett, once cried out, "The Philadelphia judges want blood. They don't respect boxers. They gotta learn to respect skill, endurance, and boxing ability. That's why I've been going overseas. It doesn't make sense to fight in your own town and get robbed."

The explanation supposedly supplied by Tress is even flimsier, however, when one considers that he was a judge in at least three previous fights in which Everett went the distance. At the minimum, this suggests that Tress was familiar with Everett's fighting style and that he knew how to distinguish effective aggression from aggressive posturing. One of the fights that Tress presided over was the one against Benjamin Ortiz, Escalera's stablemate, in 1975. That was the night that Everett got knocked down for the first time in his career. Despite that, Tress ended up scoring the fight 49-43 for Everett, which was in line with his colleagues but also somewhat generous compared to that of several writers on press row, who felt the fight was closer than what the scores indicated. Even though Ortiz was the aggressor in that fight, that did not seem to affect Tress' scorecard, which favored the defensive boxer in Everett. In any case, it seems that Tress was more aware of the merits of so-called defensive boxing than he let on in his justification of his suspect scorecard.

Of course, nobody on Everett's side thought twice to scrutinize Tress before the title fight. Peltz knew him as one of the trusted functionaries of the old guard, and Frank Gelb knew him—crucially—as a family friend; they lived in the same neighborhood. In their heads, the only way Everett could lose was if Escalera knocked him out.

When the decision was announced at the Spectrum, Gelb was ready to call Tress out on the carpet. But as he turned to look for his friend, all Gelb saw was a spry old man scampering up the aisle, bolting for the exits. Peltz remembers seeing Tress earlier that evening inside the Spectrum and being struck by how aloof he looked. When he tried greeting him, Tress barely lifted his head. "He might have lifted his hand, maybe a foot," Peltz recalled. "I don't know if he waved to me or kept walking, and I thought he was O.K., because he was a friend of the Gelb family."

By the end of the night, Peltz had levied a lifetime ban on Tress from ever judging another fight at the Spectrum as long as he was director. "What we have here is a situation where a Philadelphia fighter won by such an overwhelming margin that it is beyond discussion," Peltz said the next day. "It not only cost Tyrone a title which he earned, it cost him a great deal of money. It cost the Spectrum, Frank Gelb, and a lot of other people money. And it is my contention that the weight of this all goes into the lap of one man, Lou Tress […] I plan to press the commission to have Lou Tress suspended for life as an official in this state on the grounds that he's totally incompetent."

Not that it mattered. Tress never judged another fight again. Three years later, he died of cancer. He was never brought in for formal questioning.

"Never in our wildest dreams did we think that we were going to get screwed by the guy from Philly," Peltz said. "If I had just done a little bit of homework I would have been aware that he had been involved in a lot of bullshit decisions over the years."

Of the three scorecards that were filled out that night, Tress' was the only one marked up with a pencil, according to Peltz. How does he know? The original scorecard is in his possession today.

. . .

"TYRONE, THEY NEITHER stole your purse nor your good name. They stole the title you had so consummately won. You made a proud city even prouder by your sportsmanship-like conduct after the fight. Because you were so cool, Philadelphia fans swallowed a bitter defeat with the graciousness of true pros. Stay loose, brother. We'll be with you wherever you fight next time yelling our lungs out when you bring that championship back home to Philadelphia where it belongs." —Chuck Stone, *Philadelphia Inquirer*, December 2, 1976.

. . .

LOU TRESS WAS merely the tip of an iceberg whose depth and proportions few at the time could immediately fathom. As new details—and old names—emerged from the Stygian shadows, the word on the street among insiders was that Tress had pocketed $1,500 for his "job" on the night of November 30. It turned out that Tress had a brother who worked as a teller at a San Juan thoroughbred racetrack, a locale not exactly unknown for teeming gambling activity. The brother, moreover, was thought to be one of several goombahs under the thumb of "Honest" Bill Daly.

Although he was never formally indicted for his crimes, Daly was a key henchman for Frankie Carbo and Francis "Blinky" Palermo, the infamous gangland tandem who controlled the fight racket throughout the so-called Golden Age of the 1940s and 1950s by commandeering the International Boxing Club, Madison Square Garden, and the new profit-maker that was television. Fight fixing—and strong-arming anyone who refused to go along with their act—was their specialty. The most notorious sham the duo fabricated was in 1947, when they arranged to have Jake LaMotta take a dive against Billy Fox at the Garden.

Despite their somewhat diffident appearances, both Carbo and Palermo were sociopathic connivers at heart, each with a gory mean streak. Carbo was a top gunman for Murder Inc. and a lieutenant with the Lucchese crime family. Palermo, a numbers runner and career criminal, oversaw the Philadelphia chapter of their nefarious operations. Like Carbo, Palermo had an itchy trigger finger. Amazingly, thanks to timely congressional efforts and government witnesses, Carbo's reign of terror finally ended by the beginning of the 1960s. Eventually, he received a twenty-five-year prison sentence, although he would be released on parole after fifteen years because of health issues. Carbo died in November of 1977, of diabetes, in a Miami hospital, two weeks, incidentally, before the Escalera-Everett title fight.

By this time, the Carbo name had become encrusted in amber, as outmoded as Cinerama or Aromarama. But his grisly influence continued to find currency in Palermo, who, after serving ten years of a fifteen-year sentence behind bars, quietly slipped back into the dirty sluices of boxing. It did not take long for Palermo to link up with his old stooges. One of them was Daly. After the International Boxing Club went belly up, Daly hightailed it to Puerto Rico, where he became the eyes and ears for Palermo, and later, Don King. It was not long before Palermo began wheeling and dealing like the good old days. Indeed, by the first quarter of 1976, there were rumblings that Palermo and Daly had been spotted together in San Juan. In the week leading up to the big fight, none other than Daly was spotted making the rounds in Philadelphia. Daly even visited a certain promoter.

"The day of the fight in my office is 'Honest' Bill Daly," Peltz recalled. "He was in my office the day of the fight. Who thought of anything? We knew we were going to win the title. There was no doubt about it. So Bill Daly was here, big deal. This was 1976. Those days were over, that was my attitude."

Strange cameos continued to pop up from the underworld. A few days after the fight, Peltz crossed paths with Palermo, of all people, at the local airport. When the topic of the conversation turned to the shocking outcome of the night before, Palermo's response was to merely shrug his shoulders and quip, "You can buy Lou Tress for a cup of coffee."

Even Gelb received a strange visit from an associate of the netherworld.

"After the [same day] weigh-in I was sitting around in my hotel room relaxing before it was time to go to the fight," Gelb recounted. "There was a knock at the door and a well-known fight character came in. Let's just call him my 'mystery guest.' He said, 'Are you okay, Frank?' I told him yes and then he said, 'Are you sure you're okay?' I didn't know what he was talking about. But a few days after the fight, it hit me. I put two and two together and another piece of the puzzle fit into place. The guy was an old buddy of 'Honest' Bill Daly's. Maybe if I'd taken the hint we could have worked out some sort of deal. Who the hell knows?"

It was understood that McCall had been on unusually friendly terms with the Carbo-Palermo faction years earlier. Suspicions were further confirmed in 1978, when Palermo, evidently no longer content to stay in the shadows, applied for a manager's license with the Pennsylvania State Athletic Commission. The matter would have gone unchallenged and, more important, unnoticed had it not been for the muckraking endeavors of Tom Cushman and the *Daily News*, which shed light on this instance of sordid backroom dealing. McCall was ready to offer the permit on a golden tray. But public condemnation was brisk and buttressed by a drumfire of withering editorial barbs from the mainstream press, including Dave Anderson at the *New York Times* and Paul Zimmerman of the *New York Post*. An embattled McCall was left with no choice but to call for a public hearing. In the end, Palermo withdrew his application citing his wish to save the commission from any embarrassment. (This was hardly the first instance in which Palermo, post-incarceration, tried to prise a sliver of legitimacy from the political machine. Indeed, he was barely out of the jug when he was offered a sinecure on the corrupt Frank Rizzo-led Philadelphia Redevelopment Authority, an urban renewal project, only to have the position revoked by his superiors out of concern that his name could "taint" the reputations of his colleagues.)

And, yet, these are, in the end, circumstantial details—nothing definite, and certainly no smoking gun among them. But for Peltz, as the years have passed, the premonitions of what happened that night have hardened into fact.

"The fight was fixed," Peltz said. "The decision was fixed. Gelb would say after all these years, 'How can you say that? You weren't there when the money changed hands.' I mean, c'mon. C'mon. He would say, 'How do you know?' Well, you don't know. You don't know. But nobody is going to tell me that Lou Tress, from Philadelphia, thought Alfredo Escalera won that fight. C'mon."

In the days that followed the fight, as columnists from each of the local outlets took turns inveighing against the decision, a curious broadside appeared sandwiched between two other boxing news items in the pages of the *Inquirer*: "It is impossible for me to stand by and read the senseless comments destroying a fellow colleague and a very good friend," it read. "I had the pleasure of working with Lou Tress in many important assignments when I was a referee. The records will show that he was assigned to more important fights in our state than any other judge in the history of boxing. This was solely because he is one of the most capable and qualified judges in the boxing profession. [...] All of those who have criticized Lou Tress should take an honest look at the other officials in last Tuesday's championship fight. Lou Tress has made a great contribution for 50 years to the boxing profession and is respected by boxing notables as one of the outstanding judges in the country. In my opinion, he still is."

The apologia belonged to Zack Clayton, a soft-spoken man who was the one-time head of the Pennsylvania State Athletic Commission and former hoops phenom with all-Black teams like the Harlem Globetrotters and the Harlem Renaissance. A recent posthumous inductee of the Basketball Hall of Fame, Clayton is perhaps best known for his career as a boxing referee and judge. He has the distinction of being the first Black American to officiate a world title fight with the fourth heavyweight meeting between Jersey Joe Walcott and Ezzard Charles in 1952. He was also the third man in the ring for the "Rumble in the Jungle" extravaganza between Muhammad Ali and George Foreman in the malarial heat of Zaire (now the Democratic Republic of the Congo). Clayton was deeply embedded in the Philadelphia boxing scene, a true stalwart. So it was not surprising that he took exception to what he framed as a media hit job on his old friend and colleague. Clayton felt that the far more problematic scorecard belonged to Ray Solis, who, in the process of voting for Everett, scored nine of the rounds even, a level of equivocation that Clayton felt was far more treacherous than Tress' narrow two-point swing for Escalera. Where was that outrage? Indeed, Clayton justified Tress' scorecard by citing some ancient apocryphal judging protocol in which a close round should always be tilted in favor of the champion, in this case, Escalera. "Anywhere in the world when there is an even round in the judgment of the officials, the even round goes to the champion," Clayton declared. "Never in the history of boxing has any official called nine rounds even." In other words, to Clayton, there was no controversy about the title fight. The right man had deservedly won.

In isolation, Clayton's outré support for Tress may not have meant much of anything. But it took on new meaning as some of his more unsavory contributions in boxing came to light, none more revelatory than when Peltz was told that it was Clayton who had asked McCall to appoint Tress as the Philadelphia judge for the fight. Peltz claims to no longer remember his source—despite the fact that, at seventy-four, he is still able to recall off the top of his head the exact date of old fights and purse figures, down to the cent, with aplomb— but he swears by the information all the same. For Peltz, the *Inquirer* piece that ran the Clayton interview was proof that the ex-referee was not entirely innocent.

Although Clayton was generally well-liked by the public (He was known to bring fighters around to the local synagogues and youth groups for fundraising events), he was of a certain generation whose ideas of scrupulousness would not survive outside of the tawdry boundaries of boxing, apart from, say, a boardroom on Madison Avenue or a used car sale lot. "He did have a reputation for being dodgy," said Don Majeski, a longtime matchmaker. "He was very close with Honest Bill Daly. He was from that old school. Clayton, Bill Daly, Tress—they were all part of the old boys club."

Clayton had been embroiled in his fair share of controversies as a boxing official. In 1968, he was criticized by some for his scorecard—and his officiating—of the middleweight bout between Emile Griffith and Stanley Hayward in Philadelphia, which Hayward, the local man, won by split decision; Clayton scored it for Hayward. Gil Clancy, the trainer of Griffith, was apoplectic afterward and singled out Clayton, accusing him of favoritism by breaking up the fighters whenever Griffith, a hard-nosed grinder, was ripping shots on the inside. This prompted Clayton to quip, "Well, I'm in the ring. I can see things you can't see." The other judge who scored it for Hayward was Tress.

Another suspect moment came during the Carlos Ortiz-Carlos Teo Cruz lightweight title fight in 1968 in Cruz's homeland of the Dominican Republic. Cruz controlled the bout over fifteen rounds, scoring a knockdown along the way, to win handily on two scorecards to unseat Ortiz. Clayton, who refereed, turned in the lone dissenting vote. It is worth pointing out that Ortiz was managed by none other than Honest Bill Daly.

Clayton was also accused of favoring heavyweight Jersey Joe Walcott in his title defense against Ezzard Charles in 1952, a fight in part marred by the numerous low blow warnings that Clayton issued to Charles, even though many believed that the punches were borderline, and thus legal. It was reported at the time that Clayton was overheard urging Walcott on with the words "Come on, baby" late in the fight.

But Clayton's most infamous headscratcher came about in the 1979 Wilfred Benitez-Carlos Palomino welterweight title fight in San Juan. Clayton scored it 145-142 for Palomino, the defending champion. Once again, it was the minority verdict. "Strange, because the fight wasn't close," Michael Katz pointed out in the *New York Times*. Although Benitez would win on a split decision, Clayton's curious scorecard did not escape censure. The perpetually irascible Bob Arum of Top Rank, who promoted the fight, blew his fuse upon hearing the scorecards read ringside, shouting to the skies, "It's a fix! That's Bill Daly's man and it's a fix, and I want you all to hear it!" By that point, it was no secret that Daly was one of the many beards acting on behalf of Don King. Arum did not back down from his allegation. "We had heard rumors that Zack Clayton was under the influence of Don King and Bill Daly," Arum continued, "and they wanted Palomino to win because Benitez has the option for Top Rank and Palomino didn't." Pressed by Katz to offer up an explanation, Clayton waffled, claiming first that he thought that Palomino's superior bodywork had gone unappreciated before settling on a more homespun alibi. "Well, the sun was in my eyes," he said. (The fight was held in an open-air stadium.) Clayton would subsequently sue Arum for defamation, and the two would settle out of court, reportedly for $10,000.

If Clayton had a decent poker face, he did not show it on the night of the Escalera-Everett title fight. He sat ringside, courtesy of a rare comp ticket from Peltz. "I remember now seeing Clayton sitting in the seat I gave him at ringside and how intense he was," Peltz recalled. "I've never seen him more focused in my life. I remember exactly where he was sitting, in the neutral corner, one of those seats behind the poles, right in the corner. I happened to look over that night and seeing him leaning forward, not to the point of biting his nails, but really homing in on that fight."

Suffice to say, Peltz has few fond memories of a man who is celebrated today as a sports pioneer. "Years earlier, when

Clayton was the commissioner in the early '70s, I had a big fight at the Arena one night," said Peltz. "We sold 7,000 tickets. And the place was pretty filled. And he calls me over. 'Boy, the commissioner could sure use a bag of peanuts.' My dad was in the plumbing business, and I said, 'Dad, can you believe what this guy said to me?' And my dad said, 'I'll get one of my trucks and we'll take him three tons of peanuts and dump them on his lawn.'

Years later, however, Peltz would encounter a new wrinkle in the narrative. Before he passed away in 2010, Joe Gramby, the respected Philadelphia fight manager, told Peltz that the commissioner, Howard McCall, would not have trusted Clayton enough to follow through on the latter's advice to give Tress the Escalera-Everett assignment. That was not to say that there was no monkey business afoot. Instead, Gramby told Peltz that the pressure to select Tress came from a far more influential source than Clayton—someone with real political clout. "McCall didn't know what was going on," Gramby told Peltz in an interview published shortly before he passed away. "I did. That's what swung it: Gelb's relationship with Lou Tress. Gelb thought he had an edge. You got it right. It came from Bill Daly to Zach Clayton and Zach Clayton to Lou Tress. Tress was getting assignments at the time. It came from some politician asking Howard for a favor. Howard would have been suspicious of Zack."

No matter how one sliced and diced the numerous details, they all boiled down to one conclusion for Peltz: corruption. "All Howard McCall (commissioner) had to do that night was put Tommy Cross in there, the ex-fighter who was a judge," Peltz said. "I remember there was a restaurant inside the Spectrum called the Blue Line and I was in there the night of the fight before the show started and remember Tommy Cross coming in there and saying, 'Boy, I really hope I get appointed.' Now whether or not Tress had been appointed already and no one said anything, or McCall made the decision that night, I don't know."

Even McCall became something of a suspicious actor. In 1978, the commissioner would come under fire after rumors surfaced that he had accepted an all-expense-paid trip to Puerto Rico from Don King to watch the Jimmy Young-George Foreman heavyweight fight. The stench of corruption continued to waft through Philadelphia.

Daly, Tress, Palermo, Clayton … the dots were easy enough to connect, but their alignment only triggered more questions about the underlying motive behind such wanton subterfuge. To make sense of this morass would require bringing up a certain numbers runner from Cleveland: a burly, six-foot, four-inch man with an electrified afro, a penchant for neologisms, and a cackle that could cause flowers to wilt on the spot. "I don't think Escalera's managers had any idea of what was going on (with Tress)," said Peltz. "They weren't savvy enough themselves to go for the Pennsylvania judge. But Puerto Rico was becoming very strong on American television in the early '70s. I think Daly did it on his own—and then he delivered Escalera to King."

* * *

THE DECISION ON November 30 cast a black stain on the heart of Philadelphia boxing. Ambitions were thwarted, ideals shattered. Still, years later, Peltz would contend that the tragedy of that night—and the forces that conspired against them—could have been avoided had Everett dug his soles into the canvas a bit more. Old habits, however, are so often the toughest things to kill in a fighter. "If he had been more aggressive he would've knocked out Escalera in that fight," said Peltz, his frustration still audibly fresh. "He never went for it. Not that he didn't win ten out of the fifteen rounds, but it wouldn't have gone to the scorecards."

In the immediate aftermath of the fight, it was clear that a chapter of Philadelphia boxing had come to a close. Gelb and Peltz could no longer pretend to be carefree novitiates, frogs in a world of scorpions. Cynicism took over. They knew that their prelapsarian days of carefree indulgence were effectively over. "We were in a catatonic state," said Peltz. Gelb, an otherwise garrulous individual, became more withdrawn and harder to engage.

"He got a little hard after that, Frank," Peltz continued. "He got a lot tougher to deal with because he was so disgusted. I remember the next fight when Everett came back in February to fight Cornelio Vega, Frank said, 'If you don't want to pay him $10,000, then I'll put him in a fight at the Arena. I'm not doing any more favors anymore.' I think we paid [Tyrone] $10,000 for that fight, and we lost money on it."

"I lost interest," Gelb said. "I divorced myself from a lot of it. I used to go to the gyms several times a week and follow up with boxers—where they were, how they did—I always spoke to them, I always made sure they had everything they needed, and afterward I had no interest anymore."

On the surface, Everett seemed to take the loss better than his peers. During a private screening of the fight at the Spectrum, Peltz recalls Everett was mostly mum, save for a moment in the middle rounds showing a brief scuffle on the inside that had Escalera level with Everett's crotch. Everett beamed and blurted out, "Look, I made him suck my dick!"

Glibness aside, Everett was as disillusioned as anyone else in his camp. Months later, on the day before he was killed, Everett let on that adhering to choirboy ethics would not work to his advantage in boxing. There were too many scorpions scurrying around. "A guy walks up to me," Everett told Tom Cushman, "in the lounge of the motel one day and says 'Tyrone, you might be the best fighter in the world, but you ain't gonna win the title unless you get help. If your manager had been smart, you'd have had help in Philadelphia for the Escalera fight. Help is always available.' I told Frank about that conversation, and he froze. Frank still thinks it's possible to run around, work hard, and have everything come out the way it does in the movies. I've seen others lose decisions that were almost as bad as the ones I lost, Alfonso Evans and Matthew Franklin to name two recently, Frank's fighters. I said, 'Frank, you're a terrific guy, but you're gonna have to learn to throw a little dirt in this game to get some respect.'

"Frank spends all this money flying back and forth to Puerto Rico, talking to these people with that nice college boy attitude. They smile at him, but as soon as the door closes they say, 'Bleep that fool,' and go on doing things the way they've always done them. Frank's problem is he's playing it honest, and this is a dirty game."

"Hard as he tries, there are things about me and things about this business that Frank just doesn't understand," Everett continued. "He came from a furniture store into a world where they don't think nothing about roughing up a person. My contract runs out next year. If Frank can't turn things for me a little faster. I'll have to look in another direction. A lot of fighters are thinking that way. Frank's working against the grain. He just doesn't realize that nice people get run over in boxing."

"Maybe, that's true," Gelb reflected recently. "Maybe he did need [outside help]. Certainly the outcome of the Escalera fight certainly showed that it was a dirty business. And the proof of it on my side was that we were straight on as it could be. I heard about the stories in boxing, but I thought that was years and years in the past, never like it was when I was one of the leading managers."

◆ ◆ ◆

A WEEK AFTER the debacle, Gelb and Peltz flew to Las Vegas to plead their case for an immediate rematch with the WBC during its annual industry convention. McCall also joined, but his presence lent nothing more than a token significance. Ironically, the fact that the native judge had voted against the native fighter hurt, rather than helped, their appeal. In the end, the Everett deputation was handed another losing verdict.

"We never really had a chance in Las Vegas," Peltz recalled. "They didn't even want to see the films of the fight I brought, which is understandable. If they ordered a rematch every time there was a controversial decision, this business would be even more chaotic than it is. And in this instance they had a bout where a local judge voted against the local fighter, where the local commission had given them every imaginable headache before we could even bring the fight into the state."

What's more, the WBC's Fighter of the Year award went to none other than Escalera.

Nevertheless, Gelb, undaunted, continued to badger Escalera's managers. By February, his efforts had yielded the skeletal framework of a deal. It was agreed that after both fighters came away victorious in separate tune-ups, the rematch would take place by late May in Philadelphia. Each fighter would get a $10,000 bump from their last purses, $100,000 for Escalera, $25,000 for Everett. Contracts were inked, and both fighters came away with early stoppages in their next bouts. The rematch seemed inevitable.

But by early March, rumors were buzzing through the streets of San Juan that Escalera was at loggerheads with his managers, Filiberto Lebron and Pedro Aponte, who, whatever their foibles might have been, succeeded in raking in almost half a million dollars in purses for their client over the course of two years. That did not stop Escalera from publicly denouncing the pair in the local papers. "They no longer adequately or effectively represent me, and they are to cease any negotiations they may be engaged in concerning future fights for me," Escalera was quoted as saying.

Enter Don King.

As mentioned before, it was no secret that Daly, underworld apparatchik par excellence, enjoyed a cozy business relationship with King. Just as Arum would later accuse Clayton of colluding with Daly and King on Palomino, Lebron and Aponte fingered the tandem for trying to "pirate" Escalera. But no matter how much they kvetched to the press, the managers had no recourse. King was in, whether they liked it or not. Suddenly the legal language in the contract Gelb had drawn up disappeared like an Etch A Sketch drawing.

Was King the linchpin behind the events on November 30? Peltz certainly thinks so. But if King was involved, it was only in an indirect sense, in that it was his name that gave coherence to the disparate moving parts that led to Escalera squeaking by with a decision. But why was it important for Escalera to hold onto his title? Consider that Daly was in the business of packaging fighters and that there was no buyer of boxing chattel more rapacious or remunerative (for middlemen, at least) than King, and the tangle becomes a little less mystifying. Escalera was the ideal fighter on whom Daly could hitch his wagon since not only was he a Puerto Rican champion, but he was, significantly, a champion not tied to a particular promoter. That was partly why Escalera frequently defended his title in foreign countries and why, on this view, Daly would have viewed him ripe for the promotional picking. Everett, on the other hand, was off-limits to someone like Daly since Arum, King's bitter rival, already had options on Everett. Had Escalera lost to Everett that night, Daly would have missed out on a meal ticket, and the WBC junior lightweight would have fallen under Arum's purview, thus depriving King of an opportunity to wield his influence in that division. There was a power vacuum in boxing, and King and Arum were in a dead heat to possess as many fragments of the business as possible. (This logic would echo the argument Arum used two years later, when he accused Clayton of favoring Palomino over Benitez, since Palomino was not tied to Arum, thus, in the event that Palomino won, it would have opened up the path for Daly and King to swoop in and control a welterweight title.)

If it sounds clichéd that yet another sordid episode in boxing should involve its most infamous denizen—a figure whose diabolical urges bring to mind the cutthroat sensibilities of Machiavelli and Mephistopheles and the grift and bunkum of P.T. Barnum and Elmer Gantry—it simply underscores his astonishing vise-grip on the sport at the time.

His rise was something out of Dickens or Stendhal. After serving four years inside Ohio's Marion Correctional Institution—cheap penance for curb-stomping to death a man who had failed to fork over a $600 gambling debt—King would emerge, in a little less than three years, as the chief impresario behind the Ali-Foreman heavyweight extravaganza in Zaire. A numbers operator from the ghettos of East Cleveland was now marauding corporate boardrooms in Manhattan. He was truly an American original, a creature of unfettered capitalism who would not have been out of place with the robber barons of the Gilded Age. He got by on zeal, charm, and guile, or as he often liked to say, "Wit, grit, and bullshit." King was at once sui generis and rotten to the bone.

Even before the Escalera rematch, Frank Gelb could attest to King's gravitational pull. Gelb was the initial manager of Philadelphia heavyweight Jimmy Young. Like Everett, Young was a southpaw with a reputation for being a spoiler inside the ring. Unlike Everett, who was reliably popular with his South Philadelphia coterie, Young was simply box office poison anywhere he fought. Still, Young would go on to carve out a name for himself during the era deemed the greatest heavyweight generation in boxing due largely to two performances: his controversial decision loss to Ali in 1976 and his points win over George Foreman in 1977.

Gelb was not involved in either fight, having relinquished his managerial stake in Young shortly after Young scored a major upset over the treacherous contender Ron Lyle in 1975, in what was supposed to be a tune-up for Lyle. In theory, the win should have lifted Young to bigger fights with some of the other ranked heavyweights, but Gelb could find no interested takers. Part of the reason was Young's ugly style, which made him a nightmare for matchmakers. But the bigger issue was the fact that King had dominion over the heavyweight class. Try as he might to pitch King on an Ali-Young showdown, Gelb simply got the run-around. In the end, Gelb, out of ideas, sold his portion of Young's contract to an undistinguished duo named Jack Levin and Ray Kelly. Levin owned an electric-supply store right down the road from Gelb's furniture business in West Philadelphia, and Kelly was supposedly an Ali-camp flunky. Neither man could be said to have had worthwhile credentials in boxing, but the pair paid Gelb handsomely for his distressed asset. Almost too handsomely, in fact. Either Levin had a monopoly on lightning supply in Philadelphia, or Kelly was the highest-paid hanger-on in the history of boxing sycophants. Something, clearly, was amiss. (Gelb claims to no longer remember what he was paid, but he recently surmised it might have been around $20,000 to $30,000. However, Bob Wright, the boxing beat writer of the *Scranton Times-Tribune*, citing several unnamed sources, pinned the purse much higher at $85,000. The latter seems like the more likely figure, judging from Gelb's comment to Tom Cushman at one point that he was paid "very, very well [for Young] ... much, much, much more than [the contract] was worth.") Whatever the case, within half a year Young, now part of the King stable, found himself across the ring from Ali.

That a pair of nonentities from Philadelphia was able to maneuver a toxic heavyweight asset into the world championship should have raised eyebrows, especially with the local commission, which has the final say over managerial licenses, but McCall, despite his frequent claims of objectivity and fairness, apparently did not consider this to be something worth probing.

Though Levin and Kelly repeatedly denied his involvement, there were persistent whispers that Blinky Palermo was a key linchpin of the operation, a matter that would be publicly litigated after Cushman blew the lid off Palermo's attempt to apply for a manager's license in Pennsylvania. The Palermo connection would explain how two tenderfoots, with few bonafides, either in boxing or in the underworld, were able to link up with King.

* * *

THE REMATCH WAS penciled in for June 18 in San Juan on a Don King promoted card. But before then, both Everett and Escalera would each get a tune-up bout on the undercard of King's May 16 ABC prime time showing of the heavyweight title fight between Muhammad Ali and Alfredo Evangelista in Washington D.C. It was easily the most publicized boxing event Everett had ever been a part of, even if the main event turned out to be an abysmal stinker. After dispatching his opponent in four rounds, Everett was amped for the impending rematch. "I'll go to San Juan if I have to because I know I can beat Escalera anywhere," he said. "He looked bad here tonight. He got hit a lot and he got tired."

Also featured on the undercard, in a non-title bout, was lightweight champion Roberto Duran, then one of the biggest attractions in Latin America and a national hero in his native Panama. Both Duran and Escalera ran into each other and traded a few pleasantries, among other things, about someday fighting each other, perhaps in Philadelphia. Duran, indeed, would end up defending his title in Philadelphia later that fall, in September, against Edwin Viruet on *Wide World of Sports.* Of course, by that point, Everett was no longer around. By then, he was four months into his permanent residence: several feet beneath a grassy knoll on the outskirts of Philadelphia.

CHAPTER EIGHT

A lot of guys do forget where they came from. It's not really guys forgetting, it's guys not wanting to come back to a place where they had bad experiences. [...] I'd like it to be right in the area I grew up, around Gray's Ferry [in South Philadelphia]. The last time I was down there was the day Tyrone Everett got killed, and that's when I realized how things are really decaying there.

—EARL "THE PEARL" MONROE

M AY 26, 1977. The first stirrings of the news arrived like a thunderclap on a Thursday afternoon on the local radio. Frank Gelb was motoring down a highway on his way to Wilmington, Delaware, to pick up ring ropes to be used for a fight card he was hosting at Atlantic City later in the summer. Gelb, to the chagrin of not a few East Coast movers-and-shakers, was the point man for hosting entertainment events in the New Jersey port town, a position he had held exclusively since the early 1970s. (The state at the time only doled out a single promoter's license, which meant anyone who wanted to operate a boxing card in Atlantic City had to go through Gelb. How a furniture retailer from Pennsylvania was able to score such a political coup in another state, he would not elaborate.) With the emergence of casino gambling, thanks to the passing of a local referendum, big-time boxing would find a profitable new home and Gelb would reap the rewards. Even when the doors of the casinos eventually opened for other promoters, Gelb would go on to form powerful alliances with Donald Trump—whose deep pockets allowed Atlantic City to briefly supplant Las Vegas as the boxing capital of America in the late 1980s—and the opera singer Andrea Bocelli.

By the end of the previous winter, Gelb had shut down his Norristown furniture business and formed Gelb Productions, Inc., his foray into the promotional and television-packaging end of the sport. He rented out an office in downtown Philadelphia and roped in his father, Morris, to act as the figurehead for the new venture. He also planned to have Everett involved with the business in some capacity, perhaps as a scout for up-and-coming blue-chippers. Gelb was all in on boxing. To hell with the commodes and chiffoniers.

But the ring ropes would have to wait that Thursday afternoon. Gelb swerved onto the median strip and slammed on the brakes. As the noise coming through the radio had it, Tyrone Everett, the seemingly perpetual No. 1 contender for the junior lightweight title, was found dead, shot in the head, earlier that morning. After a few shell-shocked minutes, Gelb stepped on the pedal, got off at the nearest exit, and sped back to Philadelphia.

* * *

GELB AND EVERETT'S brother Mike were the
first to identify the body at the morgue of the University
of Pennsylvania Hospital. There was no question it was
him—stone silent, unmoving, yes, but unmistakably him.
The deceased was fully clothed but shorn of his usual glitzy
accouterments. "Where's his jewelry, his watches, his
bracelets and necklaces?" Gelb cried out. The coroner also
uncovered an empty billfold and a single dime. "He's always
had money on him," Gelb added woefully. Later in the day,
Gelb told reporter Tom Cushman, "I've been hearing in the
last few hours that this is something to do with his girl. I
mean, I realize that it was not a conventional-type situation.
It's one that runs against the moral training that I had."

The facts were these: On Thursday morning, May 26,
Tyrone Everett was found dead in the second-floor bedroom
of a two-story row house on 2710 Federal Street in South
Philadelphia. His head was buried, face-down, in the mattress,
collecting blood, while the rest of his body was sprawled on
the floor. He was still bleeding profusely when the police
turned up. As a medical expert would later testify, Everett
had expired within minutes. Because no one else was inside
the home when they arrived, the police initially believed they
were dealing with a suicide. Everett was pronounced dead
upon arrival at the hospital at 11:32 a.m.

The home in which Everett was found was not his own.
Located on a bleak, dilapidated block dotted with boarded-up
windows, it belonged to his girlfriend Carolyn McKendrick.

Just three blocks away lived McKendrick's mother, Eloise Swint, who, of all people, was the one who phoned police after she heard a shot. A note written in red was tacked onto the front door: "Take off your damn shoes. Thank you, Carol." Parked right outside the home was Everett's cherished 1976 yellow-and-brown Cadillac Coupe de Ville; red-and-white dice dangled from the rearview mirror, and the front license plate flashed the letters "Tyrone" in gold with a pair of boxing gloves bearing his initials.

The crime scene was a grim affair, notwithstanding the slaughtered body. There was blood and brain matter splattered around one of the windows through which a projectile had escaped. As the ballistics expert would later confirm, a single bullet had penetrated Everett's right nostril and exited the back of his skull. The bullet was later found across the street on the sidewalk. Police initially surmised that the weapon in question was some sort of sawed-off rifle but would later claim that it was most likely a Ruger Blackhawk, a powerful six-chamber, single-action pistol. In one of the most glaring lacunae of this case, the weapon was never recovered. Also unresolved was the vast array of drugs sitting on the dining room table of McKendrick's home. In all, there were thirty-nine packets of heroin, a small brown bag of marijuana, and fourteen pink pills of an undetermined nature. The origin and ownership of the drugs would never be determined. Like the Ruger Blackhawk, they would remain an enigma in perpetuity.

Investigators were on more solid ground as it related to the suspects, thanks to a few witnesses, although many of the nearby residents remained tight-lipped. Several neighbors claimed that they had seen both a man and a woman leaving the home shortly after the gunshot. The woman was eventually identified as McKendrick. As for the man, no one initially had a clue. Other details were harder to come by. Police would later say that they were hog-tied in their investigation because of a lack of cooperation from the locals.

But things would change for law enforcement a few days later when they got their biggest break. A twenty-one-year-old man named Tyrone Price, who lived across the street from McKendrick, claimed that he knew the name of the person who had left the scene with McKendrick. He fingered the individual as a male in his twenties. He also said that he noticed that the presumptive "third man" was holding a green trash bag, which police speculated was used to carry the murder weapon. Price, however, reportedly struggled to keep his story straight with the police. As it would turn out, Price was essentially describing himself—He had been in the room when the shooting actually occurred. Price, for all his initial flubs, would soon become the top witness for the prosecution. In the meantime, he was being held in protective custody in an undisclosed location out of fear for his safety.

The pursuit of justice took other forms. The 20th and Carpenter Street gang, arguably the biggest fans of Everett, was reportedly on the prowl looking for McKendrick and a man who had apparently quarreled with Everett the previous evening. Revenge was hot on their minds.

The morning of the murder: Homicide detectives walk
past Everett's Cadillac to McKendrick's doorsteps
as news cameramen and neighbors look on.
(PhillySport)

McKendrick was still married at the time to a local drug
dealer, Ricardo McKendrick, but it was understood that they
were no longer together. A diminutive man with a ruthless
streak, Ricardo had served several years in prison on heroin
charges. After he was released, he reportedly told police that
he tried to win his estranged spouse back but to no avail;
Carolyn McKendrick had insisted on being with her new
beau. Naturally, Ricardo was one of the first suspects that
the police rounded up, but he was quickly released after
routine questioning.

While speculation regarding Carolyn McKendrick's
potential involvement intensified, the police initially declined

to interview her. Stephen Serota, McKendrick's attorney, repeatedly told the press that his client had nothing to hide. McKendrick, however, had far from a spotless record. In 1976, she racked up two convictions stemming from weapons and narcotics charges and receiving stolen property. (Both times she received parole.)

Finally, on Tuesday, five days after the most shocking incident to hit South Philadelphia in recent memory, the police brought formal charges against Carolyn McKendrick for the murder of Tyrone Everett. With her lawyer by her side, she turned up at police headquarters shortly after 11 a.m. for her arraignment, dressed sharply in a two-piece beige suit, a white sweater, and a black raincoat, a look of elegance that complemented her pageboy cut, a decidedly démodé look in funk-driven 1977. In her hands she held a newspaper and a book. Not exactly the look of a would-be murderess. Indeed, her sartorial sophistication would not go unnoticed by the jury during the eventual trial. McKendrick and Co. put up a confident front. "There's no question in my mind that she'll be cleared of all the charges," Serota said. "Obviously, she's very upset, having been charged with a crime she had nothing to do with."

McKendrick was hit with five counts: murder, possession of the instrument of a crime, possession of an offensive weapon, knowingly and intentionally possessing a controlled substance, and possession with intent to deliver. She was freed on a $12,000 bond. The police were still hunting for a motive.

∙ ∙ ∙

SLIM AND SOIGNÉE, Carolyn McKendrick was twenty-three and a mother of two children at the time of the shooting. Most people acquainted with McKendrick held her in high esteem, including Frank Gelb. In the wake of her conviction, Gelb went so far as to praise McKendrick for her supposed salubrious influence on Everett, telling the *Daily News* that "she used to come to the gym and watch him train. She was very good." Years later, he would say that her role in the tragedy exacerbated the heartache he experienced at the time. Not only did he know McKendrick from the gym, but Gelb often hosted her, together with Everett, at his summer home in Atlantic City. "Many, many, many times Tyrone would come and stay over a weekend or whatever and there were times when he would bring Carolyn along, which I never did with any of my other fighters," Gelb said. "She was a nice, beautiful girl. My relationship with Tyrone and his family was a lot different than just being a manager or a promoter or whatever the title might have been at the time. The first time he called to say he was bringing a lady. Carolyn … she seemed like an average girl like anybody else would be. That's why it was so shocking."

To be sure, Gelb was basing his opinion of her on a small sample size. After all, he seldom even met Everett outside of the gyms, the fights, and his Atlantic City bungalow. As involved as he was with Everett's business affairs related to boxing, Gelb could not profess to know the day-to-day life his charge led away from the ring, in the so-called inner city. That was one reason why Gelb at the time struggled to reconcile his perception of Everett, a surrogate son of sorts, with the version propped up by gossip that proliferated in the wake of his death, suggesting he was a philandering drug dealer.

"I really didn't pay too much attention to any rumors that might have abounded at that time," Gelb continued. "I recall that there may have been some drugs involved with different things that they were doing in the hood as they called it. But I divorced myself from that. I wasn't aware of that. I didn't live that kind of life where I would see that happen. The way that I knew Tyrone on such a close family basis was beyond belief that he would take drugs or deal in drugs or be a part of drugs. I don't know if people would call me naive. I don't think so. Because my wife and my children lived the life that I was doing businesswise by managing fighters and right at the top of their list would have been their friendship with Tyrone."

His fellow denizen of the Main Line, however, was less surprised.

"What can I tell you, except that I'm probably not as shocked as the average person on the street who has nothing to do with boxing," Peltz told the *Daily News* hours after receiving the news. "I don't know that much about the circumstances but more than anything I have to say it's the atmosphere. The lives the fighters lead, where they come from, the people they associate with, all of it is like walking along a precipice."

"Now this," Peltz continued, "I don't know the whys of what happened but, regardless, there are injustices that were done to Tyrone Everett long before today that could be cleared up if the people who know the specifics would only care enough to come forward and reveal them. I know there's been a lot of street talk because Tyrone told me some of the talk that had to do with the first Escalera fight. That, plus what happened today, makes you say, 'What the hell am I doing in this business?'"

Incidentally, the day before he was killed, Everett met with reporter Tom Cushman to discuss the Escalera fight and to see if there were any credible hypotheses circulating in the streets about the decision. The rendezvous had been arranged after Everett had successfully negotiated a tentative rematch with Escalera. Everett was accompanied by a woman and a child, who sat at a separate table. As Cushman would soon discover in a few days, that woman was McKendrick. (He could never say if the child belonged to Everett.)

Cushman recalled one tantalizing observation Everett made on the night of the title fight. He was sharing a dressing room with a man he believed to be one of the judges. At some point in the evening, a representative from the Pennsylvania State Athletic Commission entered the dressing room to tell the man that he had been replaced. Cushman was immediately skeptical of this theory. It seemed highly unusual to Cushman that a judge would be in a fighter's locker room and, further-more, that the people supposedly masterminding this heist would issue such a short-notice change right in front of the very fighter they planned to bilk. (Peltz finds it improbable as well, since everyone involved already had full knowledge of who would be judging the fight.) Everett did not know the name of the judge that was replaced, but he assured Cushman he would notify him once he did. Cushman wrote down his home phone number on his *Daily News* business card and gave it to the boxer.

The next day an editor called to let Cushman know that Everett had been shot in the face in what he described as a gangland execution. Immediately, Cushman, who lived with his wife and children in a suburban town in New Jersey, feared the worst, that Everett's attempt to dig up the name of the mystery man had cost him his life. Anyone with the Yellow Pages at hand could find Cushman. Was he next? Cushman even wondered if he needed to hire private security. In hindsight, Cushman admitted it was a silly thought. But that concern simply reflected the feeling of dread and paranoia that permeated the Philadelphia boxing scene as a result of the circumstances on the night of November 30, 1977.

At the pizza parlor, Cushman had encountered an embittered, somewhat maudlin Everett. The Escalera fight seemed to have aged him twofold. He left Cushman with some hauntingly prescient words. "I figured I'd win the title by the time I was twenty two or twenty three," Everett said. "But now I'm twenty four and I'm still not there. It worries me. After a while your legs don't move like you want them to. You have so many disappointments you begin to lose the desire to succeed. You don't want to go to the gym that much anymore. In this game, a twenty-five or twenty-six-year-old man can be old when he's fighting a kid of nineteen."

On the same day that McKendrick was arraigned, a funeral service was held for Everett in South Philadelphia. More than 1,500 people showed up, pouring out onto the streets. Entire blocks were cordoned off to traffic to accommodate the vast swath of mourners. Bus routes had to be rerouted. A large phalanx of police officers—plainclothes and uniformed—were on hand to manage the crowd. Nurses were also dispatched to hand out paper fans. Many elderly women fainted. It had the look of a Cecil B. DeMille epic. "It was a fucking tragedy," Peltz recalled. Even the mayor was present. And, of course, Everett's lovesick fans. "The most impressive thing about the funeral was when Frank Rizzo came in to view the body with the bodyguards all around him," Gelb recalled. "He was making some kind of Catholic prayer on his own, right by the staging where Tyrone lay. That and also to see all the people that turned out. Seeing so many, many, many women crying, screaming, yelling at that funeral … All the women ran after him, always."

Thousands Pay Final Respect to People's Champ

Headline in the June 4, 1977 edition of the *Philadelphia Tribune*.
(Courtesy The Tribune)

The day before the funeral, Everett's mother, Doris, received a personal visit from Muhammad Ali and Alfredo Escalera. "His death affected me a lot, personally and emotionally," Escalera would tell the *Ring* years later. "His death created more doubts about the outcome of the fight and created more controversy. They were difficult times. I always regretted his death. He was a warrior and a champion." Fans from far-flung places such as Canada and Germany flooded

Doris with postcards and telegrams. "That all made me feel good," she said, "but I'd still rather have my son back."

Several weeks later, at the behest of Mike Everett and Matthew Franklin, Gelb hastily arranged a fight card for the express purpose of raising money for a scholarship benefit in Everett's name. The show had a lackluster turnout, and Mike appeared to have been gifted a decision. But they still managed to reel in significant donations from fighters such as heavyweight Jimmy Young, Everett's one-time stablemate, and promoters Don King and Bob Arum, both of whom reportedly chipped in as much as $500 each. But it was not long before even this act of goodwill was cast in a negative light. Rumors had it that the card had been staged to pay off Everett's allegedly numerous debts. The *Daily News* reported that Everett's phone had been pulled out of the wall of his apartment and that his Cadillac—his beloved Coupe de Ville—was being repossessed.

As far as South Philadelphia was concerned, it was the trial of the century, and the proceedings would soon take on a sensational veneer. Suddenly, there was talk that Everett, a noted teetotaler whose drink of choice was a glass of orange juice, had been using his watering hole as a front to peddle dope. "Young whites used to pull up in front of the bar and wait in their cars, and eventually Everett would come out and make the deals, and then they'd drive away," one newspaper's source was quoted as saying.

It hardly mattered whether or not the allegations against Everett were rooted in any semblance of truth. They had all the effect of casting swift—and irrevocable—damage to his name, a sadly ironic turn of events for a fighter whose instincts for self-preservation inside the ring had been second to none.

*   *   *

AT A PRELIMINARY hearing on June 15, a motive was finally unearthed that would leave a permanent stain on Everett's reputation. More than eighty people jammed the standing-room-only courtroom. Under a grant of immunity, Tyrone Price came forward and testified that he was in the room when Carolyn McKendrick pulled the trigger on her boxer-lover. The prosecution's ace witness said he was in the home that morning because McKendrick had asked him to sell some drugs, which would explain the large quantity spread out on the dining room table. McKendrick had left the house around 10 a.m. and returned forty-five minutes later. At that time, Price said he had heard a commotion coming from the second-floor bedroom and then, moments later, heard her beckoning him. "She kept asking, 'Who was in the room?' and Tyrone just stood there and laughed at her. 'I'll tell you who was here,'" Price recounted.

Everett then raised his fist as if to punch her, at which point Price said he jumped in between the couple.

"He kept telling her he was going to tell her [who had been in the bedroom]," Price said. "He kept laughing." Then, McKendrick pulled out her gun, prompting Everett to warn her that "it wasn't a plaything."

When Roger E. King, the assistant District Attorney who would go on to become one of the most formidable homicide prosecutors in Philadelphia history, asked Price directly if he saw McKendrick point the gun at Everett, Price was silent at first. With further prodding from the judge, he finally responded, "Yes ... She shot the gun." Price also admitted the drugs on the table were the ones he was planning to sell.

The hearing took a lurid turn when Serota, McKendrick's attorney, addressed the elephant in the room. An avowed gay man who admitted to being a part-time drug pusher, Price was also a cross-dresser, and a flamboyant one at that, as was evident to everybody in the courtroom that day. He went by "Terry" and spoke in a falsetto voice. According to the *Tribune*, Price was "wearing a woman's long-sleeved, see-through, pink flower-print blouse with a tan sweater tied across his shoulders, tight-fitting red slacks that revealed the outline of bikini-type panties underneath and a processed, fluffed hairstyle." But his unconventional fashion sense did not stop there. The *Tribune* also reported that Price had padded his chest and buttocks, an image that had spectators "aghast." The guise apparently was so credible that both Serota and King slipped up and referred to the witness as "she." It was all too much for mother Doris to take in, and at one point during Price's testimony, she fled the room in tears.

Given the optics, Serota wasted no time trying to discredit Price. He went straight for the jugular, despite frequent objections by King.

"Had you not just had a homosexual relationship with Mr. Everett?" Serota asked Price.

"No!" Price responded.

"You had been having a homosexual relationship with Mr. Everett for some time, hadn't you?"

"No, I wasn't!"

"Isn't it true that you are a homosexual?"

"Yes, I am."

"Were you aware of Mr. Everett's involvement with drugs, if any?"

Here King raised an objection, which Judge Latrone upheld. Serota started again.

"Did you kill Tyrone Everett?" he asked Price.

"No, I didn't. I was standing right beside Carolyn."

"Did Everett indicate to you that he was using money from his fight purses to purchase narcotics?"

King objected once more, and again Judge Latrone sustained it. Serota pivoted to his ace in the hole.

"Did you ever see Mrs. McKendrick walking around with bruises?"

"Yes, I did."

It was only the preamble, but the stage had been set for the seamiest courtroom saga to hit South Philadelphia in an eon.

As one blistering allegation after another detailing Everett's supposedly illicit tastes and trades sprang out of the Court of Common Pleas, his closest confidantes were scrambling to douse all the narrative flames. Doris Everett, for one, was quick to stomp on the drug rumors. "That's a lie," she told the *Tribune*. "Tyrone was never involved with any drugs. Fighting and the bar was his business. Drugs was not his business." Then, in a comment that hinted at Carolyn's malfeasant background, she added, "Just because he was going with that girl does not mean he was involved in drugs." Mike Everett followed up with a firm denial as well. "He would never allow himself to be involved with anything drug-wise," Mike insisted at the time. "Tyrone thought too much of his body to abuse it with stuff like that. There's no question."

Mike, moreover, was incensed that nobody in the press had bothered to highlight his brother's more virtuous qualities, including his civic-minded endeavors. "Like how he was helping my brother, Eddie," Mike said. "They shared an apartment, but Tyrone paid the rent. Nobody talked about the way he liked kids, about the Little League team we sponsored. About the recreation center he planned to open in the neighborhood so the kids would have a place to go."

"You could not find one person anywhere who knew Tyrone who would ever have said when Tyrone was alive that he was dealing in drugs," Gelb told the *Tribune*. "Now that he's dead, though, some people are saying this, and it annoys the hell outta me because it was so far out of character for Tyrone. These innuendoes make me sick. Tyrone lived so clean; he didn't smoke or drink. It takes so much to be a professional boxer, more so than any other sport, that you could not possibly fool around with drugs and be successful at it.

"He made very good money as a professional athlete, but he didn't throw it away. He owned houses and a bar and a Cadillac, and he dressed well. He would not have needed to deal with drugs to make more money. This whole situation is so foreign to my norm, I'm still in a state of shock. I guess the full brunt of it will hit me in about a week or so. What kind of a goddamn country are we living in when something like this can happen?"

Of course, the more unsettling insinuation concerned Everett's furtive sex life. But the idea that Everett was a closeted homosexual did not find much purchase among his staunchest admirers. "We don't believe all that junk," eighteen-year-old Al Grushman, a South Philadelphia resident, told the *Daily News*. "Tyrone wouldn't even smoke some grass, let alone deal (heroin). He wouldn't mess with any fags either. He had too many women. Even at this funeral, he must have left fifteen girls crying on a corner. He didn't need to mess with any fag. He was getting too much booty and nobody should fault a man for loving women. Can they?"

Everett, in short, was too alpha, too virile, too straight to be anything else but what people always knew him to be, an unapologetic sexual conquistador. "Men used to get angry because their women liked [Tyrone]," Mike once said. "They liked him because he was a fighter at the top of his career and also because of his personality." Today, Eddie Everett abides by that same line of thinking. Why would a Casanova like Everett, he says, ever pine for the same sex when he had all the women in South Philadelphia at his beck and call? "Ty had so many girlfriends," Eddie said. "He wouldn't have needed that. He had so many girlfriends that a lot of girls always fought over him. He had three kids at the time and one on the way. We was young guys having fun and enjoying life."

Indeed, at the time of his death, Everett had left behind several distraught lovers. One was his high school sweetheart Christina Smalls, a twenty-year-old from West Philadelphia. Smalls told the *Tribune* that she was Everett's fiancée and that they had been conducting an on-again, off-again relationship for the better part of six years. "We broke up five or six times, but we always got back together," she said. Smalls noted that she had been living with Everett at his Napa Street apartment but had recently moved out to be with her sick mother. She was planning on moving back in with Everett on Thursday, May 26—the same day he was murdered. "He asked me if I was coming back, and I said I'd be back Thursday night to stay," Smalls said, "but tomorrow never came." She even had a diamond engagement ring with the inscription "From Tyrone, Love. 1/15/75." When asked about McKendrick, Smalls simply responded, "He just said she was a friend of his. I gather it did get serious as time went on. I never thought it would."

Regarding Everett's alleged role as a dope trafficker, Smalls echoed what his family members said. "He never did anything like that," Smalls insisted. "There was no reason to. He was doing good." She noted, however, that in the last few weeks of his life, "he acted very different," and that when she "asked him what was wrong ... all he'd say was that he was confused. He wouldn't go into details." Years later, Eddie Everett would recall observing the same behavior from his brother.

Smalls found out about the murder the next day. "I kept saying I didn't believe it," she said. "Then I got a ride down to his mom's house, and all the relatives were there. I knew then it was reality, but it still seems like a dream with a nightmare yet to come."

Perhaps none of Everett's former lovers took the news of his death harder than twenty-four-year-old ex-girlfriend Sherry Arthur, whose picture was prominently published in the *Daily News* the day after the murder. A stream of tears is captured rolling down her right cheek as she gazes despondently off into space. "I was waiting for him," Arthur said.

"He treated me nice. After he won $10,000 at the Spectrum, that was a bad fight, he bought me a living room set and a bedroom set and a TV, and a glass table. He was dating a lot of people I knew of, but I never seen any. Women flocked around men like that, anyway. A lot of people were jealous. You know, they said, 'Oh he's not so great …' I know he used to love me. I'll bet my life on it, and I used to love him, too."

A proud, if almost smug, McKendrick next to her attorney, Serota.
(PhillySport)

Carolyn McKendrick was hardly alone in her predicament when her trial finally got underway on Tuesday, November 22. Sharon Crigler of Tacoma, Washington, Carol Ann Wilds of Evansville, Indiana, and Claudia Thacker of Port Orchard, Washington, all stood trial that November for murdering their significant others. All three would end up with lengthy prison sentences.

In courtroom 453 of Philadelphia City Hall, more than one hundred and seventy-five hawk-eyed spectators were jammed into the benches, setting off the first of what would become nine days of testimony, broken up only by Thanksgiving Day. Extra seats were brought out to accommodate the overflow. The twelve jurors—eight men and four women, four Black and eight white—had been painstakingly selected from a pool of over six hundred candidates.

In his opening arguments, Stephen Serota painted a visceral portrait of prolonged domestic abuse and jealousy, at times imitating his client's high-pitched screams during the portentous last moments of Everett's life. But Everett, Serota posited, was not the real victim here. Describing his client McKendrick as a "love slave" and a poor mother with two kids who took "merciless beatings" from her "king," Serota claimed that anything so much as a side-eye glance invited a rendezvous with Everett's fists. It was McKendrick, Serota pleaded, who was the real victim of all this, the one who had suffered mightily for her love of a world-class boxer and his "bigshot" lifestyle—the Cadillac, the jewelry, the bar. She was desperately in love with the "king of flash and glamour." But there was only so much abuse she could incur. It all had to come to a head on May 26. Suspecting that a tryst had taken place in her own home, McKendrick finally confronted Everett. When he cocked his fist at her, thereby triggering flashes of previous outbursts, Carolyn, Serota said, decided enough was enough. "He was king and everybody had to bow down to him," Serota declaimed. "When she didn't, she was beaten. Between her love for him and her fear, she lived like a slave, a true slave. I'm going to level with you. Carolyn McKendrick shot Tyrone Everett. Make no bones about it. The question is, did she have a good reason?"

Serota's account elaborated on the initial testimony offered by Price. According to Serota, McKendrick spent the previous night with Everett in her home. The following morning, she left the house to run an errand for her sister that ended sooner than she expected. When she came back, she found the chain hooked on the front door, an unusual occurrence. She yelled for Everett to open the door, and when he appeared he looked a bit frazzled, with "beads of sweat on his forehead."

Moreover, he was barefoot, which was unusual because while every other visitor was expected to take their shoes off to preserve McKendrick's new rug, Everett was allowed to keep his on. "He was king," Serota said. "He had the run of the place."

McKendrick then went upstairs to her bedroom and found the sheets curiously rumpled and clothes strewn everywhere. "What's going on here?" she cried. "Who's been here?" Everett supposedly just laughed. "It was the laugh of a little boy whose hands got caught in the cookie jar," Serota said.

That was when McKendrick bolted to other rooms of the house and eventually stumbled upon Price hiding out in a darkened bedroom. Price said he was "looking for something."

"In the dark?" Serota quoted McKendrick as asking.

Putting two and two together, McKendrick then demanded that Everett kick Price out of the home. Everett responded by threatening her. "I told you what I would do to you," he reportedly said. From there, the situation apparently spiraled out of control. "I'm not going to take another beating from you," McKendrick allegedly shouted as she pulled out a pistol from the bedroom bureau. When Everett allegedly lunged at her, she pulled the trigger "out of fear, or something else," said Serota. He added, "To this day, she doesn't know where the gun is. She ran out in her bare feet."

Not surprisingly, the prosecutor, Roger King, described the final moments differently. She pulled the trigger out of retribution, not fear or self-defense. Everett, he asserted, was "backed into a corner," holding a pillow to his chest, trying to defuse the situation. "I can explain. I will tell you," he allegedly told McKendrick. Everett, King said, never made any threatening gesture toward the defendant.

Both sides whipped up contradictory profiles of Price. Serota, referring to him as a "queen" and "flaming faggot," fought back against the characterization that he was a drug flunkey, contending that he was simply a "housekeeper, a friend" whom McKendrick paid. In King's account, Price was enmeshed in the narcotics racket and earned a percentage on whatever heroin he sold. For King, this case was only about domestic abuse insofar as it related to the abuse sustained by Everett. At its core, this was a case about unmitigated jealousy and how the sexual proclivities of one man caused one star-crossed lover to commit "an unjustified killing." "The acts of this defendant were willful, deliberate, and premeditated," King declared.

On the second day of the trial, King called some of Everett's closest friends and family to the witness stand. His brother Mike was specifically deployed to support the prosecution's thesis that McKendrick, blinded by her own jealousy, was given to bouts of vindictive rage.

According to Mike, McKendrick entered Everett's home on South 31st Street sometime in July 1976. Because the bedroom door was locked, she kicked it until the hinges fell off, only to discover Everett in bed with another young woman. Mike, who was also present in the home, came over and recalled seeing McKendrick lob one of Everett's trophies at the woman. "[Carolyn] was yelling and cussing. She said, 'Get out of here, bitch, get out of here,'" Mike recounted. In what was no doubt something of an inadvertent aid to the defense, Mike added that he held his brother back from the two women because he thought he was going to strike one of them.

In his effort to make Everett out to be a womanizer, Serota grilled Mike hard during the cross-examination, which, in turn, led to several bitter exchanges. In the end, Mike admitted that he knew that on the last night Everett spent with McKendrick, Everett had accompanied another woman to work earlier that morning.

Gelb was also sworn in as a witness. He was brought in solely to shed light on Everett's fight earnings. The manager revealed that Everett had netted $25,000 in 1976 and, up until his death, had racked up $7,500, before taxes, in the calendar period of 1977. It was a rather sober financial picture. While Gelb had frequently touted his fighter's business acumen in the past, he told the courtroom that he was against the idea of Everett purchasing a bar, citing the financial risk and the damage it could do to his image. (At the time of the trial, Everett's bar had been temporarily shut down because of building violations.) He also warned Everett about McKendrick, citing the old boxing truism that fighters should refrain from fooling around with women.

But perhaps the most electrifying moment of the day's proceedings occurred when Doris Everett took to the stand and claimed that McKendrick's husband, Ricardo, "had a contract out to have my son killed." Judge Robert A. Latrone had the allegation immediately stricken from the record. Although Serota moved for a mistrial, Latrone denied the request. Once she collected herself, Doris testified that her son had been dating McKendrick for about a year and a half—much to her objection. But Doris would not stay composed for long. At one point, the court had to call for a ten-minute recess because Doris was so overcome with grief. "Leave me alone," she screamed.

The trial took a break on Thanksgiving Day and resumed on Friday. Now, it was Terry's turn.

He showed up to the courtroom festooned in women's clothing, wearing a wig, bright globular earrings, and a tight sweater that played up his padded chest. His presence alone, like that of an ultraviolet glow stick, seemed to desecrate Everett's name, a name that took its currency from the macho code of the South Philadelphia streets, not the cabaret. Each

of Price's scandalous dis-
closures had the effect of
driving a stake through
Everett's casket.

Price, who made no
bones about his sexual
orientation, said that he
was acquainted with at
least four gay men who
told him that they had
had sexual encounters
with the boxer. However,
Price denied the charge
that he himself ever had

Tyrone Price.

such relations with Everett. On the morning of the killing,
Price said that he had seen Everett leave the house with
another woman, whom he could not identify but whom he
described as being "well proportioned." This was contrary
to the claims of the defense. Price also rejected the defense's
attempt to sanitize his background. Indeed, Price admitted
to being an out-and-out drug pusher and that, moreover, he
took his marching orders from both Everett and McKendrick,
who would furnish him with batches of heroin—the drug du
jour—which he would then go out and sell on the street. For
every "bundle" he sold, he earned a commission of $35.

Unlike the other testifiers, Price was the only known eyewitness to the shooting. As such, he was the prosecution's best
ticket to delivering a first-degree murder verdict. Conversely,
for the defense, the less reliable Price could be portrayed, the

more beneficial it would be for McKendrick. At one point during the prosecution's cross-examination, it was revealed that Price had tweaked his account of the shooting multiple times to the police. But before the matter could be delineated at length, a disturbance took place during the proceedings. In an unprecedented move, Judge Latrone cleared out the packed courtroom because he sensed that there were people in the crowd trying to intimidate Price, who could not help but stutter and hesitate before each question for at least thirty seconds. After order was restored, Price said he told the police that he had no knowledge of the shooting; in another instance, he told them that McKendrick had shot Everett in self-defense. Price claimed that one officer kept accusing him of lying and threatened to send him to Mike Everett. Serota remembers this day vividly and cites it as a sort of crux in the trial because that was when the prosecution introduced the polygraph test, which, at the time, was not admissible as evidence in a court of law in Pennsylvania. (Most jurisdictions, in fact, prohibit polygraph tests because of their unreliability.)

King: Did you tell the police one story?

Price: Yes

King: Did you change that story?

Price: Yes—because the box told me I was lying.

Serota: Objection, your honor. Obviously, he's talking about a polygraph test. That's inadmissible and I move for a mistrial.

King: Did you tell the police a second story?

Price: Yes.

King: Did you tell the police a third story?

Price: Yes.

King: Did you tell the police a fourth story?

Price: Yes, I was telling the truth.

King: And what did the box say then?

Price: The box told me I was telling the truth.

Again, as with the Doris Everett outburst, Judge Latrone would not deem this to be grounds for a mistrial—a frustrating result, as Serota would recount nearly forty years later. "They [the prosecution] used evidence that was inadmissible, and they got away with it," he said. "And to this day, I'm still pissed off at it, if you can detect the anger in my voice. The box told [Price] that he was telling the truth. The whole gist of my defense was how can you believe a word that this man said? He lied to the police three times and you're supposed to believe him?" Still, the prosecution knew that it dodged a bullet of sorts—whether they failed to properly prep their client on the admissibility of the polygraph test is not clear—and the eventual verdict, according to Serota, would owe much to this brief bungle.

The defense did not leave empty-handed that day. They were able to extract testimony from Price in support of their initial thesis: that Everett was a woman batterer. In particular, Price attested to Everett's overbearing impulses, admitting that he had seen him beat McKendrick on several occasions. He also said that Everett had even once punched him to the stomach after he told Everett that he loved McKendrick "as a sister and he got jealous." Price added that while Everett lived at McKendrick's home on Federal Street, Everett would often discourage her from bringing over friends or guests or even going over to her mother's home just down the block.

On the same day, it was also determined, according to a ballistics expert's testimony, that the murder weapon was most likely a .30 Carbine Ruger Blackhawk, a powerful single-action gun that unleashes a burst of flame upon discharge. A medical examiner testified that there were no powder-burn marks on his body, lending credence to the theory and previous testimony that Everett had been at least eight feet away when he was killed. "Eight feet" was a crucial figure for the prosecution since it suggested that Everett was not anywhere in range of hitting her with his fists, thereby weakening the defense's argument.

Nevertheless, the prosecutorial notion that McKendrick was some heartless murderess would receive significant revision in the coming days. On what was a tone-shifting fifth day of the trial, two testimonies were offered in support of the view that Everett had a violent streak, courtesy of two of McKendrick's childhood friends.

Robbin Evonne Craddock, whom McKendrick had known since middle school, described a disturbing incident that took place in McKendrick's home. Everett knocked at the front door when McKendrick came down from the second floor to greet him. At that point, Craddock, who was up on the second floor, remembers hearing McKendrick saying, "Tyrone, don't hit me anymore." Craddock then came down and alleged that she saw McKendrick holding onto the wrists of her boyfriend. After yanking his hands away, Everett started to rap her with his fists. The scuffle moved to the couch, where Craddock says Everett thrashed her around until "her face was starting to swell." McKendrick retrieved an ashtray from the floor and tried to strike him with it and ended up shattering it on his arm. At first, according to Craddock, it looked as though Everett was about to kick McKendrick, but when he noticed the broken glass shards on the floor, he picked one of them up and started nudging it sadistically in her face. "I'm going to hurt you where you prize the most—your face," Craddock recalled Everett saying. It was at that point that Craddock tackled Everett from behind and held onto his jacket, allowing McKendrick to flee the house. Outside, McKendrick took a brick and smashed out the windows and lights of Everett's Cadillac.

McKendrick dons one of her oft-mentioned luxury coats as she leaves the courthouse, while her friend and defense witness Cynthia Dill broods silently.

The other witness, Cynthia Laverne Dill, recounted further incidents in which Everett laid his hands—whether they were closed or open, Dill could never say—on his inamorata. The first occasion occurred outside an after-hours club in downtown Philadelphia in August 1976. It was after 4 a.m., and Everett was waiting for McKendrick to emerge from the club. When she did, Everett dragged her across the street and smacked her in the jaw. "Her mouth was bleeding," Dill recalled. Dill witnessed another flare-up the following December. Everett was waiting outside for McKendrick to come out of a friend's home. McKendrick had rebuffed Everett earlier that day to go shopping with Dill. When McKendrick finally appeared, Everett wanted to speak to her inside his car. Moments later, Dill witnessed McKendrick struggling to get out of the car, screaming, "Tyrone, don't hit me!" while she held onto his arms to prevent him from hitting her. According to Dill, Everett managed to strike her twice across the face anyway, causing her mouth to bleed again.

Eloise Swint, Carolyn's wheelchair-bound mother, also appeared on the witness stand. Swint recalled that shortly after the gunshot, she heard her daughter banging on her front door, calling for her. Swint had been reading her Bible. By the time she reached the door, McKendrick had fled to the home of her neighbor Lillian Williams, who would later confirm in her own testimony that McKendrick had appeared before her barefooted, frazzled, asking to use the phone.

✦ ✦ ✦

ON NOVEMBER 29, McKendrick took the stand before a standing-room-only crowd of one hundred and seventy spectators. She was in her bespoke best, wearing a "reddish-orange vest and calf-length skirt," as the *Inquirer* described her. For the past week, McKendrick was a portrait of stoic calm. She held her chin high and took notes during the testimonies. She would not have been out of place at a high-stakes poker table. But minutes into her testimony, McKendrick finally cracked, forcing Judge Latrone to order the jury out of the room.

When she was finally able to collect her emotions, McKendrick began corroborating the accounts detailed by her friends from the day before, how what began as a feverish romance seemed to switch into a domestic deathtrap with all the abruptness of a guillotine blade dropping. She said she had met Everett in the summer of 1975. Shortly thereafter, they began dating, even though she was still married to her husband Ricardo, from whom she had separated in February 1974, after three years of marriage. Everett showered her with gifts, bought her a car, fox coats, and even took her to San Francisco for his fight against Ray Lunny. "People kept telling him he was champ," McKendrick said. "As he progressed in fighting, his punches and beatings became more frequent. I couldn't count all the beatings … He wanted me to take a different role … He left the bathroom dirty, left dirty dishes, he'd say, 'I'm the champ, you do these things.' He said he would punch me in the face, tear the tissues in my arms so no one would want me. He also said he would give me kidney shots so when I urinated, blood would be in my urine."

Then, in a statement that would echo Everett's well-known, undisguised contempt for fighters with scar-ravaged faces, McKendrick added, "He said I'd look like all those other fighters, like Benny Briscoe, and how he looks over his eyes, all swollen and cut. He told me my husband or no other man would want me."

McKendrick maintained that Everett grew even more vicious right around the time he challenged Alfredo Escalera for the junior lightweight championship. "Every two weeks after that fight he'd slap and punch me," she admitted. "His attitude changed and his personality changed. He got nasty ... conceited." When pressed by Serota about why she continued to see him, McKendrick said she was in a Catch-22. "I cared for him a great deal. I didn't want to ruin his career by going to the police or filing suits," she explained.

Still, McKendrick insisted that the day before the shooting, she had pleaded with Everett to leave her home. Everett, who was spending at least three to four days out of the week holed up at her place, refused and threatened her once more with physical violence.

On the morning of May 26, McKendrick said she had left her home to help her sister repair her car in West Philadelphia. Everett had spent the previous night with her. But McKendrick returned much sooner than she had intended because another one of her other sisters ended up taking care of the task. McKendrick thought something was up when she noticed Price's keys on the floor of her bedroom and the bedsheets disheveled with clothing that belonged to both Price and Everett. McKendrick concluded that the two had engaged in sexual activity while she was out. (Later, lab results of the bedsheets did not indicate the presence of any semen stains, although that did not rule out the possibility that intercourse had taken place.) When she asked if Price was in the home, Everett denied that he was. But when McKendrick dashed into her children's darkened bedroom, she discovered Price hiding in the closet. Price, she said, told her he was searching for a pair of pants. At this point in the testimony, Serota brandished a pair of black women's underwear from his briefcase. McKendrick confirmed that the garment belonged to Price and that she had found them in her children's bedroom.

When she returned to her own bedroom demanding an explanation, Everett responded by threatening her with another beating. At that moment, McKendrick picked up the pistol resting on the dresser. McKendrick said the weapon belonged to Everett and that it was already cocked and loaded. "I told him I wasn't going to take no more beatings," McKendrick said, as she recalled holding the gun by her side some ten feet away from Everett. "I told him to leave my house. Then he put his hands up and made a gesture to come at me. When he made that movement, I fired the gun ... Then I turned and ran. I didn't know if I hit him. I thought he was coming after me."

There was less dramatic flourish when it came to the question of the bags of heroin that were found on her dining room table. On that issue, McKendrick professed total ignorance, denying King's claim that she had purchased them for distribution. Moreover, her only income, she said, was a welfare check. King pressed her about her on this point. Where, he asked, did you get the funds to buy a diamond-studded gold pendant which had Everett's initials engraved along with the words "a token of love?" McKendrick said she purchased it for $150 and paid for it in installments. Later, King would bring in a jeweler who would testify that the resale value of the pendant was $500 and that "you couldn't buy it legitimately for $150." Police also testified that they had found another bedroom in McKendrick's home stacked from floor-to-ceiling with shoes and clothing, many of which still retained their original tags.

King scored his biggest points when he needled McKendrick with a relatively simple question: "Did Tyrone Everett have to die?" She responded, "I don't know." King would have a field day with this response in his closing arguments. She should have said, "I was afraid," he would later say.

The court committed an error the next day when Judge Latrone mistakenly introduced inadmissible evidence by allowing a clerk to read aloud McKendrick's four previous criminal convictions stemming from stolen goods and possession of a firearm with a defaced serial number. Latrone asked the jury to "completely ignore, eradicate, and expunge" the charges from their minds, saying that he had no idea that gun charges would be brought up. Serota moved for a mistrial, but once again he was denied. Still, the question was ringing in everyone's ears: What was a supposedly nice woman like Carolyn doing with contraband firearms?

On December 1, after a week of skeevy, tabloid-generating testimony and heightened tensions, the defense and prosecution summed up their closing arguments to the eight-man, four-woman jury. Serota characterized his client as a "love slave" under the thumb of an abusive lover, while King referred to her as a "love queen" impaired by jealous urges. Serota went first, speaking for nearly two hours, trying to pour cold water over, among other things, the reliability of Price and the notion that Everett was defenseless.

"Don't judge her morals," he pleaded. "We are not asking you to judge her lifestyle ... What do you think of Terry Price? We ought to feel sorry for that poor man ... woman ... for that poor soul. But would we believe him? I don't believe a thing the guy says. How many times did he change his story on the witness stand?

"The question has come up that he did not have a weapon. Didn't he? Aren't a fighter's fists weapons? ... And the eight feet [of distance separating Tyrone and Carolyn]? Eight feet is less than half the size of a boxing ring."

King, a riveting orator who sprinkled references to Grantland Rice and Shakespeare during his final pronouncements, protected his key testifier. "A witness is a witness is a witness, and you take him as you find him," King said. "If a crime occurred in a court, you'd get lawyers and judges. So I make no apologies for Tyrone Price ... If he can see and he can talk, who is anyone in this courtroom to say that we should disregard him?

"What was she protecting herself from at that distance? Did all of a sudden Mr. Everett become Plastic Man and have the ability to reach eight to ten feet? The defense made much to do about a love slave in opening remarks. You saw the manner in which this love slave lived? Is this a love slave or a love queen? Is this the love slave who made trips to San Francisco and other places as the honored guest of Tyrone Everett? Is this the love slave who got fox coats and a car? Does she look like a love slave or a fashion model? ... Have you met any love slaves that can afford a maid?"

King urged the jury to return a first-degree murder verdict. Calling McKendrick a "human lie-detector," he stated that under McKendrick's heavily skewed moral compass, a perceived lie was essentially punishable by discharging hot metal into the human brain. "Twenty-four years went up in smoke [that] comes out of the muzzle of a seven-inch gun," King concluded. "Was this act justified? I submit, No."

• • •

ON FRIDAY, DECEMBER 3, the jury convened for two-and-a-half hours to resolve the central cause of dis-agreement: Did Carolyn McKendrick act out of fear for her own life when she shot Tyrone Everett on the morning of May 26? Or did she act out of malice? About an hour before reaching a verdict, the jury asked Judge Latrone to clarify the legal definitions of first-degree and third-degree murder, and voluntary and involuntary manslaughter—a sign, perhaps, of some indecision.

At 4:50 p.m., before a jittery, jam-packed City Hall courtroom that included the presence of fourteen sheriff's deputies, the jury finally produced their answer: murder in the third degree. It was the least serious of homicide charges; it stipulates that while there was malicious intent to inflict bodily harm, there was no intention to take a life. The jury, clearly, did not hold the greatest confidence in the testimony provided by Price. That was little consolation, of course, for the defendant. McKendrick hardly batted an eye when the verdict was revealed. But moments later, as Judge Latrone was reading her rights to appeal for a new trial, her mask came undone, and she burst into tears. "I don't know what you're saying," she sobbed. McKendrick was led away in handcuffs as she contemplated a five-to-ten-year sentence. Although McKendrick's bail was set at a steep $35,000, her older sister, Ruby Tilghman, would post the ten percent ($3,500) required for her temporary release. She would have until the following Friday—the start day of her incarceration—to make arrangements for her children.

'Love slave' mother of 2 guilty of killing boxer over gay friend

Headline in the Dec. 10, 1977 edition of the *Philadelphia Tribune*.
(Courtesy The Tribune)

Outside the courtroom, the Everett family heaved a cathartic sigh. "Justice has finally been done," Doris cried. While the jury also found McKendrick guilty of possession of an instrument of crime, they had acquitted her of all three heroin charges. "I'm not surprised. Justice was done," King said of the verdict. But King knew that they had come up short, noting that it was "kind of a sign of leniency on the jury's part that they came back with third degree."

As for Serota, he was apoplectic. Before the verdict, he told the jury that he would do handsprings out of the courtroom if they came back with involuntary manslaughter. Now he was disparaging them, calling them "intellectually dishonest." "This was a complete overreaction by the jury to the fact that Tyrone Everett was a celebrity," Serota fumed at the time. "If he was a nonentity, she'd be a free woman today."

Serota would immediately appeal on the basis of ten "major errors" he believed had been committed by the prosecution and the court. But the case would never go anywhere, getting batted away for good by the Supreme Court in 1983. "We had nothing to lose," Serota said of the appeal attempt recently. "We had gotten away with all the other stuff—what I mean is that we had been acquitted on all that stuff. The only thing that was an issue was this conviction for third-degree murder. Now, the polygraph was not admissible in Pennsylvania. And when I took that on appeal to the Supreme Court, the Chief Justice Robert Nix Jr. said, 'That's a minor error, that's a trivial error.' Yeah, right. That's why the prosecution got back a guilty on anything."

Indeed, despite his outward anger at the time, Serota knew he had wrung out an improbably favorable outcome for his embattled client. Today, he maintains that the case went as well as it possibly could have. "I am not even sure it was not a win," Serota said. "It was a reasonable verdict. There were drugs involved. Stolen items. She was charged with all of that. All of those got thrown out. And instead of the first degree that the prosecutor was thinking, and probably should have gotten, she ended up with third degree and five years. Like I said, I'm not sure that it wasn't a win."

It has been decades since Serota, long retired from his law practice, last spoke to Carolyn.

"Beautiful woman," Serota said of his old client. "I thought the world of her. Whether she got involved in anything, I won't get into that. But as far as the person that I knew, I thought the world of her. She thanked me for the defense that I put up. She was very satisfied with my performance. I liked that.

"If you get in touch with her, give her my love."

CHAPTER NINE

Guile, deceit, and bile for so many years.

—GEORGE SEFERIS

WITH THE JUDICIAL process having run its course, Courtroom 453 returned to its usually modest levels of attendance, newspapers began hunting for their next nail-biter, and in street corners around the city, the name Tyrone Everett no longer rattled off tongues as it once did. The alleged perpetrator was now behind bars, and the victim's family could finally move on. Like everything else, the McKendrick trial became just another memory in the relentless march of time—obscured, then forgotten. But the aftertaste of one of the most disturbing chapters in South Philadelphia history was as bitter as a raw quince, and it lingered stubbornly in the mouths of those closest to the tragedy. In the wake of the trial, there was an uncomfortable number of unanswered questions, which could not be properly pursued in the court of law and continued to proliferate, like flies swirling around carrion, in the days and years after the official verdict was read.

Whatever happened to the murder weapon, the presumed Ruger Blackhawk?

To whom did the thirty-nine polybags of heroin on the dining table belong?

Who did McKendrick call on the phone at her friend's home immediately after the shooting?

Where did McKendrick get the money to afford all those clothes and jewelry?

What was the nature of Everett's sexuality? Was he gay? Bisexual?

Who was the man that tried to intimidate Price in the courtroom?

But the more one tried to trace this Ariadne's thread, the more convolutions one would encounter. That McKendrick was directly responsible for Everett's death did not ease the churnings of the conspiratorial mind. Indeed, the murkiness surrounding the case gave ballast to numerous alternative theories, the most prominent and enticing of which argued that McKendrick was not the shooter—that she was, in fact, covering for somebody else who had actually pulled the trigger. Far from being the provenance of some arcane forum thread, this happens to be the view shared by many in the South Philadelphia community today, including members of the Everett family.

"I don't believe that for one minute that Carolyn killed him," Eddie said recently. "I know when he got shot, she left, she ran. If you said it was self-defense, why run? Why leave the house and then turn yourself in? Because you gotta get an alibi. I don't believe that for one second … The witness, what else is he going to say? Who gonna believe him? Whatever happened, I believe she might have taken the rap. I believe she probably might have taken the rap and it would have been the best thing [for her] for having done it."

Eddie's mother said as much at the time of the tragedy.

"There's more to this than what's being said," Doris told the *Tribune* shortly after Carolyn was charged. "Carol was alright. She wouldn't have shot Tyrone in no jealous rage. She's not that type of person. She's scared to reveal who did it. There had to be other people involved, but the police have not investigated this thoroughly as they should. You can't tell me that she was carrying around a rifle. And what about that guy who ran out of the house with a plastic bag?"

In the June 4, 1977, issue of the *Tribune*, roughly one week after Everett's death, reporter Len Lear penned an article in which he cited several unnamed sources insisting that Carolyn was "going to take the fall to protect the real killer." Although he had trouble recollecting the trial, Lear confirmed that one of the sources he most likely spoke to was Tommy Cross, a former Philadelphia boxer whom the *Tribune* kept on retainer to be their eyes and ears on the street. Cross occasionally supplied the metro desk with the heartbeat of the ghetto, and the tragedy on Federal Street fell right into his purview. (Cross was also the ex-fighter that Peltz had spotted milling around at the Spectrum on the night of Escalera-Everett.)

"There's no way that story put out by the police makes any sense," the source (Cross) said. "That story about her killing Tyrone because of another woman is so ridiculous, it's laughable. Anyone who knew them would know how crazy that story is. Carolyn knew all about his other women just like everybody else did, and she accepted it. After all, she's married herself, so she didn't have much room for complaint. She was told, though, that if she doesn't take the rap, she'll wind up just like Everett—in a wooden box. She was told she'll get a good deal and get out in a few years and then be well taken care of. She's still a young woman, and that's a lot better than being a dead hero. These people are not playing games. It's been made clear to her that they would eliminate her."

The official evidence suggested otherwise.

"Not true, just street talk," Serota would say years later in another interview. "The details of the way it was told, by both Price and Carolyn McKendrick, are too involved. She knew too much. In my opinion, her story fit all the physical evidence too well to be bullshit. You want to know what I think happened? Well, I'll tell you: She came home and Everett was balling a fag. She got bent out of shape and told Everett to get the hell out of the house. She was incensed. He came at her and threatened her. He obviously could have hurt her. You could call it a lovers' spat, I guess. But at that point, I think she just wanted to end the relationship." Asked if he knew of any concrete examples supporting Everett's alleged sexual habits, Serota offered a somewhat cryptic answer. "Women, men, yep," he said recently. "That's what the rumor was. There was probably more than one rumor. Yeah, I don't know—I do know something, but I can't go into it."

Still, the fact that McKendrick ended up with a far less punitive sentence—five years—than originally foreseen supplied more grist for the rumor mill. But who exactly were "these people" that were supposedly working the marionette strings on McKendrick? All signs pointed to her husband, Ricardo McKendrick, who was just finishing up a short stint in prison for heroin distribution when he allegedly discovered that his wife was shacking up with the biggest sporting name in South Philadelphia.

Short and bespectacled, with a thick mustache, Ricardo did not cut an especially imposing profile. In fact, from a physical standpoint, he matched up evenly with Everett, although he lacked the latter's natural good looks and charisma. "If you've ever seen Rick in person, he would remind you of Sammy Davis Jr.," said John W. King, a Temple University instructor who grew up knowing the McKendricks. "He's about five-five. All of about one hundred thirty pounds. He's not a physically intimidating man, yet he had a reputation in the streets where you certainly didn't want to mess with him or his people." There was a good reason for that.

Ricardo's run-ins with the law started early in life, on exceptionally grisly terms. In 1966, when he was a fifteen-year-old sophomore, Ricardo was responsible for shooting four classmates in a basement at South Philadelphia Public High School; he also stabbed another student at the same school the day before. Two of the gunshot victims suffered flesh wounds, while another was struck in the chest and in critical condition. All of the victims were thought to be members of the juvenile street gang, the 13th Streeters. According to the *Inquirer*, Ricardo told gang control experts that he had been harassed by them, claiming at one point that they had cut him with a knife; he was simply trying to retaliate. Moreover, his bloody foray was also something of a family affair, as he enlisted the help of his brothers, Harold and King McKendrick, both of whom were also arrested for their alleged involvement in the shooting.

But Ricardo's fiendish ambitions would quickly outgrow the strictures of a schoolyard. The start of the 1970s saw heroin become the narcotic of choice in South Philadelphia, and Ricardo became one of the top street purveyors of the illicit substance. Simultaneously, he became an object of fear within the Black community. When Doris accused him of having a contract out on her son's life during her stricken courtroom testimony, she was addressing the elephant in the room—Ricardo was reported to have attended every day of the trial—zeroing in on a suspicion that was on everyone's mind, but which nobody dared to utter. The supposition that Ricardo had had a hand in the death of her son made for an appealing, convenient hypothesis, after all, for on that interpretation, the motive was all too easily supplied: Jealous husband enlists triggerman to mow down wife's flashy—and abusive—lover. Ricardo was one of the first suspects that the police rounded up for questioning, but he was quickly released, presumably because he produced an ironclad alibi.

It is unlikely, in any case, that Ricardo would have been the one to squeeze the trigger. The veteran Philadelphia boxing trainer Georges James would later tell a writer that he was chatting casually with Ricardo on a street corner at the very moment a bullet went through Everett's head. Of course, for people like Doris and Eddie, the whole point was that Ricardo was operating from behind the curtain. Serota, however, poured cold water over any theory involving Ricardo. "Rickie was in love with [Carolyn]," Serota said. "I doubt he would have done anything to her that would implicate her. That's bullshit. Ricky was a streetwise guy." Streetwise is one way to put it. There were rumors that the original hitman declined to follow through with his assignment because he was so taken with Everett's outsize status in South Philadelphia.

If there is one undeniable yet woefully minimalized element in this maze of smokescreens, it is heroin. After all, thirty-nine carefully packaged cellophane packets of smack primed for allocation do not appear on a dining room table out of thin air, even if a court of law decided to sweep the issue under the rug. While he initially denied Everett's involvement in drug trafficking, years later, Mike would offer a more nuanced response in which he conceded that his brother was probably in on the heroin action on some level. According to Mike, his brother was always thinking of ways to diversify his income—that same industriousness of spirit that Gelb had often heralded as one of Everett's finest features as an individual. "Tyrone never would do any drugs himself," Mike would later say, per Tom Cushman. "I know him, and he couldn't have fought the way he did taking drugs. But he probably was fronting people to buy drugs. Once you start making a little money, you get a little greedy and look for ways to invest it and make some more. That's what Carolyn was into. That's the life we were leading back then." Indeed, in 1978, Mike himself would be charged for selling heroin to undercover cops. He was rounded up during a sweeping federal narcotics raid in South Philadelphia involving fourteen other suspects, two of them members from Ricardo's own family: seventeen-year-old Venda and eighteen-year-old Novick McKendrick.

The McKendricks, admittedly, were something of a familiar presence on the police blotter. On April 14, 1978, the *Inquirer* carried a piece with the headline: "Brother-in-Law Joins Carolyn Among Rank of Killers." The older sibling of Ricardo (whom he had assisted in the school shooting), Harold McKendrick, was serving a life sentence for the cold-blooded murder of a fellow South Philadelphian. But the in-laws of Carolyn McKendrick were hardly the only ones in her extended family who were accustomed to stirring up trouble. Not to be outdone, plenty of members in her own immediate, fourteen-sibling family, the Swints, made garish headlines throughout the 1970s and beyond, making their mark on the dim streets of South Philadelphia as memorably as the McKendricks.

In 1972, Carolyn McKendrick's brother Earl Swint, twenty-one, was nabbed by authorities during the same heroin shakedown that involved Ricardo. Another brother, Bobby Lee Swint, was arrested alongside Ricardo the day Ricardo went on his shooting spree at the school cafeteria. Apparently, Bobby was not only a classmate but a close ally.

In June 1977, a day after McKendrick received her murder charge, her brother, Matthew Swint Jr., was sentenced to life in prison for first-degree murder. Years earlier, Swint had allegedly interrupted a card game at an after-hours club looking to get back at an individual who had wronged him earlier in the day. He ended up pumping a bullet into the back of a bystander and another at his intended victim, striking him in the head. But Swint, driven by some deep-seated malevolence, did not stop there. He then picked up his maimed target by the collar and drilled him, point-blank, with a parting shot to the neck.

Around the same time, McKendrick's twenty-five-year-old half-brother, Nathaniel Swint, also popped up in the papers for the wrong reasons. "Nate" was already doing time at Graterford Correctional Institution for fatally stabbing a man, when one day he escaped custody during evening classes at a community college (as part of a prison outreach program), stole a station wagon, and went on a drunken joy ride before crashing the car in a nearby town. He was eventually apprehended later that night.

No doubt, the collective rap sheets on the Swints and the McKendricks ran long. But if their criminal backgrounds, however harrowing, seem to consist of violence committed on a helter-skelter basis, nothing could be further from the truth. In 1970, while he was briefly out on bail after receiving a second-degree murder conviction, Nate had been involved in another shooting at a party that consumed the life of his brother, Robert. Alas, it was not some clip joint flare-up. Robert Swint was one of the first casualties of what would later become known to the public as the Black Mafia, an almost unspeakably ruthless criminal organization that came to power in the late 1960s. Moreover, Swint's assailant was none other than the notorious Robert "Bop Daddy" Fairbanks, a founding member of that group and who had actually registered the group's first murder the year before by taking out another co-founder whom he had suspected of swindling him during a bust-out dice game.

Made up of a combination of violent, hard-bitten street thugs and Nation of Islam loyalists, the Black Mafia lorded over every main street and back alley in Black Philadelphia throughout the late 1960s and 1970s. Truly, no form of slaughter was beneath them. When a .38-caliber bullet through the head would not suffice, there were always other methods at hand, like decapitation, immolation, and the sawing off of hands. What's more, they rarely discriminated when it came to their proposed targets. Men and women, drug kingpins and retail employees, and, yes, even children were all sent to an early grave by the Black Mafia. By the end of their reign of terror, the Black Mafia had racked up a body count of more than forty individuals. The group's bloodthirsty inclinations were reflected in their key founders, Sam Christian and Ronald Harvey, two of the most pitiless, spine-tingling thugs in Philadelphia crime history.

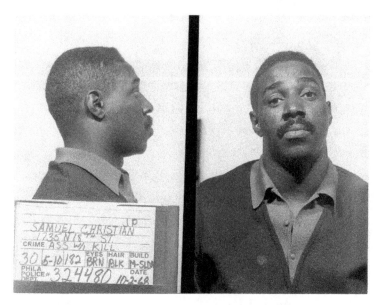

Mugshot of Sam Christian.
(Courtesy Sean Patrick Griffin)

Unlike Ricardo, Christian and Harvey provoked fear on the basis of their physical makeup alone—both were nearly six feet tall and weighed over two hundred pounds. They were brutes straight out of central casting for a Blaxploitation flick. "To a lot of young bloods on 52nd Street or South Street, Sam Christian is Shaft, Superfly, and Bad Leroy Jones rolled into one," claimed one article. With comic-book personas like theirs, a muzzling effect soon took place in Black Philadelphia. The slightest mention of their names had would-be witnesses thinking twice about taking the stand. Lowlifes and street hustlers were constantly looking behind their backs. At the peak of their authority, Christian, an ex-Black Panther who once fired bullets into a crowd at a voter registration drive to settle a score, and Harvey, both managed to carve out a spot on the FBI's Most Wanted list. And yet as deranged as Christian, Harvey, and the rest of the congregants that made up the Black Mafia were, the lust for violence was not the only attribute that made them unusual in the crime landscape of the 1970s.

RONALD HARVEY

Mugshot of Harvey, who broke into the FBI's Ten Most Wanted fugitive list at #321.
(Courtesy Federal Bureau of Investigations)

Unlike the street gangs that dominated the underworld scene—20th and Carpenters, 12th and Oxford, the Moroccos, the Clymers, Mongo Nation, et al.—the Black Mafia was more than simply a collective of riffraff throwing their weight around in the asphalt jungle of Philadelphia. As their self-styled nomenclature suggests, the Black Mafia had an organizational substructure that belied their freebooting veneer. What started out as an extortion ring that oversaw cathouses and the numbers game quickly morphed into an all-out heroin trafficking operation with unsettling ties to the legitimate world; they had the ear of municipal and civil rights leaders, a go-to stable of shrewd defense lawyers, and, perhaps most astonishingly, access to federal pork barrels. They were, in other words, a full-blown, well-oiled syndicate, the Black American answer to La Cosa Nostra and the Irish Mob. Extortion, contract killings, armed robbery, loan sharking, credit card fraud, welfare fraud, prostitution, drug peddling—there was no malfeasance under their blighted sun that was off-limits for the Black Mafia. "Often gangs in Philadelphia were brotherhoods, but they weren't really organized," said Tyree Johnson, who covered the crime beat for the *Daily News* during the heyday of the Black Mafia. "They [the Black Mafia] were organized. In North Philly, West Philly, the violence was unplanned. In South Philly, the gang violence was planned. If they wanted to get someone, they got him. That's why the leadership of the Black Mafia really came from South Philly and the drug dealing and the stuff like that. When it comes to organized crime, South Philly was more organized, more disciplined, and unfortunately, more violent."

Just how organized? The Black Mafia took minutes during their weekly meetings, which included a fully fleshed-out attendance roster and bylaws (nineteen points, in all). Members were patted down before the start of each session, and most, save for the elite, were barred from bringing weapons or drugs. Dues were $5 per week, and absences were punished with a $15 fine; three absences invited disciplinary action. All these layers of red tape represented a degree of administrative formality unusual for even the most organized crime syndicates, according to Sean Patrick Griffin, the author of *Black Brothers Inc.*, the first serious study to lay out and conceptualize the extensive machinations of the Black Mafia, with the aid of reams of revelatory court and law enforcement documents and firsthand interviews. "The Black Mafia's predilection for bureaucracy was [...] novel—and perilous, because the underworld requires a delicate balance between organization, to increase the probability of illicit ventures, and dis-organization, to avoid becoming too predictable, and thus an easier target for competitors and law enforcement," noted Griffin.

A noticeably unfazed Harvey being hauled away for the alleged murder of notorious Philadelphia drug kingpin and politician "Major" Coxson; by his side, ace Black Mafia attorney Nino V. Tinari.
(Courtesy the Special Collections Research Center. Temple University Libraries. Philadelphia, PA.)

Both Nate Swint and Ricardo McKendrick were key players within this frightening fraternity. Inevitably, members of their families were drawn into their seedy orbit. That Carolyn Swint married a McKendrick suggests there was a concerted effort to keep their growing fiefdom in-house. Indeed, Ricardo's sister, Sarah, was also married to another prominent figure in the Black Mafia, Russell Barnes, who made his bones as a flamboyant contract killer. To bolster his standing in the group, Barnes once shot a man three times in the back at a bar where a party was taking place. Despite the plethora of witnesses, the only credible one, the one who had the gumption to take the witness stand, was the dead man's sister, Velma. Barnes eventually gunned her down as well before she could testify, an act that essentially led to his acquittal.

Barnes' alleged witness-victim, Velma, lying slumped in the doorway of her home.
(Courtesy Sean Patrick Griffin)

Close-up of the bullet holes in Velma's screen door.
(Courtesy Sean Patrick Griffin)

"[Carolyn and Ricardo] come from very interesting families," said John W. King, the son of Black Mafia member John W. Griffin, whom he chronicles in his book *The Breeding of Contempt*. "That's why I use the analogy of the Genoveses and the Gambinos because there were a lot of intermarriages with the Italians to consolidate power. These guys saw the opportunity to do the same. It wasn't looked at this way because they were always relegated to being these neighborhood gangsters. So there was a lot of activity among those particular families: The Swints, the McKendricks, and, of course, the Barneses. If they were white people we would be talking about them like the Gottis and the Gambinos and the Genoveses, and so forth. But Black people don't get that sort of notoriety."

In the Black quarters of South Philadelphia, everyone knew of the Swints, the McKendricks, and the Barnes, and the rule of thumb was that you kept your head down and your lips sealed. That the residents on Federal Street, where Carolyn McKendrick lived and Tyrone Everett died, were hardly forthcoming to police officials in the aftermath of the shooting was certainly part and parcel of the general distrust Black civilians had at the time (and, alas, still do) toward the city's police force, which received its cues from police chief-turned-mayor Frank Rizzo, a man many felt epitomized the phrase "police brutality." But their reticence was also a natural reaction to the entrenched culture of fear propagated by the Black Mafia, a culture in which—as Russell Barnes showed—witnesses and cop collaborators were summarily snuffed out before they could appear before a jury. The media was not immune from this either. One reporter was allegedly picked out as a marked man by the Black Mafia after he wrote an unfavorable story about some of their so-called civic-minded ventures within the community.

While investigative reports by crusading journalists named Jim Nicholson and Mike Leary of the *Inquirer* and Tyree Johnson of the *Daily News* helped lift the lid on the undertakings of the Black Mafia, the group did not exist in the broader public consciousness until much later—that is, in the mid-aughts, with the emergence of Griffin's definitive book on the group. In fact, there is good reason to believe that without that publication, the existence of the Black Mafia as an entity and social phenomenon would have remained purely the topic of street lore. What accounted for this blackout? Part of it may be rooted in a kind of cultural soft racism. The idea that there was a mobilized criminal organization run by African Americans on par with, say, the Italian mafia went against the entrenched public perception that Black crime was strictly of an ad-hoc variety. Somehow, despite the numerous articles that cropped up within the Philadelphia/South New Jersey media sphere covering the Black Mafia throughout the 1970s, the term would never stick. For example, books on the Nation of Islam published in the 1990s describe the Black Mafia as either "Philadelphia Muslims" or "Muslim Mafia," which, while not necessarily incorrect as descriptors, shows that the term had not only lost its currency, but that much of the original reporting on the Black Mafia had seemingly vanished from any meaningful mainstream discourse, whether in the media or in academia.

As Griffin himself found out in the aftermath of the publication of his book, the very utterance of the term "Black
Mafia" had certain racial connotations that gave pause to
the editors at institutions like the *Inquirer* and the *Daily
News*, not a few of whom apparently believed that the Black
Mafia was a bugaboo created by the Rizzo-era police, even
though award-winning reporters at their own papers, like
Nicholson, had sourced their stories beyond law enforcement
records. Another factor was the pressure in newsrooms to
hew to matters of political correctness. In 2007, Griffin asked
a reporter at the *Inquirer* why their coverage of Shamsud-
din Ali—a powerful Black Mafia member who at the time
had just been caught up in a corruption probe involving
then-mayor John Street, one of the biggest political scandals
to hit Philadelphia in recent memory—repeatedly left out
his Black Mafia credentials, and the answer apparently had
to do with fears that adding such racially-charged context
could be a detriment to Street's chances in the upcoming
mayoral election.

The question of optics had implications for how the
Everett murder trial was covered by the Philadelphia press.
In short, none of the local newspapers delved into Carolyn
McKendrick's tantalizing associations with the underworld. Whether the press covering the trial were aware of her
unsavory affiliations and simply kept those details out of their
coverage, of course, is a difficult matter to parse. At the time,
Ricardo was simply portrayed as a relatively anodyne figure,
a middling drug pusher who had done some time. However,
it is worth pointing out that the reporters covering the trial

had colleagues in other departments who had reported on the Black Mafia, including at the *Inquirer, Daily News,* and the *Evening Bulletin,* throughout the mid-1970s. Was it a failure of cross-communication? In any case, the absence of the Black Mafia context would shape the story of Tyrone Everett for decades to come. Indeed, by the time that journalist Bob Ingram came to write his feature story on the aftermath of Everett's death, in the late 1980s, for *PhillySport,* the Black Mafia as a term had receded from public memory. Case in point, in Ingram's piece, there is no mention of the Black Mafia even though a significant portion of it deals with Eddie Everett conveying his suspicions that Ricardo was somehow involved in the murder of his brother. When asked about this omission recently, Ingram professed he had never heard of the Black Mafia while he was working on the story.

In hindsight, had the role of the Black Mafia been fore-grounded early on, some of the most salient unknowns regarding the Tyrone Everett murder case would have seemed less spectacular. There would have been a realization that Carolyn McKendrick was something of a mafia princess and why certain questions regarding, say, her extensive luxury wardrobe or the drugs on her dining room table, may have had nothing to do with Everett and everything to do with her own background. But these questions were not asked at the time, and it has had consequences for the way in which the tragedy is regarded today. Those who lived through the Everett case tend to remember only the drugs, his supposed homosex-uality, the cross-dressing dope peddler—in other words, all the sensationalized tidbits—but they are almost always entirely clueless about the gang subtext. Ask someone about Tyrone Everett today and you are likely to be met with the common refrain, "He was the guy that was caught in bed with another guy, right?"

```
PLEDGE MY LIFE AND SOUL AS PAYMENT SHOULD I EVER HAVE AN ILLICIT
CARNAL RELATIONSHIP WITH A FAMILY MEMBERS WIFE,SWEETHEART,
BETROTHED, OR MOTHER KNOWINGLY, (EXCEPT IN CASES WHEN ONE IS A
KNOWN PROSTITUTE.) I PROMISE AND SWEAR THAT I WILL NOT SURPLANT
NOR UNDERMIND ANOTHER FAMILY MEMBER IN ANY OF HIS LAUDIBLE
UNDERTAKINGS, NOR WILL I BETRAY KNOWINGLY IN ANY MANNER WHATSO-
EVER. I SWEAR BY MY OWN LIFE THAT I WILL NOT COMMUNICATE ANY
INFORMATION TO ANY LAW-ENFORCEMENT OFFICIAL OR ANY ONE ELSE
IN ANY WAY, THAT WHICH WOULD ENDANGER THE SAFETY OR FREEDOM OF
ANOTHER FAMILY MEMBER, NOR WILL I WRITE, PRINT, DRAW, SCRIBBLE,
OR OTHERWISE ATTEMPT TO MAKE LEGIBLE, INTELLIGIBLE, OR UNDER-
STANDABLE, ANYTHING TO ANY PERSON OR PERSONS THAT WOULD HARM
OR JEOPARDIZE ANOTHER MEMBERS FREEDOM. I PROMISE TO ALWAYS
ANSWER ALL SIGNS AND SUMMONS SENT ME BY THE FAMILY, AND THAT I
WILL DO ALL WITHIN MY POWER TO SUSTAIN THE FAMILY AND SEE TO IT
PROSPERING. I PROMISE AND SWEAR THAT I WILL OBEY ALL ORDERS
AND COMMANDS ISSUED ME BY A FAMILY MEMBER IN EXECUTIVE POSITION
OR ANY OTHER POSITION OF AUTHORITY HIGHER THAN MY OWN. I PROMISE
AND SWEAR THAT I WILL OBEY ALL LAWS, RULES, AND REGULATIONS OF
THE FAMILY, AND NEVER LET SHAME, HUMILIATION, DISGRACE, OR
SCANDAL BE BROUGHT UPON THE FAMILY BECAUSE OF ME. I REALIZE
THAT THIS RACIST CAPITALISTIC SOCIETY IS UNJUST & UNFAIR TO MY
```

Second page of the Black Mafia "oath."
(Federal Bureau of Investigations)

It was only with Griffin's *Black Brothers Inc.* that proper weight was given to a phenomenon that had been treated previously like a discursive footnote. In doing so, it introduced the unsettling notion there had been in the urban Black underbelly of Philadelphia during the 1970s, an entity with sadistic tendencies as far-reaching as Gilles de Rais but with the structural solidity of a corporation.

• • •

THAT THE BLACK Mafia arose out of the civil rights maelstrom of the 1960s, when the peaceful sit-ins of Martin Luther King Jr chafed against the militant-minded sorties of Huey Newton and Malcolm X, was, of course, hardly a coincidence. The novel forms of Black solidarity that burst onto the national scene were a belated, unbridled response to the nearly century-long subjugation and disenfranchisement of Black people under Jim Crow, and the Black Mafia was, in its own crooked, self-destructive way, merely one expression. In a sense, the soil in Philadelphia had long been tilled with the anger and resentment necessary for its germination. The nation's symbolic cradle of liberty, Philadelphia had failed to integrate the large influx of Black people who came up from the South during the Great Migration (largely in two waves, after 1914 and in the period between 1940 and the early 1970s), leading to large swaths of Black citizenry being cordoned off from the city's mainstream. As early as the late 1890s, when Philadelphia boasted perhaps the largest number of African Americans in the North, a young sociologist named W.E.B. Du Bois observed how Black Philadelphians were caught up in a vicious cycle in

which racism and the continual lack of economic opportunities conspired to keep them grounded as second-class
citizens. It was the ideal breeding ground for resentment
and lawlessness. He chronicled his findings in his now
landmark study, *The Philadelphia Negro*:

"Here is a large group of people—perhaps forty-five
thousand, a city within a city—who do not form an integral
part of the larger social group. This in itself is not altogether
unusual; there are other unassimilated groups: Jews, Italians,
even Americans; and yet in the case of the Negroes the segregation is more conspicuous, more patent to the eye, and so
intertwined with a long historic evolution, with peculiarly
pressing social problems of poverty, ignorance, and labor,
that the Negro problem far surpasses in scientific interest and
social gravity most of the other race or class questions."

Later on, Du Bois writes, "Without doubt there is not in
Philadelphia work of the kind that the mass of Negroes can
and may do, to employ at fair wages the laborers who at present
desire work. The result of this must, of course, be disastrous,
and give rise to many loafers, criminals, and casual laborers."

What is remarkable about this passage is that it could
describe the same inner-city neighborhood of Philadelphia
more than sixty years later, when the Black Mafia first began
applying their machinations against a backdrop of violent
race riots.

America in the 1960s was a tinderbox in perpetual dry
season. More than seven hundred fifty riots broke out between
1964 and 1971. In all, two hundred twenty-five people were
killed and nearly thirteen thousand injured, to go along with

more than fifteen thousand acts of arson. Detroit, Newark, Harlem, and Watts—sites of the most notorious outbreaks—became permanent fixtures in the public imagination. The year 1967 may have been the Summer of Love for the flower children, but for the angry, jobless, and downtrodden, many of whom were Black, it was the year of the Long, Hot Summer, and riots were their untethered response to decades of systemic repression, what Martin Luther King Jr., the most famous evangelist for nonviolent protest, described as "the voice of the unheard."

The common denominator for many of these riots was that they were triggered by varying instances of police brutality. In July 1967, in Newark, New Jersey, two police officers pummeled a Black cab driver after handing out a traffic ticket, sparking a six-day long bloodshed that left twenty-six people dead and millions of dollars in real estate damage. Later that month, in Detroit, a police raid of a sub-rosa bar led to the bloodiest riot of them all. A five-day circus of bloody confrontation eventually saw forty-three people killed and more than twenty-five hundred stores looted and burned down.

There were few recorded deaths in the Columbia Avenue Riot of North Philadelphia on the night of August 28, 1964, and for that reason, perhaps, it is seldom mentioned in the same breath as Detroit or Newark or Watts or, for that matter, any of the riots spawned in the aftermath of the assassination of King in 1968. But the tumult that took place in North Philadelphia in 1964 was traumatic in its own right. What it lacked in fatalities, it made up for in sheer intensity and structural devastation as one of the worst racial upheavals in the city's history. In all, three hundred thirty-nine people were injured, another three hundred were arrested, more than six hundred storefronts were looted and gutted, many of which would never return, and there were at least two recorded deaths. To this day, some of those streets bear the vestiges of that destruction. It began innocuously, when two patrolmen sought to break up a squabble between an inebriated married couple who were parked on the intersection of Columbia Avenue and 22nd Street, a busy commercial section noted for its rambunctious nightlife. But their involvement only escalated the domestic dispute, which, in turn, had the effect of attracting scores of other Black bystanders who were less than enthused with the optics of two white cops seemingly bearing down on a Black man and woman. Suddenly, bricks were flying through the air, smashing through the windows of the police cars. But the kicker occurred when, in a clear sign of how frayed race relations were at the time, a well-known Black militant falsely claimed that a white officer had beaten a pregnant Black woman. The rumor hurtled its way down every street block, compelling hundreds to converge on Columbia Avenue with vengeance on their minds. The riot took days to quell. In all, more than eighteen hundred policemen were dispatched. "They tore up the whole North Philly, Ridge Avenue, all of the stores," recalled Eddie, whose family lived in North Philadelphia at the time. "I mean it was crazy. We was just kids. Maybe nine, ten. To see a riot is crazy. To actually live to see a riot, I mean, a lot of people haven't seen a riot. We were little kids, but we had seen a riot and, yeah, it was ugly. No, it wasn't a good time to grow up."

The Columbia Avenue Riot foregrounded Philadelphia's increasingly divisive cop problem, which was simultaneously a race, class, and urban space problem. Depending on which side of the fence you were on, there was either not enough policing or too much of it. The deputy commissioner at the time was the star of the Philadelphia police department and future Philadelphia mayor Frank L. Rizzo, a girthy, swaggering, cock-of-the-walk Italian American who favored the liberal use of the nightstick and firmly believed that the police response to the Columbia Avenue Riot had been woefully inadequate; not enough heads had been bashed in, apparently. Quick to profanity, Rizzo would drop boorish lines such as, "I'm gonna be so tough as mayor, I'm gonna make Attila the Hun look like a faggot," and "Get their black asses," which was a directive he allegedly hurled at a few hundred subordinates during a peaceful demonstration led by Black junior high and high school students. Rizzo, no doubt, was a cop's cop—and even that may be an understatement. He personified law and order, as exemplified by a notorious photograph in which he is seen standing outside a banquet wearing a tuxedo with a nightstick protruding from his jacket. His peers called him "The General" or the "Cisco Kid," which seems appropriate because Rizzo, a high school dropout from South Philadelphia, was, in 1964, a glaring anachronism. He did not have the inclination nor the frame of mind to deal with the encroaching liberal order helmed by the civil rights movement other than to regard it as a threat that needed to be extinguished.

Law and order: Frank Rizzo pictured here in his infamous get-up.
*(Courtesy the Special Collections Research Center. Temple
University Libraries. Philadelphia, PA.)*

Nevertheless, Rizzo exerted a Messianic presence to a wide swath of the Philadelphia population, especially with the blue-collar, predominantly white working-class who found his tough-on-crime, law-and-order rhetoric refreshingly appealing. By commandeering this powerful coalition, as a Democrat, no less, Rizzo would win two terms as mayor of Philadelphia in the 1970s. If there is something to be said for Rizzo's macho-maniacal outlook, it is that he was devoid of pretense; he practiced what he preached. His political instincts helped lay down a blueprint for the populist stances of many a Republican president, from Ronald Reagan to Donald Trump. Indeed, Richard Nixon, whose own ascent was conterminous with Rizzo's, regarded the so-called toughest cop in America as the very face of his much cherished and ballyhooed silent majority.

Rizzo, suffice to say, was no friend of Philadelphia's Black community, which had been worn down by his hard-edged "supervision" over the years. For example, during his time as police chief, he was infamous for implementing—and defending—"turf dropping," a virulent practice whereby instead of arresting and jailing Black males suspected of crimes, they were rounded up and "dropped" into ostensibly hostile white enclaves. The Black community's trust in the police was further eroded in 1970 when Rizzo ordered a raid on multiple Black Panther compounds throughout the city that led not only to a significant arms confiscation but a humiliating and emasculating PR blow for the Black Panthers, whose members were strip-searched with their hands against a wall and undergarments down by their ankles, a moment that was preserved for posterity thanks to the presence of a few photographers working on a tip. The next day all the local newspapers, and eventually many national outlets, slapped an image of the naked Black militants on their front page. Although Rizzo was not present for the raid, he would be associated with that chapter for the rest of his political career. Because he treated the pursuit of civil liberties as an existential menace to the police, Rizzo's strong-arm approach to anything that had the whiff of rebellion meant there could never be any honest, conciliatory attempt to bridge the gap between Black people seeking improvement to their conditions and a white police force eager to preserve the status quo. As Timothy Lombardo argues in *Blue-Collar Conservatism: Frank Rizzo's Philadelphia and Populist Politics*, this dynamic created a mutually reinforcing situation in which "civil rights activists and African American leaders viewed the police as the sum of its whole, as an institution with a record of damaging effects on their communities. As white police officers in predominantly Black neighborhoods tended to see residents as potential criminals and viewed civil rights activism as a threat, residents came to fear and resent the police."

The schism between the Black public and the police was merely one chapter in a larger narrative about the crumbling integrationist ideals undergirding the civil rights movement. By the mid-1960s, a new Black nationalism was in full bloom, one that found its most eloquent spokesperson in the charismatic firebrand Malcolm X. As Harold Cruse, the rancorous social critic, put it bluntly at the time, "The Negro Integrationist runs afoul of reality in pursuit of an illusion." Distrust of government also loomed large, and it was clear for many Black Americans that President Lyndon B. Johnson's

"Great Society" program, which arose out of a fundamental, but seemingly outmoded, belief in a universal world order, had no place in their lives. Hence, there was considerable appetite for separatist ideologies and Black nationalist organizations like the Nation of Islam and the Black Panthers gained considerable traction promulgating the pitfalls of racial harmony. (In the 1970s, this ideology produced lethal permutations in fringe vanguard groups such as the Black Liberation Army and the Symbionese Liberation Army.)

Black nationalism saw one of its more perverse manifestations in the Black Mafia, whose emergence in the late 1960s in retrospect seems less like an aberration and more of an inevitable byproduct of the culture wars at that time. Though the concept posed a convenient rhetorical cover for their illicit operations, the group, at least as its high priests were concerned, clung to ideas of racial separatism with genuine fervor. There was a religious side to this that was deeply intertwined with the racial. Many of the foundational members of the Black Mafia, including Sam Christian and Ronald Harvey, were committed disciples of the Nation of Islam, the radical Islamic sect led by a near-illiterate son of a sharecropper-turned Baptist lay minister, Elijah Muhammad, who famously preached that white people were "blue-eyed devils." Though relatively small in numbers, the NOI punched above its weight thanks to their two most famous devotees: Malcolm X and Muhammad Ali, whose collective celebrity ensured the group a secure place in the zeitgeist of the '60s and '70s. Like the Black Mafia, the Nation of Islam inspired both respect and fear. Even as intimidating a fighter as Sonny Liston, no stranger to the mafia, was rumored to have been deathly afraid of the Black Muslims, which, according to a widely peddled conspiracy theory, was the reason why he went down from Ali's "phantom punch" during their 1965 rematch in Lewiston, Maine. Not everyone in the Black Mafia was Muslim. In fact, many of the low-to-mid-ranking foot soldiers and affiliates had little desire to pick up the Qur'an, which was fine. Although they would be barred from a leadership position within the hierarchy and would have to fork over a higher cut of their drug profits, they would find themselves more respected—and feared—than ever by operating under the Black Mafia banner, an incalculable benefit for an agnostic hustler with ambition such as Ricardo McKendrick.

The union between criminals in Philadelphia's Black Muslim community and the Black Mafia was a match made in underworld heaven, occurring sometime in 1969, on the heels of a heated escalation between the two sides to corner Philadelphia's burgeoning heroin market. As fierce as the Black Mafia were, they were heavily outnumbered by the no less ornery Black Muslims. The Black Mafia knew, moreover, that engaging in a bloody turf war with the Muslims would not only decimate their own ranks but also attract the attention of authorities. At the time, a government crackdown on street gangs led to a peace treaty signed by almost all the warring factions. The question of how they were to carry out felonious endeavors under the radar became a preeminent concern for the Black Mafia. The Nation of Islam provided the ideal disguise. According to Griffin, the sprawling network of Muslim Mosques—not only in Philadelphia where there were five, but across the nation in urban capitals—operated as an underground network, giving the Black Mafia a safe space to store their munitions and, when the heat was on, to shelter members who were on the run. Because high-ranking Black Mafia members Christian and Harvey were already committed, Mosque-attending Muslims—Harvey, in particular, was once described as a "religious fanatic"—the basis for a profitable partnership was already in a sense outlined in the sand. In fact, both Christian and Harvey were conscripted into the Fruit of Islam (FOI), the much-feared militant arm of the Nation of Islam. The Black Mafia now had the resources and the clout to keep all the small-time straggling street gangs in line, expand their territory, and ramp up their extortion racket.

The headquarters for the Philadelphia Muslim community was the mosque known as Temple No. 12. While it was established by Malcolm X in the early 1960s, Temple 12 would be most strongly associated with the two-faced NOI minister Jeremiah Shabazz (né Jeremiah Pugh), a pivotal figure of the Philadelphia crime scene who was essentially responsible for rubberstamping many of the high crimes of the Black Mafia. For every swaddling disquisition Shabazz gave on moral uprightness, somewhere on a Philadelphia street corner, another "brick" was sold with his imprimatur. Though Shabazz was the one who helped shepherd a young Cassius Clay into the fold of the NOI, he was also the one who, in what should have been a verboten act against the articles of his faith, cut deals with the KKK back when he still helmed an NOI mosque in Atlanta. Apparently, as long as the green tinge of a dollar bill was involved, Shabazz was more than willing to be color-blind. Shabazz's lust for filling his coffers had crippling consequences for the NOI at large. In

Occasionally referred to as the "Godfather of the Black Mafia,"
Jeremiah Shabazz was a powerful figure in the underworld who
had the ear of both Muhammad Ali and NOI leader Elijah
Muhammad, whose likeness here hangs over Shabazz's head.
*(Courtesy the Special Collections Research Center. Temple
University Libraries. Philadelphia, PA.)*

The Messenger: The Rise and Fall of Elijah Muhammad, author
and NOI expert Karl Evanzz argued that Temple 12 was the
main gateway for the NOI's entry into hard crime, and that the
goings-on at the chapter imperiled the parent organization at
a time when its most powerful devotee (Malcolm X) had been
slayed and whose head (Elijah Muhammad) was in physical
decline. "The most serious threat to the NOI wasn't misfeasance
by the FBI or the growth of black nationalist organizations, but
came from the Philadelphia mosque headed by the Messenger's
lifelong friend Jeremiah X Pugh," Evanzz wrote.

In any case, with the Black Muslims backing their pursuits,
the Black Mafia could now skate through the Philadelphia
underworld with virtually unchecked powers, amping up
their extortion to include above-board businesses, not just
gambling dens. They were untouchable, a fact that goes a
long way in explaining the brazenness of some of their most
heinous pursuits. According to Griffin, the situation was such
in Philadelphia that one could "park a car in a rough neighborhood with the windows down and the keys in the ignition
and only needed to place a copy of *Muhammad Speaks* on the
dashboard to ensure no one would touch it." The alliance also
immunized the Black Mafia from outside scrutiny. Given the
group's quasi-religious status, police had to think twice about
pursuing a case involving the Black Mafia, lest a civil rights
backlash drown them in bad PR. Griffin again: "The merger
afforded the Black Mafia the opportunity to create a more
powerful political problem for authorities, for it was no longer
simply race but religion too that could be exploited as needed. In
addition to the public relations challenges the alliance presented

to authorities, the syndicate now routinely attempted to exploit the legal system [...] By the time Sam Christian and the rest of the Black Mafia were formally incorporated into the Mosque, the foundation for underworld success was laid. Temple 12 was thriving under Jeremiah Shabazz and exploiting the militant strand of the Black pride movement that rationalized many dubious acts under a ends-justifies-the-means philosophy, or as Malcolm X once famously put it, 'By any means necessary.'"

The Black Mafia took those words to heart. Indeed, they were essentially codified in a one-and-a-half-page pledge that all prospective Black Mafia members were required to sign prior to joining the group. Their Manichean and martyristic worldview is distilled in the following passage: "I realize that this racist capitalistic society is unjust and unfair to my peers and that it may be that as I carry out the functions of the family, protecting and standing for the principles that we believe and know are right, that I may fall mortally wounded and give my life in service. If this should be my lot I am assured that I will not be buried as a criminal or vagabond, but that I shall receive all the honors due a freedom fighter and fallen hero."

Two spine-chilling deeds put these words into action.

On a languorous Monday afternoon on January 4, 1971, when most people were still coming down from their New Year high, eight members of the Black Mafia decided to pillage a furniture store in North Philadelphia. But the loot, which did not amount to much, was an ancillary concern for the gang. The owner of the store, Harry Dubrow, had allegedly refused to fork over the "street tax," and the Black Mafia was looking to address the insolence the only way they knew how. In the end, at least three people were shot, one of whom was killed, another burned, while more than twenty employees were bound up with tape and electrical cords, pistol-whipped, and had gasoline doused all over them. Fortunately, the store did not go down in a blaze, thanks to several employees who were able to worm their way out of the restraints and contain the situation. Senseless, abrupt, and altogether ghastly, the Dubrow's Furniture Store Robbery was the quintessential Black Mafia crime, serving no other utility than to bolster their street cred and enlarge their web of fear. "I have seen many crimes in my long police career, but this is the most vicious one I have ever come across," said Police Commissioner Frank Rizzo.

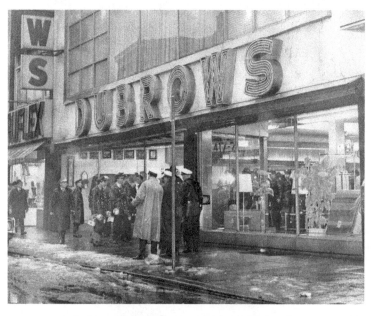

Police processing the carnage inside Dubrow's.
(Courtesy the Special Collections Research Center. Temple University Libraries. Philadelphia, PA.)

The Black Mafia was not finished, however. In 1976, while the lead architect of the robbery and Black Mafia co-founder Robert "Nudie" Mims was in the midst of appealing charges, two employees from Dubrow's, Lou and Yetta Gruby, were slain in their own home in a sleepy suburb in Northeast Philadelphia. Nothing of any value had been taken from their home.

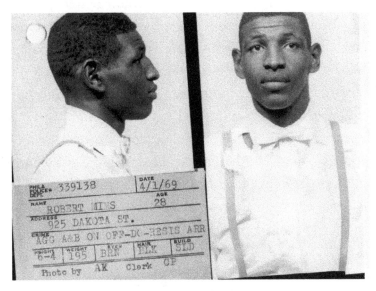

Mugshot of Nudie Mims.
(Courtesy Sean Patrick Griffin)

Lou was one of the few witnesses who fingered Mims and had not held back during his testimony. Although the police would never solve the case, experts had little doubt that it was a Black Mafia hit job.

Yet as heartless and barbaric as the Dubrow's Robbery was, it paled in comparison to the infamous Hanafi Muslim

Massacre that took place in Washington D.C. two years later. The Hanafi Muslims were followers of Hamaas Abdul Khaalis, a former NOI devotee who decided to strike out on his own and form his own Sunni sect after feuding with Elijah Muhammad. Khaalis despised Muhammad and made no secret about it. In 1972 he disseminated an open letter in which he not only castigated Muhammad but hurled shots at NOI founder Wallace D. Fard, claiming, among other heresies, that Fard was really a white man "who served seven-and-a-half years in jail for stealing a carload of junk in Gary, Indiana, and for raping a seventeen-year-old so-called white girl." Word of the blasphemy traveled quickly. Considering that the NOI was not inclined to turn the other cheek, as the assassination of Malcolm X demonstrated, this was an audacious move on Khaalis' part. Eventually, a fatwa of sorts was issued, calling for his head. As for the matter of carrying out the reprisal, that responsibility would fall on the hefty shoulders of Philadelphia's version of Murder, Inc., the peerless Temple No. 12.

* * *

ON JANUARY 18, 1973, a troop of Black Mafia cat's-paws, including the psychopathic Ronald Harvey, drove down to the D.C. headquarters of the Hanafi sect, a building that was donated by the Hanafi's most visible convert, NBA center Kareem Abdul-Jabbar. Harvey suggested that they also ransack the place, thinking there would be untold riches. The mission, in fact, would turn out to be a flop for the Black Mafia: they failed to kill Khaalis and ended up plundering a measly $1,000 in cash. But they left behind a scene of carnage that recalled the still-fresh Manson Family murders. By some quirk of fate, Khaalis was out shopping that day. When he returned home, he found his wife, Bibi, and son, Daud, shot dead. His daughter, Amina, would survive, despite being shot six times, twice in the head. In all, seven people were killed. As far as mass murders go, from a purely quantitative standpoint, this was perhaps a modest toll. But what distinguished this bloodbath from others was the disturbing revelation that five of the victims were children, including a nine-day-old who was submerged in a bathtub. When the authorities arrived, one police officer initially mistook the nine-day-old for a "doll." Infanticide, to be sure, was never part of the original plan, but Harvey had apparently insisted on it. When his cohorts, who evidently did not share his sadistic impulses, asked him why it was necessary to kill off the babies since they would be too young to act as credible witnesses, Harvey allegedly responded, "Because the seed of the hypocrite is in them."

The Black Mafia was no one-trick pony. At the same time they were letting their bloodlust reign unchecked over their faculties, the group was also busy finessing an elaborate PR ruse in the world of grant applications. Under the shell corporation Black Brothers Inc., the Black Mafia sought to present themselves as a social service collective aimed at alleviating the various ills of the Philadelphia ghetto, and especially that of gang violence. The top officers of Black Brothers Inc., however, were exclusively Black Mafia members, all with troubling rap sheets. They rented out office space, adorned their windows with posters warning against drug dealers and gangsters, and had a personnel hierarchy similar to any other non-profit organization. As Griffin has noted, the Black Brothers probably contributed to the reduction of gang violence, but mainly because most of the small-time gangs in Philadelphia had already been subsumed under Black Mafia leadership.

The ploy was successful, at least initially. The Black Brothers Inc. presented the kind of human interest and social justice angle that would tickle the liberal fancy. In fact, the *Philadelphia Daily News* ran a largely positive story about the Black Brothers Inc. after their grand opening in the fall of 1973, although their subsequent reporting would be far more skeptical. That the Black Mafia was able to pull the hood over the mainstream press speaks to the prevailing attitudes toward social remedy programs that were in vogue at the time.

Gang violence in Philadelphia reached appalling levels in the mid-1960s, to the point that many progressive activists and politicians felt the need to explore more radical avenues. Philadelphia District Attorney Arlen Specter offered one such social experiment. Called Safe Streets, the program sought to provide one-stop-shop "safe spaces" for at-risk youth and juveniles. Specter went directly to President Nixon to present his plan and successfully received funding to open up two branches. The North Philadelphia branch of Safe Streets was initially run by supposedly reformed gang member Clarence Fowler, who would eventually adopt the Muslim name Shamsud-din Ali. Fowler, to little surprise, was a Black Mafia member and one of the feared captains of Temple

12's paramilitary arm, the Fruit of Islam. His stint would be cut short when he was indicted on a murder charge in the early 1970s that would later be overturned. (Decades later, Fowler would become the step-father of Mike Tyson.) There were other offshoots to the Black Brothers as well, like the mundane-sounding Council for Youth and Community Development. The political climate, in short, paved the way for the Black Mafia to front these non-profits with career criminals with virtually no blowback, since that was precisely the goal behind these social uplift measures.

Not surprisingly, most people within the community were far more skeptical of the Black Brothers Inc. They knew that the people decrying gang violence were the same ones extorting and terrorizing small businesses. Instead of allaying the concern of the residents, the social outreach initiatives commandeered by the Black Mafia had the dual effect of ramping up the locals' suspicions of both state and street authorities. "The problem with government officials lending support to the syndicate's anti-gang front group was that it confused and intimidated people," Griffin said. "Many assumed the syndicate had paid off the authorities, since it was difficult for citizens to grasp violent cons being openly embraced by these officials. It mattered little to the victimized Black community that the Black Mafia's political connections in the criminal justice system were part of a legitimate, though failing, progressive reform effort. Witnesses and victims in Black Mafia's cases, already fearful of testifying against this vicious cast of characters, were further dissuaded from cooperating with police, and the result was the strengthening of the syndicate's extortion enterprise."

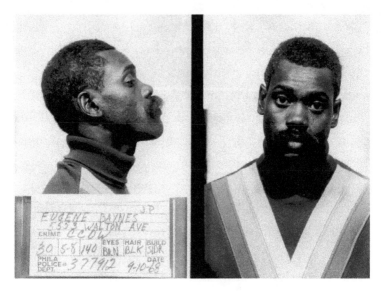

Mugshot of "Bo" Baynes.
(Courtesy Sean Patrick Griffin)

Such accounts attesting to the Black Mafia's bald-faced practice of chicanery and brute force against its own people should remove any doubt that the group was interested in anything other than its own personal gain. Some partisan observers, however, had apparently deluded themselves into thinking that their seemingly unslakable thirst for moolah and menace was justifiable so long as they could argue that those impulses were in the service of political and racial empowerment. At least one has suggested, amazingly, that violence played a negligible role within the group. In 2007, the documentary television series *American Gangster*, produced by the Black Entertainment Television Network, ran an episode devoted to the Black Mafia featuring founding member Eugene Carl "Bo" Baynes, a Philadelphia native who was once an enforcer for Philly Groove Records, the famed soul music label most famous for introducing the Delfonics. Baynes, who was sentenced to nearly thirty years in prison in 1974, defended the group on the grounds of Black autarky. "We kept the Black dollar in the community to take care of ourselves, to build schools," Baynes said. "We did that. We built schools for our babies, had businesses to take care of our families. We was together. We had a common interest. We wanted to do better and be better and take charge of our life. That was the message ... I found brotherhood. I never was a criminal. I wasn't looking for that. That wasn't what I went there to look for. If [crime] was present I couldn't say."

* * *

IN THE YEARS that he was making his mark on the Philadelphia boxing scene, Tyrone Everett portrayed himself as a man from the streets but not of it. He had fallen into some grisly situations here and there, but he claimed he had avoided the fray for the most part.

Still, Everett was wedded to the underworld in at least one concrete sense. He had been a former member of the notorious 20th and Carpenter gang and would maintain something of a friendly relationship with his old posse throughout his boxing career. As mentioned earlier, the 20th and Carpenters were among Everett's most dedicated fans and attended all of his fights in Philadelphia. When news broke that Everett had been shot, it was reported that the Carpenters were on the hunt for the alleged perpetrator.

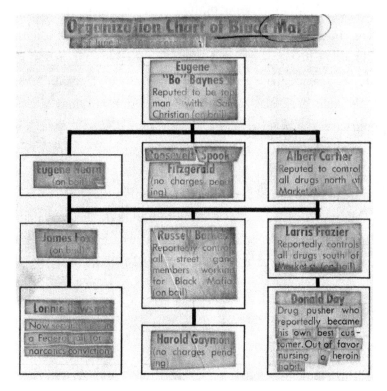

Early law enforcement attempt to chart out Black Mafia hierarchy.
*(Courtesy the Special Collections Research Center. Temple
University Libraries. Philadelphia, PA.)*

One of the most influential members of 20th and Carpenter
was named James Fox. According to Griffin, Fox was a 1966
graduate of Edward Bok Vocational High School, the same
alma mater as Everett, who would graduate a few years after Fox.
Although he participated in one of the first anti-gang services
to pop up in Philadelphia, Fox began to act differently once
the social service became a front for the extortion operations
of Temple 12, i.e., the Black Mafia. "The once subdued All-
American boy began wearing flashy suits and slouch hats, and

drove in expensive Cadillacs and Lincoln Town Cars," Griffin noted. "He became a frequent spectator at boxing matches, often in the company of several women." Russell Barnes, the feared Black Mafia contract killer, was Fox's best friend.

This fact becomes more alluring when one considers that the 20th and Carpenters had a fractious relationship with the Black Mafia. Unlike the other small-time outfits in South Philadelphia, the combative 20th and Carpenters did not pay fealty to the Black Mafia. At the height of their feud, the journalist Tyree Johnson recalled witnessing the extraordinary image of teenage boys on their bicycles taking aim at snazzily dressed men sitting in their Cadillacs. It was something out of Peter Pan and the lost boys. That was the 20th and Carpenters, in parvo.

• • •

BY THE LATE 1970s, right around the time when Everett was wading into the final chapter of his life, the Black Mafia was starting to lose its hold on the drug trade in Philadelphia. Internecine warfare and lengthy prison sentences to its top leaders had decimated their ranks. For the first time, law enforcement had reams of evidence to back up their claims in court without necessarily requiring eyewitness testimony. By the mid-1980s, the Black Mafia, both as an organized criminal force and object of terror, was effectively finished. Some of the most prominent leaders of the Black Mafia were permanently defanged through prosecution and would find themselves hurtling toward a life of obscurity; Sam Christian, for example, would spend most of his later life behind bars before quietly passing away in a nursing home in 2016. Some of his other colleagues were savvier in finding ways to continue plying their trade in the underworld, the most successful of whom was Shamsud-din Ali, formerly known as Clarence Fowler.

A respected imam with unusually deep political connections, Ali (as Fowler) beat a murder charge from 1970 after his conviction was overturned by the Pennsylvania Supreme Court (once again, presumably due to a lack of credible witnesses). Subsequently, he changed his name and took over for Jeremiah Shabazz as the head honcho of Temple 12. In 2004, Ali sprang up in national headlines when a federal probe slapped him, his wife, and five accomplices with a 48-count racketeering indictment. Ali eventually served seven years in federal prison before being released in 2013. In true Black Mafia spirit, Ali had no shortage of friends in both high and low places and moved between both circles with relative ease. He hobnobbed with prominent municipal politicos and bankers on the one hand and consorted with drug wholesalers on the other. Ali was already on the FBI radar in the late 1990s for his alleged kickbacks to senior officials connected with Philadelphia Mayor John Street. In a move that perfectly illustrates Ali's unique two-way profile, Street tapped Ali to serve on a board devoted to improving prison life for Philadelphia inmates back in 1999. There could not have been a more apt hire since it was no secret that Ali had enormous pull in the Black Muslim world. Jimmy Binns, Ali's lawyer, once described to the *Inquirer* what it was like when his client walked into Graterford Prison, one of the unofficial seats of Black Muslim power: "It was as though President George

Bush was going to visit the troops in Baghdad." Ali also has considerable ties to the boxing world, even beyond his relationship with Muhammad Ali. (There is a photograph that cropped up not too long ago on the Internet that shows Shamsud-din and Black Mafia member Nudie Mims posing with the heavyweight boxer sometime in the late 1970s.) His daughter, Lakiha "Kiki" Spicer Ali, happens to be the (third) wife of Mike Tyson. Tyson's promoter, Don King, no stranger to the nefarious side of life, once reportedly warned Tyson to "stay away from her. Don't go talking to that girl. Leave these people alone. These are not the people to mess with."

Ricardo McKendrick is the other high-level Black Mafia member to erupt in the headlines during the 2000s, albeit for different reasons. Unlike Shamsud-din Ali and his shrewd networking abilities, McKendrick's shtick was good old-fashioned drug hustling. Like Ali, his business was also a family business. In 2008, when he was fifty-six, McKendrick and his thirty-six-year-old son, Ricardo "Li'l Rick" McKendrick Jr., were arrested after the FBI seized from the duo more than six hundred pounds of cocaine, an amount that the prosecutor would later describe as the biggest drug bust in recent Philadelphia history. "If this were an HBO series, like *The Wire*, nobody would believe one South Philadelphia family could have so many convicted drug traffickers, killers, and murder suspects in it," reporter Kitty Caparella wrote in her lede for the *Daily News*. "And that's not all: There's also a North Philadelphia preacher and a federal civil-rights trial lawyer in the family. Such is the life of one-time Black Mafia gangster, Ricardo McKendrick Sr., 56, who at 5-foot-5, heads the clan." The bounty, estimated to be worth

$28 million, was discovered in McKendrick's Federal Street
rowhouse—mere blocks away from the home where Tyrone
Everett was killed thirty years prior.

**Ricardo McKendrick, left, middle row, posing with
fellow Black Mafia members at a black-tie event.**
*(Courtesy the Special Collections Research Center. Temple
University Libraries. Philadelphia, PA.)*

"Rick was living in Federal Street basically as a single
man," John King recalled. "That was the running joke. He
had young women running in and out of [his home] because
Jr. had fixed up the place pretty nice. Li'l Rick put about
$50,000 worth of renovation in the house. It's kind of like
if you've ever seen the movie *Coming to America*. It was a
beautiful place when I saw the place around '90 to '92. There
was a spiral staircase—and we're talking about a South Philly

rowhouse. This is where Rick Sr. was living. So he had a little palace in the ghetto, essentially." Because the court records were sealed, it is not clear if McKendrick Jr. cooperated with federal authorities and thus, helped lessen his father's sentencing, but the understanding among most educated observers is that Jr. most likely had struck some sort of plea bargain with federal officials. Jr. was sentenced to nine years, while his father, who was staring down a mandatory life sentence, received ten. Noted Philadelphia crime author and journalist George Anastasia wrote in the *Inquirer*, "If either McKendrick has flipped, investigators will have access to inside information about the movers and shakers who populate Philadelphia's highly secretive and violent drug underworld."

John King offered his two cents on the proceedings. "I don't know how much time [Li'l Rick] got, but I know he made the big sacrifice because his father would have gotten life without parole if he had not made a deal," King explained. "I knew he got a reduced sentence. Li'l Rick basically gave up his suppliers because there was a deal on the table, from what I heard, and that if he did that they could plea out his father. Because his father wasn't a minor player, but he also wasn't the main target. Li'l Rick was. They knew who his father was. They had him on the record for years. They knew they could leverage him. So what I'm thinking is wherever Rick may be in terms of his incarceration—and he may still be incarcerated—his mom may have moved to be closer."

Lil Rick's mom, of course, is Carolyn McKendrick.

"Carolyn has cleaned her reputation. She's a mother. She's a businessperson. I guess people don't sort of think about her that way when they think about her," King continued. "Where Carolyn is today depends on what happened to the McKendricks after the drug bust [in 2008], because I'm assuming her son turned in evidence to the feds and that may have meant that he had to go into the [Witness Protection] program, so she could be with him."

As always, there was one more rumor, at least according to Eddie Everett.

The story goes that shortly before his death, Everett met up with Ricardo to try and hash out their difficulties, presumably about Carolyn McKendrick. What's more, Eddie remembers his brother behaving strangely in the days before that fatal May morning. "I picked up something from [Tyrone] when he came to me one time, and I think he was afraid," Eddie said. "Something was different. I think he was scared for his life. But he kept it to himself. He didn't tell us. He didn't want us to get involved. He wanted to handle the situation himself.

"The rumors were that [Ricardo] McKendrick and him had talked. Before he died he feared for his life. He might have been threatened. He was [acting] different ... but we knew he was in an environment with a lot of drugs and his relationship with Carol was surrounded by drugs and violence; all the other girls were more clean-cut and nice. With Carol he had a more dangerous relationship, so I just know that at some point I got a sense that there was something wrong, and I think it was because he was in that environment. He put himself into a dangerous situation."

Although Eddie declined to elaborate on what Ricardo and Everett talked about, he had recounted the substance of that alleged conversation years before to Bob Ingram in a 1989 issue of *PhillySport* magazine. "[Ricardo] and Tyrone sat and talked, and Tyrone said, 'I'm not going to mess around with your wife anymore,'" Eddie told Ingram, "but Rickie had heard all these rumors in jail, and he was embarrassed and his pride was hurt because he was this big drug dealer."

It was a classic love triangle, with one twist: The beloved appeared to piss off not just the husband but the lover, as well.

"Carol was more interested in Tyrone [than Tyrone was in her], which hurt her pride," Eddie continued. "And you couldn't control Tyrone; he did what he wanted to and that might have motivated her and whoever else was involved to see him dead. Her pride was hurt, and she would go to any extent to see him hurt. And if things went wrong, Carolyn would fly into rages. One time she came over and tore up the apartment Tyrone and me lived in. She couldn't control him, and she might have got to the point where she wanted to see him dead. He was making her look bad in front of all her drug people. And Rickie had put a contract out on Tyrone, I heard, and the hit man gave him the money back and said, 'I can't kill this guy.'"

Whatever the veracity of such scuttlebutt, it gives one a glimpse of how Everett was perceived in his community. According to King, Everett's megawatt appeal likely meant that for someone in the standing of Carolyn McKendrick,

leaving her husband was not a particularly trepidatious prop-
osition. "What I know about all of them, how do I say this
nicely … a lot of women who dated hustlers in Philadelphia
[back in the 1970s] there was some level of opportunism,"
King explained. "He was on the rise, Mr. Everett. Very
notable guy, nice-looking guy, so women liked him."

Yet the optics never looked good for the brazen fighter.
Eddie only wishes he could have caught on to his brother's
disturbances sooner. "If you did research on Ricardo
McKendrick, and you're dealing with a woman that's married
to him, dealing with somebody who's in this syndicate with
drugs, then that's not good," Eddie says today. "But we didn't
know much about the Swints and the McKendricks at the
time. But if you put two and two together, if you brought
up the McKendricks and the Swints, then you had your
answer. Had I known what I knew afterward, I would have
had a talk with [Tyrone], like, 'Are you crazy? What are you
doing?' Tyrone put himself into a very dangerous situation
[getting involved with Carolyn]. That's like messing with
Scarface's girl or the Godfather's wife. You're between two
mafia families. They were vicious families."

It is no doubt ironic that for someone who was so pre-
ternaturally aware of the dangers inside the ring, as if a
radar had been outfitted into his brain alerting him to every
punch that crossed his breathing space, Everett appeared
to be something of a klutz outside of it, be it in the streets
or, fatally, in the bedroom. Recall that two of Carolyn
McKendrick's best friends and Everett's brother Mike all
testified that they had witnessed the boxer strike McKendrick

on multiple occasions. This fact raises several questions: Was Everett aware of McKendrick's cutthroat affiliations? If so, did Everett proceed to beat her despite this knowledge? Did he feel so invincible that he could mess around with the wife of a Corleone, no matter their supposed estrangement?

"The Swints weren't Sam Christian—they didn't have that kind of reputation—but they were respected," King said. "They were feared, more importantly. So people really didn't fuck with them, to be quite honest. So, again, when I think back about this, it boggles the mind [that Tyrone would have beaten Carolyn]. Clearly, Tyrone did not have a good sense of who Carolyn's people were and the fact that her husband had been in one of the most gruesome murders in Philadelphia mafia history. That he's alleged to have beaten her is interesting. Both of them are small guys. It's really kind of interesting if the story is true that Tyrone would put his hands on Carolyn."

Sam Christian may have been in a league of his own when it came to committing blunt acts of atrocity, but Ricardo himself was long rumored to have been involved in an especially harrowing homicide in 1973, the "gruesome murder" to which King referred. The victim in this case was fellow Black Mafia member George 'Bo' Abney, whose body was found on a highway but whose head was discovered swaddled in a pillowcase on the steps of a downtown Philadelphia bar. According to police reports obtained by Griffin, Abney likely met his gruesome fate because he had been skimming from the drug proceeds that he was required to fork over to the Black Mafia—the obligatory street tax.

But Abney, who was at that point becoming a major player within the syndicate, was a hard-headed man and had little intention of giving his betters their full cut. Like clockwork, the Black Mafia put Abney's life on the market, with some sources suggesting that Ricardo, along with Russell Barnes, volunteered to carry out the contract. The pair supposedly had tried to drown Abney in a bathtub (sound familiar?), but after failing to do so—Abney was a physically powerful man—they moved to decapitate him instead. No suspects were ever apprehended, and the case remains unsolved.

"It's inconceivable to me—unless Tyrone had an ego where he thought he was invincible—that he would [have beaten Carolyn]," King continued. "Because it sounds like from everything that I read that there was a lot of mistreatment of Carolyn, which justifies her actions, not necessarily murdering him, but certainly justifies her wanting to hurt him—beyond the homosexuality. The fact that it was alleged that [Tyrone] beat her ... This guy must have been suicidal. The fact that she was a Swint alone should have made him think twice about that."

Whether she was abused or not, Eddie continues to maintain that Carolyn McKendrick was not the perpetrator, that she had simply been chosen as the fall guy for the Black Mafia (although Eddie never once used that appellation throughout multiple conversations). Indeed, for the past forty years, Eddie has not changed his tune about what he thinks happened that May morning in 1977. He never attended a single day of the trial because he suspected the truth, whatever that was, would never come to light within the confines of a courtroom. "I knew better," he said. "I didn't go because it just didn't add up." The Black Mafia notwithstanding, Eddie could never accept the idea that McKendrick was capable of lifting a pistol to his Everett's head, no matter the circumstances, in part because of how much he believed she loved his brother.

"She was crazy about him, and she wanted to be with him," Eddie recalled. "I saw them together in cars and she loved being around him, being in his presence and the attention she got when she was with him. She was totally in love with him. She's a beautiful woman and Tyrone was sought after by a lot of women, and some were in love with Ty. I think she probably didn't want to be with her husband anymore."

Despite his disappointment with the judicial process, Eddie never seriously entertained the idea of waging any kind of personal retaliation against the Black Mafia since he was already well aware of the fate that awaited those who went up against them. "At that time, me and Mike were upset," Eddie explained. "The family was upset. But when you're dealing with the McKendricks you're dealing with someone that has money, power, and hitmen ... It could have been either revenge or more lives would have been lost if my side of the family or me and Michael wanted to take revenge. They was so big in the mafia that any potential witnesses would be killed. Any retaliation would have been more bloodshed and my mom losing another son. I don't think that's what Tyrone wanted. Ricky McKendrick still has power today."

Tyrone Everett was the brightest fixture in South Philadelphia for a moment—Halley's comet, as Tom Cushman once put it. But his light has long fizzled out. A dark haze continues to obscure the final days of his life.

"I never believed she did it. So that's where the story ends with me," Eddie said.

He paused, then continued.

"Only Carol knew what happened that day."

EPILOGUE

SHE WAS REDUCED to something of a cipher in the years that followed. Occasionally, her name would spring up in scholarly feminist research on domestic violence. Carolyn McKendrick became, in short, a statistic.

But the last time McKendrick resurfaced in the public realm, on her own accord, was in 1990, in the form of a letter that she sent to the *Inquirer* that was subsequently published in the March 9 edition. Tucked away between an editorial on public housing and prison crowding, the letter, all of 139 words, was in response to the newfangled item pricing scanners that supermarkets across Philadelphia were starting to adopt at the time. It reads as follows:

As a person who does the shopping for my household, I am definitely in favor of City Council's ordinance for prices on individual items in supermarkets.

Individual item price tagging will make my shopping much easier. It will eliminate the probability of my overspending my budget by allowing me to do comparative shopping. It will cut back on the amount of time I normally waste scouting to find the item price.

I shudder to think what senior citizens are going through, shopping under these conditions. No wonder that they have a program set up where younger adults shop for them. I am 36 years of age, in healthy condition and this practice wears me down.

Even if it does boost the public's collective food bill by a few dollars, it would be well worth it in the long run.

Carolyn Swint
Philadelphia

"As a person who does the shopping for my household … It will eliminate the probability of my overspending my budget … I shudder to think what senior citizens are going through … I am 36 years of age, in healthy condition and this practice wears me down …" The measured cadence of the prose, the favoring of streamlined methods, the preternatural concern for the elderly, and the sense of civic responsibility all strike up an image of a person who is deeply ensconced within the boundaries of respectable society and committed to observing the rites of domesticity. Her days are probably humdrum, quotidian. At this stage in her life, she is supposedly running a hair salon in—where else?—South Philadelphia. It is virtually impossible to detect from these words that the author spent half a decade cooped up in a gray cell of a correctional facility for the cold-blooded murder of her beloved boyfriend.

• • •

Summer, 2020.

"You keep calling me," the voice huffed on the other line. "If you don't stop, I will call the police. I don't want anything to do with that family."

After months of repeated attempts to reach her had gone unheeded, Dawn Edge finally picked up the phone one summer day. The conversation was over as soon as it began, and her sternly-worded warning, pointed yet so completely cryptic at the same time, seemed like an appropriate parting shot to what at that point had been a largely futile undertaking to locate Carolyn McKendrick.

A lawyer for the Equal Employment Opportunity Commission in Philadelphia, a federal agency, Edge popped up in the local papers back in 2008, after the infamous drug bust that ensnared her husband, Ricardo McKendrick Jr., and her notorious father-in-law. Nearly twelve years later, she still had the same occupation and the same publicly available office phone number. Clearly, Edge was no longer with Li'l Rick, and, what's more, she seemed to have washed her hands of her extended family, the McKendrick clan. Noli me tangere. Once again, the winding, circuitous trail to reach Carolyn McKendrick led to yet another cul-de-sac.

By that point, hardly anyone who knew McKendrick from the 1970s was in contact with her, and the ones that supposedly were wanted first to see a Cash App transfer pop up in their bank accounts. As one gentleman from South Philadelphia who claimed to have grown up with the Everetts and the Swints put it, "You gotta pay up, brother. You know how it is," in response to an invitation to speak on the record.

Only Carolyn McKendrick had the skeleton key that could unlock the strongbox of secrets. Without her side of events, the story would always remain jarringly incomplete.

But, in a propitious turn of events, after all recognizable options had thoroughly been exhausted, one more last-ditch effort yielded some fruit. A message was left with a deacon of a church attended by one of McKendrick's sisters. A few days later, a phone call arrived from an unknown number using a Philadelphia area code. It was Carolyn McKendrick.

The conversation took place on a weekday afternoon. It lasted for about half an hour. It was cordial, if a tad surreal. The voice on the other line was calm, articulate, and evenly modulated. McKendrick spoke slowly, as though she were dipping into cold waters, and chose her words with precision. One thought of those perfectly tailored outfits she was often photographed wearing at the trial and that carefully crafted letter about the efficacy of supermarket item scanners; she seemed to speak just as she wrote.

After the customary small talk, McKendrick noted that this was the first time anyone had ever reached out to her to get her side of the story. She appreciated the gesture. But the subject in question, never more tantalizing than in that moment, would have to wait for another day. She needed some time to think it over, to find out for herself if she was ready to open up about what really happened forty-five years ago on Federal Street. She wanted to check in with her children first and gauge their response. Whatever she decided on, she said she would get back in touch to relay her answer. There was no reason to doubt her.

A week passed and then another, then another, then another … but the call never came. Three messages were left on her phone; all went unanswered. The trail went cold again.

• • •

HISTORIC EDEN CEMETERY is a sprawling 53-acre property situated in the Philadelphian suburb of Collingdale. Founded in 1902, it is the resting place for more than 93,000 people, mainly African Americans. Eden, in fact, is widely regarded as the largest cemetery devoted to African Americans in the United States, and not a few of its residents have left their mark in history. Abolitionist icon William Still, one of the prime movers of the Underground Railroad, is buried there. So is John B. Taylor Jr., the first Black American track-and-field athlete to win an Olympic gold medal, as well as Octavius Catto, the prominent 19th-century civil rights activist who was tragically gunned down in the streets by a deranged Irish partisan, and Marian Anderson, the celebrated opera singer whose gifted voice reached Super Bowl-sized audiences on the radio in the latter first-half of the 20th century.

The body of Tyrone Everett is also interred there, but for the longest time, he was practically a non-entity. For some thirty-odd years, his gravesite remained unmarked, bereft of a headstone to distinguish it from the tawny-green patch of grass of its environs. The only way you could find his plot would have been to inquire with the local office, obtain the coordinates, and have a groundsman lead you to the spot. Everett may have been nothing less than the unofficial pope of South Philadelphia in the mid-1970s, but there was nothing in his final resting place to suggest the staggering nature of that reputation.

John DiSanto, a longtime Philadelphia fight fan, spotted this incongruence one day and decided that it had to change. It was 2005, and he had just started a website called PhillyBoxingHistory.com, a one-stop digital repository for all things related to Philadelphia boxing and its rich fistic past. Although he had never seen Everett fight live growing up, DiSanto reached pugilistic maturity at the tail end of the Golden Age, and thus he was able to witness the rise of many of Everett's peers in Matthew Saad Muhammad, Jeff Chandler, Tyrone Crawley, and scores of other popular Eastern seaboard fighters that defined the Philadelphia boxing scene of the 1980s. DiSanto had been in the library reading up on old microfilm news clippings, when he came across an article describing the swarming assembly at Everett's funeral. When DiSanto reached out to the Everett family to get their blessing for a proper headstone, he was met with unanimous approval.

Doris Everett just had a couple of requests. She wanted a photo of her son to be adorned on the headstone and also have space on the same headstone reserved for herself; she wanted to be buried next to her son. In the end, DiSanto put up $1,500 of his own money for the stone slab.

Mike, Doris and Eddie Everett.
(Courtesy John DiSanto)

The dedication took place on a sunny December day in 2005. It was the start of what would become a more formal venture. In the ensuing years, as he essentially morphed into the de facto custodian of Philadelphia's boxing heritage, DiSanto helped install markers for other notable boxers who were buried into unidentified plots, including Eddie Cool,

Gypsy Joe Harris, Garnet "Sugar" Hart, and, most recently, Matthew Saad Muhammad, perhaps the most exciting fighter to appear in the city during the late 1970s. It turns out there is a whole potter's field worth of unspecified graves concerning Philadelphia's boxing heroes from yesteryear.

The gravestone is a warm blue granite. Etched at the top is "Everett" in large capital letters. Doris, who passed away several years after the dedication of the stone, is represented on the right, with the years of her birth and death inscribed below her first name and a small picture of herself above it. On the left, her son is featured in identical fashion. His portrait, framed in an oval, is cropped from a photograph that was taken shortly before his death—the same photograph, incidentally, that served as the basis for one fan's idealized artistic rendition, with angel wings and a halo. But there is little about this face, despite the obvious facts of its youth, that could be construed as cherubic. The eyes are coal-black, insolent, with a hint of anxiety bubbling beneath the surface. It is a serious, unsmiling face, the look of someone who knew, perhaps, that he was on borrowed time.

Brooklyn, New York
August 2022

ACKNOWLEDGEMENTS

THIS BOOKS OWES its genesis to my friend and mentor Carlos Acevedo, who first suggested that a little-known Philadelphian lightweight contender could be a worthwhile subject to delve into. Thanks also to Carlos for his unerring editorial hand and encouragement throughout this project.

Thanks to Russell Peltz, Frank Gelb, and Eddie Everett for their time and willingness to speak to me on numerous occasions. Their insight and first-person accounts of Everett were crucial, given the paucity of secondary sources.

Thanks to Sean Patrick Griffin, whose groundbreaking scholarship on the Black Mafia tilled the soil for my own research. Thanks also to John W. King, who, as both a South Philadelphia native and son of a high-ranking Black Mafia member, offered a unique perspective.

This book benefited from materials gathered at the Special Collections Research Center at Temple University in Philadelphia.

Thanks to my sister, Sunjin, for her patience and assiduousness in designing the cover for this book.

And, finally, thanks to Kristen, whose gracious counsel and tenacity throughout the revisionary process saved this writer from embarrassment every step of the way. Love you, dearest.

If there are any errors in this book, they are not the responsibility of any of the aforementioned.

SOURCES

BOOKS

Anderson, Elijah. *Code of the Street: Decency, Violence, and the Moral Life of the Inner City.* New York: W.W. Norton & Company, 1999.

Atlas, Teddy, Bert Sugar. *The Ultimate Book of Boxing Lists.* Philadelphia: Running Press, 2011.

Callis, Tracy, et al. *Philadelphia's Boxing Heritage.* Charleston: Arcadia Publishing, 2002.

Collins, Nigel. *Boxing Babylon: Behind the Shadowy World of the Prize Ring.* Citadel Press, 1990

Cushman, Tom. *Muhammad Ali and the Greatest Heavyweight Generation.* Cape Girardeau: Southeast Missouri State University Press, 2009.

Doveed, Linder. *Ringside: Interviews with 24 Fighters and Boxing Insiders.* Jefferson: McFarland & Company, 2016.

Du Bois, W.E.B. *The Philadelphia Negro: A Social Study.* Philadelphia: University of Pennsylvania Press, 1995.

Evanzz, Karl. *The Messenger: The Rise and Fall of Elijah Muhammad.* New York: Pantheon, 1999.

Griffin, Sean Patrick. *Black Brothers, Inc.: The Violent Rise and Fall of Philadelphia's Black Mafia.* London: Milo Books, 2007.

Jones, Ann. *Women Who Kill.* New York: Holt, Rinehart, and Winson, 1980.

Lane, Roger. *The Roots of Violence in Black Philadelphia, 1860-1900*. Cambridge: Harvard University Press, 1989.

Lombardo, Timothy J. *Blue-Collar Conservatism: Frank Rizzo's Philadelphia and Populist Politics*. Philadelphia: University of Pennsylvania, 2018.

Nash, Gary B. *Forging Freedom: The Formation of Philadelphia's Black Community, 1720-1840*. Cambridge: Harvard University Press, 1991.

Oppenheim, Gabe. *Boxing in Philadelphia: Tales of Struggle and Survival*. Maryland: Rowman & Littlefield, 2015.

Paolantonio, S.A. *Frank Rizzo: The Last Big Man in Big City America*. Philadelphia: Camino Books, 1994.

Wolfinger, James. *Philadelphia Divided: Race and Politics in the City of Brotherly Love*. Chapel Hill: The University of North Carolina Press, 2011.

INTERVIEWS

John DiSanto
Eddie Everett
Frank Gelb
Sean Patrick Griffin
Tyree Johnson
John W. King
Len Lear
Don Majeski
J Russell Peltz
Mike Rossman

Augie Scimeca
Stephen Serota
Greg Sirb

NEWSPAPERS

Courier-Post
New York Times
Philadelphia Bulletin
Philadelphia Daily News
Philadelphia Inquirer
Philadelphia Tribune
Scranton Times-Tribune

PERIODICALS

Jet
PhillySport
Sports Illustrated

VIDEOS

Everett vs. Escalera Fight (Author's personal collection)
Library of Congress
"Philly Black Mafia: Do For Self" (BET, *American Gangster*)

WEBSITES

Philly Boxing History
Philadelphia Inquirer
National Public Radio
RingTV

ABOUT THE AUTHOR

Sean Nam is a contributor to BoxingScene.com and the British weekly boxing magazine Boxing News. A former boxing writer for USA Today, he is a full member and co-vice president of the Boxing Writers Association of America. He is also a member of the International Boxing Research Organization. *Murder on Federal Street* is his first book. He lives in Brooklyn, New York.

ABOUT THE FOREWORD WRITER

Carlos Acevedo is the author of *The Duke: The Life and Lies of Tommy Morrison* and *Sporting Blood: Tales from the Dark Side of Boxing*. He is the editor of Hannibal Boxing and a member of the Boxing Writers Association of America. From 2009 to 2016, he was the editor of The Cruelest Sport. His work has appeared in The Ring, Boxing News, HBO Boxing, Undisputed Champion Network, Remezcla, and Boxing Digest. His stories "A Darkness Made to Order," "A Ghost Orbiting Forever," and "The Duke of the West Side" all won first place awards from the BWAA. He lives in Brooklyn, New York.

Printed in the USA
CPSIA information can be obtained
at www.ICGtesting.com
BVHW042137210823
668756BV00001B/4